Microsoft

Deploying
SECURE
802.11 WIRELESS
NETWORKS with Microsoft
WINDOWS

Joseph Davies

PUBLISHED BY
Microsoft Press
A Division of Microsoft Corporation
One Microsoft Way
Redmond, Washington 98052-6399

Library of Congress Cataloging-in-Publication Data
Davies, Joseph (Joseph Glenn), 1962-
     Deploying Secure 802.11 Wireless Networks with Microsoft Windows /Joseph Davies.
          p. cm.
     Includes index.
     ISBN 0-7356-1939-5
     1. Wireless LANs.   2. IEEE 802.11 (Standard).   3. Computer networks--Security
measures   4. Microsoft Windows (Computer file).   I. Title.

TK5105.78.D36   2003
004.6'8--dc21   2003054031

Printed and bound in the United States of America.

1 2 3 4 5 6 7 8 9   QWT   8 7 6 5 4 3

Distributed in Canada by H.B. Fenn and Company Ltd.

A CIP catalogue record for this book is available from the British Library.

Microsoft Press books are available through booksellers and distributors worldwide. For further information about international editions, contact your local Microsoft Corporation office or contact Microsoft Press International directly at fax (425) 936-7329. Visit our Web site at www.microsoft.com/mspress. Send comments to *tkinput@microsoft.com*.

Acquisitions Editor: Martin DelRe
Project Editor: Jean Trenary
Technical Editors: Tim Upton and Ray Horak

Body Part No. X09-71495

For Katie:
Lux quae tam splendide fulget.

Contents

PART II   Wireless Network Deployment

PART III Troubleshooting Wireless Networks

Introduction

Welcome to *Deploying Secure 802.11 Wireless Networks with Microsoft Windows*, your complete source for the information you need to design and deploy 802.11-based wireless networks for Microsoft Windows wireless clients using Windows 2000–based or Windows Server 2003–based servers for the authentication infrastructure. This book includes overview explanations of the various technologies involved in deploying a secure wireless solution, step-by-step instructions about how to deploy various types of wireless configurations for both the enterprise organization and the Small Office/Home Office (SOHO), and discussions of troubleshooting tools and common connectivity and authentication problems.

In today's world, the term security needs to be defined. Here is a definition that you should use when thinking about secure wireless connections:

Security is not binary. It is not a switch or even a series of switches. It cannot be expressed in absolute terms. Do not believe anyone who tries to convince you otherwise. Security is relative—there is only more secure and less secure. Furthermore, security is dynamic—people, process, and technology all change. The bottom line is that all of these factors make managing security difficult.

—Ben Smith and Brian Komar, *Microsoft Windows Security Resource Kit*,
Microsoft Press, 2003.

Deploying Secure 802.11 Wireless Networks with Microsoft Windows describes the combination of technologies in Windows that supports the strongest set of industry standards for secure wireless access that were available at the time of the writing of this book.

How This Book Is Structured

Deploying Secure 802.11 Wireless Networks with Microsoft Windows is structured to provide a conceptual overview of not only wireless networking but also all the other components of the authentication infrastructure such as Remote Authentication Dial-In User Service (RADIUS) and certificates. Many companies have not implemented RADIUS or a public key infrastructure (PKI), so this book takes the time to explain them in detail and how they apply to the authentication and authorization of wireless connections. It then describes the steps of deploying secure wireless connections using certificate and password-based authentication in a large organization as well as SOHO and public access wireless networks. Finally, it describes how to troubleshoot wireless problems from the wireless client, the wireless AP, and the authentication infrastructure.

Part I, "Wireless Network Technology and Components," provides an introduction to the various elements of secure wireless networking. To understand how to deploy and troubleshoot a secure wireless network, you must have an understanding of the underlying technologies and how they work. These technologies include 802.11 wireless LAN networking, wireless security, the various Windows wireless clients, and the elements of the authentication infrastructure. This background is provided in Part I, which includes the following chapters:

- Chapter 1, "IEEE 802.11 Overview," briefly describes the advantages of wireless LAN networking and then describes the IEEE 802.11 standards including 802.11b, 802.11a, and 802.11g; components of wireless networking; and operating modes.

- Chapter 2, "Wireless Security," provides an overview of how authentication, confidentiality (encryption), and data integrity are supported with both the original 802.11 standard and the new Wi-Fi Protected Access (WPA) standard. Authentication with the 802.1X standard is also discussed.

- Chapter 3, "Windows Wireless Client Support," details the support for wireless networks provided in Windows XP (prior to Service Pack 1 [SP1]), Windows XP SP1 and later, Windows Server 2003, and Windows 2000 (with Microsoft 802.1X Authentication Client). The Wireless Zero Configuration (WZC) service and the set of configuration dialog boxes for each operating system are described in detail. This chapter also discusses the manual configuration of wireless settings and the automated configuration using the Wireless Network (IEEE 802.11) Policies Group Policy extension.

- Chapter 4, "RADIUS, IAS, and Active Directory," presents a detailed look at Remote Authentication Dial-In User Service (RADIUS), a protocol and infrastructure for providing authentication, authorization, and accounting for network connections. Internet Authentication Service (IAS) is the Microsoft implementation of a RADIUS server and proxy. This chapter describes the configuration dialog boxes for IAS global settings, remote access policies, and connection request policies. Finally, this chapter presents an overview of the Active Directory directory service and how user accounts, computer accounts, and groups are used to provide wireless access.

- Chapter 5, "EAP," details the Extensible Authentication Protocol (EAP) and its support in Windows for secure authentication of wireless access. This chapter provides detailed explanations of EAP-Transport Layer Security (EAP-TLS) and Protected EAP-Microsoft Challenge Handshake Authentication Protocol version 2 (PEAP-MS-CHAP v2) with their corresponding client and server-side configuration dialog boxes in Windows.

- Chapter 6, "Certificates and Public Key Infrastructure," presents an overview of public key encryption and the role of certificates in providing authentication. This chapter includes discussions of PKI, certification authorities, certification hierarchies, certificate revocation and validation, and how Windows supports certificates using the Certificates snap-in and Certificate Services.

This chapter also details the various methods of obtaining a user or computer certificate on a Windows wireless client or an IAS server.

After you understand the basic concepts and components of secure wireless networking, the next step is to begin the planning and deployment of secure wireless connectivity in your organization. Part II, "Wireless Network Deployment," provides you with the information you need to plan and deploy your secure wireless network solution. Part II includes the following chapters:

- Chapter 7, "Wireless AP Placement," includes wireless LAN design guidelines such as wireless access point (AP) requirements, signal propagation modifiers and sources of interference, and the number of wireless APs needed. This chapter then gives you step-by-step instructions on how to deploy your wireless APs to provide adequate coverage for all desired areas.

- Chapter 8, "Intranet Wireless Deployment Using EAP-TLS," provides detailed step-by-step instructions on how to deploy the authentication infrastructure (PKI, Active Directory, and IAS) and wireless clients for EAP-TLS authentication.

- Chapter 9, "Case Study: The Microsoft Wireless Network," details the history, design and deployment considerations, and phases of the deployment of the wireless network that is in place at the Microsoft Corporation. This chapter also provides details on the authentication infrastructure, including domains, PKI, and IAS RADIUS proxies and servers.

- Chapter 10, "Intranet Wireless Deployment Using PEAP-MS-CHAP v2," provides detailed step-by-step instructions on how to deploy the authentication infrastructure (certificates, Active Directory, and IAS) and wireless clients for PEAP-MS-CHAP v2 authentication.

- Chapter 11, "Additional Intranet Wireless Deployment Configurations," details the following additional wireless configurations: Internet access for business partners, cross-forest authentication, using RADIUS proxies to scale authentications, and using both EAP-TLS and PEAP-MS-CHAP v2 authentication.

- Chapter 12, "Secure Wireless Networks for the Home and Small Business," provides detailed step-by-step instructions on how to deploy a secure wireless network in a SOHO using either infrastructure mode or ad hoc mode, and either Wired Equivalent Privacy (WEP) or WPA.

- Chapter 13, "RADIUS Infrastructure for Public Place Deployment," details the configuration of RADIUS proxies and servers for a wireless Internet service provider (WISP) that is offering public wireless access to its own customers or wireless users that have a benefactor (another telecommunications provider or a private organization).

After you deploy secure wireless networking, you must know how to troubleshoot the common problems with obtaining wireless connectivity. Part III, "Troubleshooting Wireless Networks," includes the following chapters:

- Chapter 14, "Troubleshooting the Windows Wireless Client," describes the troubleshooting tools available to gather troubleshooting information on a Windows wireless client and provides a discussion of common connectivity and authentication problems that can be solved from the Windows wireless client.

- Chapter 15, "Troubleshooting the Wireless AP," describes the typical troubleshooting tools provided with wireless APs to gather troubleshooting information and discusses common connectivity and authentication problems that can be solved from the wireless AP.

- Chapter 16, "Troubleshooting the Authentication Infrastructure," describes the troubleshooting tools provided with Windows to gather troubleshooting information for IAS and discusses IAS-authentication, certificate-validation, and password-validation problems that can be solved from the authentication infrastructure.

Part IV, "Appendixes," includes the following:

- Appendix A, "Wireless Deployment Best Practices," is a single location for the best practices for all the elements of a secure wireless deployment, as described in Chapters 1–16.

- Appendix B, "Wireless ISPs and Windows Provisioning Services," is a brief overview of the upcoming Wireless Provisioning Services update for Windows XP wireless clients, which attempts to solve various security, automated configuration, and consistency issues that WISPs and public wireless users now have to face.

- Appendix C, "Setting Up Secure Wireless Access in a Test Lab," provides detailed step-by-step instructions on how to configure secure wireless access using IEEE 802.1X and PEAP-MS-CHAP v2 and EAP-TLS authentication in a test lab using a wireless AP and four computers.

Additional Resources

Deploying Secure 802.11 Wireless Networks with Microsoft Windows is primarily a deployment book, not a technical reference. It is designed to provide enough background information so that you can understand the basic workings of the various technologies to plan and deploy secure 802.11-based wireless networking. There are many topics that, for a completely thorough treatment, would fill their own books. For more detailed technical or deployment information about specific elements of wireless deployment, such as RADIUS, Active Directory, or PKI, see the following Web sites:

- Internet Authentication Service: *http://www.microsoft.com/ias*

- Active Directory: *http://www.microsoft.com/ad*

- Windows 2000 Security Services: *http://www.microsoft.com/windows2000 /technologies/security/default.asp*

- Windows Server 2003 Security Services: *http://www.microsoft.com /windowsserver2003/technologies/security/default.mspx*

For the latest information about support for 802.11 wireless networking in Windows, see the Microsoft Wi-Fi Web site at *http://www.microsoft.com/wifi.*

Conventions Used in This Book

Throughout the book, you will find special sections set aside from the main text. These sections draw your attention to topics of special interest and importance or to problems that implementers invariably face during the course of a deployment. These features include the following:

Note This feature is used to underscore the importance of a specific concept or to highlight a special case that might apply only to certain situations.

More Info When additional material is available on a subject, whether in other sections in the book or from outside sources such as Web sites or white papers, the links to these extra sources are provided in the More Info features.

Caution The Caution feature points out the places where you can get yourself into trouble if you do something or fail to do something. Pay close attention to these sections because they could save you a great deal of aggravation.

Tip This feature directs your attention to advice on timesaving or strategic moves.

Best Practices Getting the most stable performance and the highest quality deployment often means knowing a few ins and outs. The Best Practices features are where you'll find such pieces of knowledge.

Planning There are times when an ounce of prevention through planning is worth many hours of troubleshooting and downtime. Such times merit the Planning feature.

Part I
Wireless Network Technology and Components

Chapter 1
IEEE 802.11 Overview

Before getting into the technical details of the Institute of Electrical and Electronic Engineers (IEEE) 802.11 standard, it is helpful to review the benefits of wireless LAN networking, which include the following:

- Wireless connections can extend or replace a wired infrastructure in situations where it is costly, inconvenient, or impossible to lay cables. This benefit includes the following:

    - To connect the networks in two buildings separated by a physical, legal, or financial obstacle, you can either use a link provided by a telecommunications vendor (for a fixed installation cost and ongoing recurring costs) or you can create a point-to-point wireless link using wireless LAN technology (for a fixed installation cost, but no recurring costs). Eliminating recurring telecommunications charges can provide significant cost savings to corporations.

    - Wireless LAN technologies can be used to create a temporary network, which is in place for only a specific amount of time. For example, the network needed at a convention or trade show can be a wireless network, rather than deploying the physical cabling required for a traditional Ethernet network.

    - Some types of buildings, such as historical buildings, might be governed by building codes that prohibit the use of wiring, making wireless networking an important alternative.

    - The wiring-free aspect of wireless LAN networking is also very attractive to homeowners who want to connect the various computers in their home together without having to drill holes and pull network cables through walls and ceilings.

- Increased productivity for the mobile employee. This benefit includes the following:

    - The mobile user whose primary computer is a laptop or notebook computer can change location and always remain connected to the network. This enables the mobile user to travel to various places—meeting rooms, hallways, lobbies, cafeterias, classrooms, and so forth—and still have access to networked data. Without wireless access, the user has to carry cabling and is restricted to working near a network jack.

- Wireless LAN networking is a perfect technology for environments where movement is required. For example, retail environments can benefit when employees use a wireless laptop, palmtop, or computer to enter inventory information directly into the store database from the sales floor.

- Even if no wireless infrastructure is present, wireless laptop computers can still form their own ad hoc networks to communicate and share data with each other.

- Easy access to the Internet in public places.

Beyond the corporate campus, access to the Internet and even corporate sites can be made available through public wireless "hot spot" networks. Airports, restaurants, rail stations, and common areas throughout cities can be provisioned to provide this service. When the traveling worker reaches his or her destination, perhaps meeting a client at the corporate office, limited access can be provided to the user through the local wireless network. The network can recognize the user from another corporation and create a connection that is isolated from local corporate network but provides Internet access to the visiting user. Wireless infrastructure providers are enabling wireless connectivity in public areas around the world. Many airports, conference centers, and hotels provide wireless access to the Internet for their visitors.

Note In all these wireless LAN scenarios, it is worth noting that today's standards-based wireless LANs operate at the same speeds that were considered state of the art for wired networks just a few years ago. For example, IEEE 802.11b, a prevalent wireless LAN technology, operates at a maximum of 11 megabits per second (Mbps), or about 30 to 100 times faster than standard dial-up technologies. This bandwidth is certainly adequate to deliver acceptable throughput for a number of applications or services. In addition, ongoing advancements with these wireless standards continue to increase the bit rate, with speeds of up to 54 Mbps.

Although IEEE 802.11 wireless LAN technologies provide these benefits, they also introduce security challenges with regard to who is allowed to connect and how they must send wireless traffic. These security challenges and their solutions are described in detail in Chapter 2, "Wireless Security."

IEEE 802.11 Standards

IEEE 802.11 is an industry standard for a shared, wireless LAN that defines the physical (PHY) layer and Media Access Control (MAC) sublayer for wireless communications. Figure 1-1 shows the relation of the IEEE 802.11 standard relative to the IEEE 802 specification and the Open Systems Interconnection (OSI) reference model.

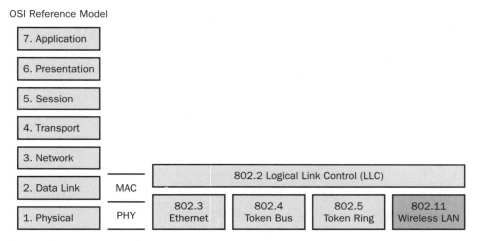

Figure 1-1. *The IEEE 802.11 standard.*

802.11 MAC Sublayer

At the MAC sublayer, all the IEEE 802.11 standards use the carrier sense multiple access with collision avoidance (CSMA/CA) MAC protocol. A wireless station with a frame to transmit first listens on the wireless frequency to determine whether another station is currently transmitting (*carrier sense*). If the medium is used, the wireless station calculates a random backoff delay. After the random backoff delay, the wireless station again listens for a transmitting station. By instituting a random backoff delay, multiple stations that are waiting to transmit do not end up trying to transmit at the same time (*collision avoidance*).

The CSMA/CA scheme does not prevent all collisions, and it is difficult for a transmitting node to detect that a collision has occurred. Depending on the placement of the wireless access point (AP) and the wireless clients, distance or radio frequency (RF) barriers can also prevent a wireless client from sensing that another wireless node is transmitting (known as the *hidden station* problem).

To better detect collisions and solve the hidden station problem, IEEE 802.11 uses acknowledgment (ACK) frames and Request to Send (RTS) and Clear to Send (CTS) messages. ACK frames indicate when a wireless frame is successfully received.

When a station wants to transmit a frame, it sends an RTS message that indicates the amount of time it needs to send the frame. The wireless AP sends a CTS message to all stations, granting permission to the requesting station and informing all other stations that they are not allowed to transmit for the time reserved by the RTS message. The exchange of RTS and CTS messages eliminates collisions due to hidden stations.

802.11 PHY Sublayer

At the physical (PHY) layer, IEEE 802.11 defines a series of encoding and transmission schemes for wireless communications, the most prevalent of which are the Frequency Hopping Spread Spectrum (FHSS), Direct Sequence Spread Spectrum (DSSS), and Orthogonal Frequency-Division Multiplexing (OFDM) transmission schemes. Figure 1-2 shows the 802.11, 802.11b, 802.11a, and 802.11g standards that exist at the PHY layer. These standards are described in the sections that follow.

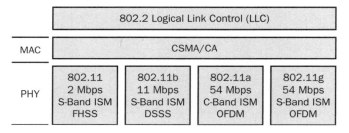

Figure 1-2. *The standards for 802.11 at the PHY layer.*

> **More Info** This book does not describe the details of IEEE PHY encoding and transmission techniques or the details of 802.11 frame formats and MAC management. For more information, see *802.11 Wireless Networks, The Definitive Guide* by Matthew S. Gast, Sebastopol, CA: O'Reilly & Associates, 2002.

IEEE 802.11

The bit rates for the original IEEE 802.11 standard are 2 and 1 Mbps using the FHSS transmission scheme and the S-Band Industrial, Scientific, and Medical (ISM) frequency band, which operates in the frequency range of 2.4 to 2.5 GHz. Under good transmission conditions, 2 Mbps is used; under less-than-ideal conditions, the lower speed of 1 Mbps is used.

802.11b

The major enhancement to IEEE 802.11 by IEEE 802.11b is the standardization of the physical layer to support higher bit rates. IEEE 802.11b supports two additional speeds, 5.5 Mbps and 11 Mbps, using the S-Band ISM. The DSSS transmission scheme is used in order to provide the higher bit rates. The bit rate of 11 Mbps is achievable in ideal conditions. In less-than-ideal conditions, the slower speeds of 5.5 Mbps, 2 Mbps, and 1 Mbps are used.

Note   802.11b uses the same frequency band as that used by microwave ovens, cordless phones, baby monitors, wireless video cameras, and Bluetooth devices.

802.11a

IEEE 802.11a (the first standard to be ratified, but just now being widely sold and deployed) operates at a bit rate as high as 54 Mbps and uses the C-Band ISM, which operates in the frequency range of 5.725 to 5.875 GHz. Instead of DSSS, 802.11a uses OFDM, which allows data to be transmitted by subfrequencies in parallel and provides greater resistance to interference and greater throughput. This higher-speed technology enables wireless LAN networking to perform better for video and conferencing applications.

Because they are not on the same frequencies as other S-Band devices (such as cordless phones), OFDM and IEEE 802.11a provide both a higher data rate and a cleaner signal. The bit rate of 54 Mbps is achievable in ideal conditions. In less-than-ideal conditions, the slower speeds of 48 Mbps, 36 Mbps, 24 Mbps, 18 Mbps, 12 Mbps, and 6 Mbps are used.

802.11g

IEEE 802.11g, a relatively new standard at the time of the publication of this book, operates at a bit rate as high as 54 Mbps, but uses the S-Band ISM and OFDM. 802.11g is also backward-compatible with 802.11b and can operate at the 802.11b bit rates and use DSSS. 802.11g wireless network adapters can connect to an 802.11b wireless AP, and 802.11b wireless network adapters can connect to an 802.11g wireless AP. Thus, 802.11g provides a migration path for 802.11b networks to a frequency-compatible standard technology with a higher bit rate. Existing 802.11b wireless network adapters cannot be upgraded to 802.11g by updating the firmware of the adapter—they must be replaced. Unlike migrating from 802.11b to 802.11a (in which all the network adapters in both the wireless clients and the wireless APs must be replaced at the same time), migrating from 802.11b to 802.11g can be done incrementally.

Like 802.11a, 802.11g uses 54 Mbps in ideal conditions and the slower speeds of 48 Mbps, 36 Mbps, 24 Mbps, 18 Mbps, 12 Mbps, and 6 Mbps in less-than-ideal conditions.

802.11 Wireless LAN Components

IEEE 802.11 wireless LAN networking consists of the following components:

- Stations

- Wireless APs

- Ports

These components are shown in Figure 1-3.

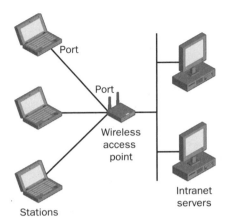

Figure 1-3. *The components of 802.11 wireless LAN networking.*

Stations

A *station* (STA) is a computing device that is equipped with a wireless LAN network adapter. A personal computer equipped with a wireless LAN network adapter is known as a *wireless client*. Wireless clients can communicate with each other either directly or through a wireless AP. An STA can be stationary or mobile.

Wireless Access Points

A wireless AP is a networking device equipped with a wireless LAN network adapter that acts as a peripheral bridge device to extend a traditional wired network to include STAs. An AP contains the following:

- At least one interface that connects the AP to an existing wired network (such as an Ethernet backbone).

- Radio equipment with which it creates wireless connections with wireless clients.

- IEEE 802.1D bridging software, so it can act as a transparent bridge between the wireless and wired networks.

The wireless AP is similar to a cellular phone network's base station—wireless clients communicate with the wired network and other wireless clients through the wireless AP, and wireless APs are stationary.

Ports

A *port* is a logical channel of a device that supports a single point-to-point connection. For IEEE 802.11, a port is an association—a logical entity over which a single wireless connection is made. A typical wireless client or wireless AP has multiple ports and can support multiple simultaneous wireless connections.

The logical connection between a port on the wireless client and a port on a wireless AP is a point-to-point bridged LAN segment, similar to an Ethernet-based network client connected to an Ethernet switch. All frames sent from a wireless client—whether unicast, multicast, or broadcast—are sent on the point-to-point LAN segment between the wireless client and the wireless AP. For frames sent by the wireless AP to wireless clients, unicast frames are sent on the point-to-point LAN segment, and multicast and broadcast frames are sent to all connected wireless clients at the same time.

IEEE 802.11 Operating Modes

IEEE 802.11 defines the following operating modes:

- Infrastructure mode

- Ad hoc mode

Regardless of the operating mode, a Service Set Identifier (SSID), also known as the wireless network name, identifies the wireless network. The *SSID* is a name configured on the wireless AP (for infrastructure mode) or an initial wireless client (for ad hoc mode) that identifies the wireless network. The SSID is periodically advertised by the wireless AP or the initial wireless client using a special 802.11 MAC management frame known as a *beacon frame*.

Infrastructure Mode

In *infrastructure mode*, there is at least one wireless AP and one wireless client. The wireless client uses the wireless AP to access the resources of a traditional wired network. The wired network can be an organization intranet or the Internet, depending on the placement of the wireless AP.

A single wireless AP supporting one or multiple wireless clients is known as a Basic Service Sets (BSS). A set of two or more wireless APs connected to the same wired network that defines a single logical network segment bounded by a router (also known as a *subnet*) is known as an Extended Service Sets (ESS). The *distribution system* is the wired network that connects the wireless APs in an ESS to each other and to the larger wired network. An ESS is shown in Figure 1-4.

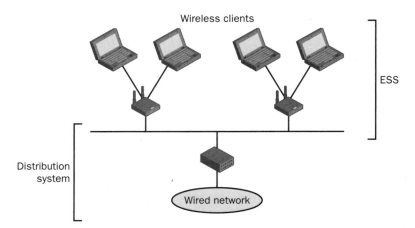

Figure 1-4. *Infrastructure mode and an ESS.*

When a wireless network adapter is turned on, it begins to scan across the wireless frequencies for wireless APs and other wireless clients. (*Scanning* is an active process in which the wireless adapter sends Probe-Request frames on all channels of the ISM frequency range and listens for the Probe-Response frames sent by wireless APs and other wireless clients.) After scanning, a wireless adapter chooses a wireless AP with which to associate. This choice is made automatically by using the SSID of a known or preferred wireless network and the wireless AP with the best signal strength (the highest signal-to-noise ratio). Next, the wireless client negotiates the use of a logical wireless port with the chosen wireless AP. This process is known as *association*.

The wireless client's configuration settings determine whether the wireless client prefers to connect with infrastructure or ad hoc mode networks. By default, a Windows XP or Windows Server 2003 wireless client prefers infrastructure mode wireless networks over ad hoc mode wireless networks.

If the signal strength of the wireless AP is too low, if the error rate is too high, or if instructed by the operating system, the wireless client scans for other wireless APs to determine whether a different wireless AP can provide a stronger signal to the same wireless network. If so, the wireless client negotiates a connection with that wireless AP. This process is known as *reassociation*.

Note Every 60 seconds, Windows XP and Windows Server 2003 instruct the wireless network adapter to scan for the available wireless APs.

Reassociation with a different wireless AP can occur for many different reasons. For example, the signal can weaken because the wireless client moves away from the wireless AP or the wireless AP becomes congested with too much other traffic. The automatic switching by wireless clients to less congested wireless APs tends to distribute the load of wireless network traffic across the available wireless APs, increasing the performance for other wireless clients.

As a wireless client moves its physical location, it can associate and reassociate from one wireless AP to another, maintaining a continuous connection during physical relocation. For example, for Transmission Control Protocol/Internet Protocol (TCP/IP), a wireless client is assigned an Internet Protocol (IP) address when it connects to the first wireless AP. When the wireless client roams within the ESS, it creates wireless connections with other wireless APs, but keeps the same IP address because all the wireless APs are on the same subnet.

When the wireless client roams to a different ESS, however, the IP address configuration is no longer valid. For a Windows XP or Windows Server 2003 wireless client, a reassociation is interpreted as a media disconnect/connect event. This event causes Windows XP and Windows Server 2003 to perform a Dynamic Host Configuration Protocol (DHCP) renewal for the IP configuration. Therefore, for reassociations within the ESS, the DHCP renewal refreshes the current IP address configuration. When the Windows XP or Windows Server 2003 wireless client reassociates with a wireless AP across an ESS boundary, the DHCP renewal process obtains a new IP address configuration that is relevant for the logical IP subnet of the new ESS.

Ad Hoc Mode

In *ad hoc mode*, wireless clients communicate directly with each other without the use of a wireless AP, as shown in Figure 1-5.

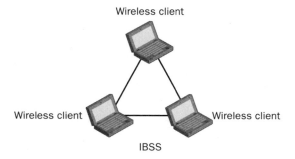

Figure 1-5. *Wireless clients in ad hoc mode.*

Ad hoc mode is also called *peer-to-peer mode*. Wireless clients in ad hoc mode form an Independent Basic Service Set (IBSS). One of the wireless clients, the first wireless client in the IBSS, takes over some of the responsibilities of the wireless AP. These responsibilities include the periodic beaconing process and the authentication of new members. This wireless client does not act as a bridge to relay information between wireless clients.

Ad hoc mode is used to connect wireless clients together when there is no wireless AP present. The wireless clients must be explicitly configured to use ad hoc mode. There can be a maximum of nine members in an ad hoc 802.11 wireless network.

Summary

Wireless LAN networking provides many benefits to network computing by eliminating the cost and effort required for traditional cabling and making network connectivity easier and more mobile. The standard for wireless LAN networking is the family of IEEE 802.11 specifications, which describe the PHY layer and MAC sublayer for wireless data encoding, signaling, and sending wireless frames. The most prevalent 802.11-based wireless LAN technology at the time of the publication of this book is 802.11b, which has a maximum bit rate of 11 Mbps and uses the S-Band ISM. IEEE 802.11 wireless LANs can be used in an infrastructure mode, in which wireless APs provide a bridge to a wired network, or an ad hoc mode, in which wireless clients form their own wireless network.

Chapter 2
Wireless Security

Wireless networks broadcast their network data using radio signals. Unlike wired networking technologies such as Ethernet, it is difficult to control access to the wireless networking media. For example, with wired networks you must have physical access to a network jack. If you use wireless networks, you do not even need to be in the building; you can access the wireless network from across the street. The difference between wired and wireless networks is illustrated in the following comparison:

- With wired networks, the medium is private. You do not have to worry about who is connecting because the assumption is that unauthorized users cannot gain access to a network plug. You also do not have to ensure that the traffic is made confidential because the traffic is sent over a private cabling system that is not accessible to unauthorized users.

- With wireless networks, the medium is public. Anyone with the proper wireless equipment that is within association range can connect. The network traffic must also be made confidential because the unauthorized user can receive wireless frames without being present in physically securable areas.

Therefore, for wireless LANs, security is a required element of the technology, its implementation, and its deployment. Properties of secure communications for wireless networks consist of the following:

- **Authentication** Before being allowed to exchange data traffic with the wireless network, the wireless network node must be identified and (depending on the authentication method) must submit credentials that can be validated.

- **Encryption** Before sending a wireless data packet, the wireless network node must encrypt the data to ensure data confidentiality.

- **Data integrity** Before sending a wireless data packet, the wireless network node must include information in the packet so the receiver can determine that the contents of the packet were not modified in transit.

Wireless Security with the IEEE 802.11 Standard

The original IEEE 802.11 standard defined authentication, encryption, and data integrity for wireless traffic. As we will discuss, the original authentication, encryption, and data integrity proved to be relatively weak and cumbersome for widespread public and private deployment. Subsequent sections of this chapter describe the additional standards that provide stronger authentication methods and discuss enhancements to the originally defined encryption and data integrity methods or replacements for them.

Authentication

IEEE 802.11 defines the following types of authentication, discussed in the following sections:

- Open system authentication
- Shared key authentication

Open System Authentication

Open system authentication does not provide authentication, only identification using the wireless adapter's Media Access Control (MAC) address. This authentication is used when no authentication is required, and it is the default authentication algorithm that uses the following process (shown in Figure 2-1):

1. The authentication-initiating wireless client sends an Open System Authentication Request message, which contains the MAC address as the source address of the 802.11 frame.

2. The receiving wireless node responds with an Open System Authentication Response message that indicates either success (the authentication-initiating wireless client is authenticated) or failure.

Open System Authentication Request

Open System Authentication Response

Figure 2-1. *Open system authentication.*

Some wireless APs allow you to configure a list of MAC addresses of wireless clients that are authorized. However, this does not provide security for a wireless network because an attacker can easily capture wireless packets and then use the MAC address of a valid wireless client as its own.

Shared Key Authentication

Shared key authentication verifies that an authentication-initiating station has knowledge of a shared secret, which is similar to preshared key authentication for Internet Protocol security (IPSec). The 802.11 standard currently assumes that the shared secret is delivered to the participating wireless clients by means of a secure channel that is independent of IEEE 802.11. In practice, this secret is a sequence of characters typed during the configuration of the wireless AP and the wireless client.

Shared key authentication uses the following process (shown in Figure 2-2):

1. The authentication-initiating wireless client sends a Shared Key Authentication Request frame.

2. The authentication-enforcing wireless node responds with a Shared Key Authentication Response frame that contains challenge text.

3. The authentication-initiating wireless node responds with a Shared Key Authentication Request frame that contains an encrypted form of the challenge text, which is encrypted using Wired Equivalent Privacy (WEP) (the encryption method used on 802.11 wireless networks) and the shared key authentication key.

4. The authentication-enforcing wireless node decrypts the encrypted challenge text in the Shared Key Authentication Request frame using WEP and the shared key authentication key. If the decrypted challenge text matches the originally sent challenge text, the authentication-enforcing wireless node sends a Shared Key Authentication Response frame that indicates authentication success. Otherwise, the authentication-enforcing wireless node sends a Shared Key Authentication Response frame that indicates authentication failure.

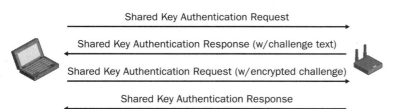

Figure 2-2. *Shared key authentication.*

Because the shared key authentication secret must be manually distributed and typed, this method of authentication does not scale appropriately in large infra-structure mode networks (for example, corporate campuses and public places).

Another serious problem with shared key authentication is that for configuration simplicity, the shared key authentication key is the same as the WEP encryption key used to encrypt all data between the authentication-initiating wireless client and the authentication-enforcing wireless node. The shared key authentication exchange includes a plaintext (the challenge text) and a ciphertext (the encrypted challenge text) exchange with an indication of success. An attacker can capture a successful shared key authentication exchange and determine the shared key authentication key, which is also the WEP encryption key, through cryptanalysis methods. When the WEP encryption key is determined, the attacker has full access to the wireless network and can begin attacking wireless nodes. Therefore, the use of shared key authentication is highly discouraged, even for Small Office/Home Office (SOHO) wireless networks.

More Info For more information about SOHO wireless networks, see Chapter 12, "Secure Wireless Networks for the Home and Small Business."

Encryption and Data Integrity

Due to the broadcast nature of wireless LAN networks, eavesdropping and remote sniffing of wireless LAN frames is very easy. Wired Equivalent Privacy (WEP) is defined by the IEEE 802.11 standard and is intended to provide a level of data confidentiality and integrity that is equivalent to a wired network.

WEP

WEP provides data confidentiality services by encrypting the data sent between wireless nodes. Setting a WEP flag in the MAC header of the 802.11 frame indicates that the frame is encrypted with WEP encryption. WEP provides data integrity by including an integrity check value (ICV) in the encrypted portion of the wireless frame.

WEP defines two shared keys:

- **Multicast/global key** The *multicast/global key* is an encryption key that protects multicast and broadcast traffic from a wireless AP to all of its connected wireless clients.

- **Unicast session key** The *unicast session key* is an encryption key that protects unicast traffic between a wireless client and a wireless AP and multicast and broadcast traffic sent by the wireless client to the wireless AP.

WEP encryption uses the RC4 symmetric stream cipher with 40-bit and 104-bit encryption keys. Although 104-bit encryption keys are not specified in the 802.11 standard, many wireless AP vendors support them.

Note Some implementations that advertise the use of 128-bit WEP encryption keys are just adding a 104-bit encryption key to the 24-bit initialization vector (IV) and calling it a 128-bit key. The IV is a field in the header of each 802.11 frame that is used during the encryption and decryption process.

WEP Encryption Process

To encrypt the payload of an 802.11 frame, the following process is used (shown in Figure 2-3):

1. A 32-bit ICV is calculated for the frame data.

2. The ICV is appended to the end of the frame data.

3. A 24-bit IV is generated and appended to the WEP encryption key.

4. The combination of [IV+WEP encryption key] is used as the input of a pseudo-random number generator (PRNG) to generate a bit sequence that is the same size as the combination of [data+ICV].

5. The PRNG bit sequence, also known as the *key stream*, is bit-wise exclusive ORed (XORed) with [data+ICV] to produce the encrypted portion of the payload that is sent between the wireless access point (AP) and the wireless client.

6. To create the payload for the wireless MAC frame, the IV is added to the front of the encrypted[data+ICV], along with other fields.

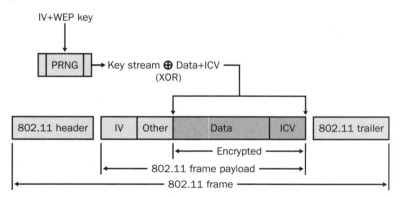

Figure 2-3. *WEP encryption process.*

WEP Decryption Process

To decrypt the 802.11 frame data, the following process is used (shown in Figure 2-4):

1. The IV is obtained from the front of the 802.11 frame payload.

2. The IV is appended to the WEP encryption key.

3. The [IV+WEP encryption key] is used as the input of the same PRNG to generate a bit sequence of the same size as the combination of the data and the ICV. This process produces the same key stream as that of the sending wireless node.

4. The PRNG bit sequence is XORed with the encrypted[data+ICV] to decrypt the [data+ICV] portion of the payload.

5. The ICV calculation for the data portion of the payload is run, and its result is compared with the value included in the incoming frame. If the values match, the data is considered to be valid (sent from the wireless client and unmodified in transit). If they do not match, the frame is silently discarded.

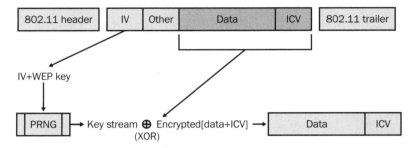

Figure 2-4. *WEP decryption process.*

Although the secret key remains constant over a long duration, the IV is changed periodically and as frequently as every frame. The periodicity at which IV values are changed depends on the degree of privacy required of the WEP algorithm. The ideal method of maintaining the effectiveness of WEP is changing the IV after each frame.

Security Issues with the IEEE 802.11 Standard

The main problem with WEP is that the determination and distribution of WEP encryption keys are not defined. WEP keys must be distributed by using a secure channel outside of the 802.11 protocol. In practice, WEP keys are text strings that must be manually configured using a keyboard for both the wireless AP and wireless clients. Obviously, this key distribution system does not scale well to an enterprise organization and is not secure.

Additionally, there is no defined mechanism to change the WEP encryption keys either per authentication or periodically for an authenticated connection. All wireless APs and clients use the same manually configured WEP key for multiple sessions. With multiple wireless clients sending a large amount of data, an attacker can remotely capture large amounts of WEP ciphertext and use cryptanalysis methods to determine the WEP key.

The lack of a WEP key management protocol is a principal limitation to providing 802.11 security, especially in infrastructure mode with a large number of stations. Some examples of this type of network include corporate and educational institutional campuses and public places such as airports and malls. The lack of automated authentication and key determination services also affects operation in ad hoc mode, in which users may wish to engage in peer-to-peer collaborative communication in areas such as conference rooms.

The security issues that exist with the original 802.11 standard are the following:

- Rogue wireless APs.

- No per-user identification and authentication.

- No mechanism for central authentication, authorization, and accounting.

- Some implementations derive WEP keys from passwords, resulting in weak WEP keys.

- No support for extended authentication methods. For example, token cards, certificates/smart cards, one-time passwords, biometrics, and so on.

- No support for key management. For example, rekeying global keys and dynamic per-station or per-session key management.

The solution for these shortcomings of the originally defined IEEE 802.11 standard is the IEEE 802.1X standard.

Authentication with the IEEE 802.1X Standard

The IEEE 802.1X standard defines port-based, network access control used to provide authenticated network access for Ethernet networks. This port-based network access control uses the physical characteristics of the switched LAN infrastructure to authenticate devices attached to a LAN port. Access to the port can be denied if the authentication process fails. Although this standard was designed for wired Ethernet networks, it has been adapted for use on 802.11 wireless LANs.

Elements of 802.1X

IEEE 802.1X defines the following terms, as described in the following sections:

- Port access entity

- Authenticator

- Supplicant

- Authentication server

Figure 2-5 shows these components for a wireless LAN network.

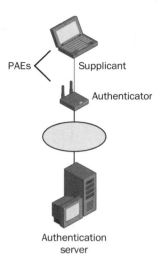

PAEs {
Supplicant

Authenticator

Authentication
server

Figure 2-5. *The components of IEEE 802.1X authentication.*

- **Port access entity**   A LAN port, also known as *port access entity (PAE)*, is the logical entity that supports the IEEE 802.1X protocol that is associated with a port. A PAE can adopt the role of the authenticator, the supplicant, or both.

- **Authenticator**   An *authenticator* is a LAN port that enforces authentication before allowing access to services accessible using that port. For wireless connections, the authenticator is the logical LAN port on a wireless AP through which wireless clients in infrastructure mode gain access to other wireless clients and the wired network.

- **Supplicant**   The *supplicant* is a LAN port that requests access to services accessible using the authenticator. For wireless connections, the supplicant is the logical LAN port on a wireless LAN network adapter that requests access to the other wireless clients and the wired network by associating with and then authenticating itself to an authenticator.

  Whether for wireless connections or wired Ethernet connections, the supplicant and authenticator are connected by a logical or physical point-to-point LAN segment.

- **Authentication server**   To verify the credentials of the supplicant, the authenticator uses an *authentication server*, which checks the credentials of the supplicant on behalf of the authenticator and then responds to the authenticator, indicating whether or not the supplicant is authorized to access the authenticator's services. The authentication server can be the following:

- **A component of the access point.** In this case, the AP must be configured with the sets of user credentials corresponding to the supplicants that will be attempting to connect (it is typically not implemented for wireless APs).

- **A separate entity.** In this case, the AP forwards the credentials of the connection attempt to a separate authentication server. Typically, a wireless AP uses the Remote Authentication Dial-In User Service (RADIUS) protocol to send a connection request message to a RADIUS server.

Controlled and Uncontrolled Ports

The authenticator's port-based access control defines the following different types of logical ports that access the wired LAN via a single physical LAN port:

- **Uncontrolled Port** The *uncontrolled port* allows an uncontrolled exchange between the authenticator (the wireless AP) and other networking devices on the wired network—regardless of any wireless client's authorization state. Frames sent by the wireless client are never sent using the uncontrolled port.

- **Controlled Port** The *controlled port* allows data to be sent between a wireless client and the wired network only if the wireless client is authorized by 802.1X. Before authentication, the switch is open and no frames are forwarded between the wireless client and the wired network. When the wireless client is successfully authenticated using IEEE 802.1X, the switch is closed, and frames can be sent between the wireless client and nodes on the wired network.

The different types of ports are shown in Figure 2-6.

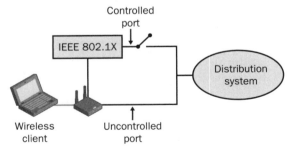

Figure 2-6. *Controlled and uncontrolled ports for IEEE 802.1X.*

On an authenticating Ethernet switch, the wired Ethernet client can send Ethernet frames to the wired network as soon as authentication is complete. The switch identifies the traffic of a specific wired Ethernet client using the physical port to which the Ethernet client is connected. Typically, only a single Ethernet client is connected to a physical port on the Ethernet switch.

Because multiple wireless clients contend for access to the same channel and send data using the same channel, an extension to the basic IEEE 802.1X protocol is required to allow a wireless AP to identify the secured traffic of a particular wireless client. The wireless client and wireless AP do this through the mutual determination of a per-client unicast session key. Only authenticated wireless clients have knowledge of their per-client unicast session key. Without a valid unicast session key tied to a successful authentication, a wireless AP discards the traffic sent from the wireless client.

EAP over LAN

To provide a standard authentication mechanism for IEEE 802.1X, the Extensible Authentication Protocol (EAP) was chosen. EAP is a Point-to-Point Protocol (PPP)-based authentication mechanism that was adapted for use on point-to-point LAN segments. EAP messages are normally sent as the payload of PPP frames. To adapt EAP messages to be sent over Ethernet or wireless LAN segments, the IEEE 802.1X standard defines EAP over LAN (EAPOL), a standard encapsulation method for EAP messages.

802.1X and 802.11 Security Issues

The current solutions provided by the use of 802.1X for the security issues that exist with 802.11 are the following:

- **Rogue wireless APs.** The best solution for rogue wireless APs is to support a mutual authentication protocol such as EAP-TLS or PEAP-MS-CHAP v2. With EAP-TLS or PEAP-MS-CHAP v2, the wireless client ensures that the wireless AP is a trusted member of the secure wireless authentication infrastructure.

- **No per-user identification and authentication.** The adaptation of IEEE 802.1X for wireless connections and its use of EAP enforce a user-level authentication before allowing wireless frames to be forwarded.

- **No mechanism for central authentication, authorization, and accounting.** By using RADIUS in conjunction with IEEE 802.1X, RADIUS servers provide authentication, authorization, and accounting services for wireless connections.

- **Some implementations derive WEP keys from passwords, resulting in weak WEP keys.** By using IEEE 802.1X and EAP-TLS as the authentication method, public key certificates, not passwords, are used to perform authentication and derive encryption key material. By using IEEE 802.1X and PEAP-MS-CHAP v2, passwords are used to derive encryption keys; however, the password credential exchange is encrypted within a TLS channel.

> **More Info**   For more information about EAP-TLS and PEAP-MS-CHAP v2, see Chapter 5, "EAP." For more information about public key certificates, see Chapter 6, "Certificates and Public Key Infrastructure."

- **No support for extended authentication methods (for example, token cards, certificates/smart cards, one-time passwords, biometrics, and so on).**   IEEE 802.1X uses EAP as its authentication protocol. EAP was designed to be extensible for virtually any type of authentication method. For more information, see Chapter 5.

- **No support for key management (for example, rekeying global keys and dynamic per-station or per-session key management).**   By using IEEE 802.1X and either the EAP-TLS or PEAP-MS-CHAP v2 authentication methods, random unicast session keys are derived for each authentication. Rekeying can be done either by the wireless client, by reauthenticating, or by the wireless AP, which changes encryption keys and sends the new keys to wireless clients using EAPOL messages.

Wi-Fi Protected Access

Although 802.1X addresses many of the security issues of the original 802.11 standard, issues still exist with regard to weaknesses in the WEP encryption and data integrity methods. The long-term solution to these problems is the IEEE 802.11i standard, which is an upcoming standard that specifies improvements to wireless LAN networking security. The 802.11i standard is currently in draft form, with ratification expected by the end of the first quarter of 2004.

While the new IEEE 802.11i standard is being ratified, wireless vendors have agreed on an interoperable interim standard known as Wi-Fi Protected Access (WPA). The goals of WPA are the following:

- **To require secure wireless networking.**   WPA requires secure wireless networking by requiring 802.1X authentication, encryption, and unicast and global encryption key management.

- **To address the issues with WEP through a software upgrade.**   The implementation of the RC4 stream cipher within WEP is vulnerable to known plaintext attacks. Additionally, the data integrity provided with WEP is relatively weak. WPA solves all the remaining security issues with WEP, yet only requires firmware updates in wireless equipment and an update for wireless clients. Existing wireless equipment is not expected to require replacement.

- **To provide a secure wireless networking solution for SOHO wireless users.**   For the SOHO, there is no RADIUS server to provide 802.1X authentication with an EAP type. SOHO wireless clients must use either shared key authentication (highly discouraged) or open system authentication (recommended) with a single static WEP key for both unicast and multicast traffic. WPA provides a pre-shared key option intended for SOHO configurations. The pre-shared key is configured on the wireless AP and each wireless client. The initial unicast encryption key is derived from the authentication process, which verifies that both the wireless client and the wireless AP have the pre-shared key.

- **To be forward-compatible with the upcoming IEEE 802.11i standard.** WPA is a subset of the security features in the proposed IEEE 802.11i standard. All the features of WPA are described in the current draft of the 802.11i standard.

- **To be available today.** WPA upgrades to wireless equipment and for wireless clients were available beginning in February 2003.

WPA Security Features

WPA contains enhancements or replacements for the following security features:

- Authentication
- Encryption
- Data integrity

Authentication

With 802.11, 802.1X authentication is optional; with WPA, 802.1X authentication is required. Authentication with WPA is a combination of open system and 802.1X authentication, which uses the following phases:

- The first phase uses open system authentication to indicate to the wireless client that it can send frames to the wireless AP.

- The second phase uses 802.1X to perform a user-level authentication.

For environments without a RADIUS infrastructure, WPA supports the use of a pre-shared key; for environments with a RADIUS infrastructure, WPA supports EAP and RADIUS.

Encryption

With 802.1X, rekeying of unicast encryption keys is optional. Additionally, 802.11 and 802.1X provide no mechanism to change the global encryption key that is used for multicast and broadcast traffic. With WPA, rekeying of both unicast and global encryption keys is required. The Temporal Key Integrity Protocol (TKIP) changes the unicast encryption key for every frame, and each change is synchronized between the wireless client and the wireless AP. For the multicast/global encryption key, WPA includes a facility for the wireless AP to advertise changes to the connected wireless clients.

TKIP   For 802.11, WEP encryption is optional. For WPA, encryption using TKIP is required. TKIP replaces WEP with a new encryption algorithm that is stronger than the WEP algorithm, yet can be performed using the calculation facilities present on existing wireless hardware.

TKIP also provides for the following:

- The verification of the security configuration after the encryption keys are determined.

- The synchronized changing of the unicast encryption key for each frame.

- The determination of a unique starting unicast encryption key for each pre-shared key authentication.

AES   WPA defines the use of the Advanced Encryption Standard (AES) as an optional replacement for WEP encryption. Because adding AES support through a firmware update might not be possible for existing wireless equipment, support for AES on wireless network adapters and wireless APs is not required.

Data Integrity

With 802.11 and WEP, data integrity is provided by a 32-bit ICV that is appended to the 802.11 payload and encrypted with WEP. Although the ICV is encrypted, it is possible through cryptanalysis to change bits in the encrypted payload and update the encrypted ICV without being detected by the receiver.

With WPA, a new method known as *Michael* specifies a new algorithm that calculates an 8-byte message integrity code (MIC) with the calculation facilities available on existing wireless hardware. The MIC is placed between the data portion of the 802.11 frame and the 4-byte ICV. The MIC field is encrypted along with the frame data and the ICV.

Michael also provides replay protection through the use of a new frame counter field in the 802.11 MAC header.

Required Software Changes for WPA Support

WPA requires software changes to the following:

- Wireless APs

- Wireless network adapters

- Wireless client software

Wireless Access Points

Wireless APs must have their firmware updated to support the following:

- New WPA information element

  Information elements are included in the 802.11 beacon frames to advertise the wireless APs' capabilities, such as supported bit rates and security options. To advertise their capability to perform WPA, wireless APs send beacon frames with a new 802.11 WPA information element that contains the wireless AP's WPA capabilities.

- WPA two-phase authentication: Open system followed by 802.1X (EAP with RADIUS or WPA pre-shared key)

- TKIP

- Michael

- AES (optional)

To upgrade your wireless APs to support WPA, obtain a WPA firmware update from your wireless AP vendor and upload it to your wireless APs.

Wireless Network Adapters

Wireless network adapters must have their firmware updated to support the following:

- New WPA information element

  Wireless clients must be able to process the WPA information element in beacon frames and respond with a specific security configuration.

- WPA two-phase authentication: Open system followed by 802.1X (EAP or WPA pre-shared key)

- TKIP

- Michael

- AES (optional)

To upgrade your wireless network adapters to support WPA, you might have to upload a WPA firmware update to your wireless network adapter.

For Windows wireless clients, you must obtain an updated network adapter driver that supports WPA. For wireless network adapter drivers that are compatible with Windows XP (SP1 and later) and Windows Server 2003, the updated network adapter driver must be able to pass the adapter's WPA capabilities and security configuration to the Wireless Zero Configuration (WZC) service.

Microsoft has worked with many wireless vendors to embed the WPA firmware update within the updated wireless adapter driver. Because of this, updating your

Windows wireless client consists of simply obtaining the new WPA-compatible driver and installing it. The firmware is automatically updated when the wireless network adapter driver is loaded into Windows.

Wireless Clients

Wireless client software must be updated to allow for the configuration of WPA authentication (including pre-shared key) and the new WPA encryption algorithms (TKIP and AES).

You must obtain and install a new WPA-compliant configuration tool from your wireless network adapter vendor for wireless clients running the following:

- Windows 2000

- Windows XP (SP1 and later) and Windows Server 2003, and using a wireless network adapter that does not support the WZC service

For wireless clients running Windows XP (SP1 and later) and Windows Server 2003, and using a wireless network adapter that supports the WZC service, you must install the WPA Wireless Security Update in Windows XP—a free download from Microsoft. The WPA Wireless Security Update in Windows XP enhances the wireless network configuration dialog boxes to support new WPA options. To download the WPA Wireless Security Update in Windows XP, go to *http://support.microsoft.com /?kbid=815485.*

> **More Info**   For additional information about how to configure WPA encryption and authentication options for a Windows wireless client, see Chapter 3, "Windows Wireless Client Support."

Supporting a Mixed Environment

To support the gradual transition of a WEP-based wireless network to WPA, it is possible for a wireless AP to support both WEP and WPA clients at the same time. During the association, the wireless AP determines which clients are using WEP and which are using WPA. The disadvantage of supporting a mixture of WEP and WPA clients is that the multicast/global encryption key is not dynamic. All other security enhancements for WPA clients are preserved.

Recommended Security Configurations

The following are the recommended combinations of encryption and authentication for secure wireless networking in an organization:

- WEP and EAP-TLS

- WEP and PEAP-MS-CHAP v2

- WPA/TKIP and EAP-TLS

- WPA/TKIP and PEAP-MS-CHAP v2

More Info For more information about deploying these security configurations for an organization intranet, see Chapter 8, "Intranet Wireless Deployment Using EAP-TLS," and Chapter 10, "Intranet Wireless Deployment Using PEAP-MS-CHAP v2."

For the SOHO wireless network without a RADIUS server, the following combinations of encryption and authentication are recommended:

- WEP with a static WEP key and open system authentication
- WPA/TKIP and WPA with pre-shared key

More Info For more information about deploying these security configurations for a small business or home, see Chapter 12.

Attacks on Wireless Networks

Wireless networks are vulnerable to various types of attacks. The following describes the different types of attacks and how to mitigate them:

- **Association attack** Occurs when an attacker attempts to use up all the available ports on a wireless AP. When all the ports are used up, the wireless AP denies association requests from legitimate wireless clients, which is a denial of service (DoS) attack on a wireless AP. Because the attacking wireless node must first authenticate, SOHO wireless networks with open system authentication are the most vulnerable to association attacks. The best defense against association attacks is to either deploy your wireless APs so the coverage areas do not extend outside buildings, or configure your wireless APs to quickly abandon associations that have not been authenticated.

- **WEP key determination attack** Occurs when an attacker captures encrypted text or the shared key authentication exchange and uses cryptanalysis to determine the WEP encryption key. The best way to mitigate WEP key determination attacks is to use 802.1X and either EAP-TLS or PEAP-MS-CHAP v2 for per-authentication unicast encryption keys. Change the encryption key periodically from the client by reauthenticating, or (from the wireless AP side) by configuring the wireless AP to change the encryption key. Alternately, upgrade your wireless network components to use WPA.

- **WEP bit flipping attack** Occurs when an attacker intercepts a wireless frame, changes bits in the frame, updates the encrypted ICV in the frame, and sends it as the original wireless node. This attack is possible with WEP encryption. To prevent WEP bit flipping attacks, upgrade your wireless network to use WPA.

Summary

This chapter described the requirements for security on wireless networks in terms of authentication, data confidentiality (encryption), and data integrity. The original 802.11 standard defined two types of authentication (open system and shared key) and WEP, which provides encryption and data integrity. The security methods used by the original 802.11 standard proved to be relatively weak and did not scale for large wireless networks. The 802.1X standard was adapted for 802.11 wireless networks to provide much stronger authentication and automated encryption key management. WPA, a software upgrade for wireless equipment, replaces WEP encryption with TKIP and WEP data integrity with Michael. Using 802.1X, WPA, or both can mitigate the most common attacks against wireless networks.

Chapter 3
Windows Wireless Client Support

Current versions of Microsoft Windows have extensive support for IEEE 802.11 wireless LANs. This chapter describes that support in detail and the wireless network configuration dialog boxes that are used to configure IEEE 802.11 and 802.1X settings for the following Windows operating systems:

- Windows XP (prior to Service Pack 1 [SP1])
- Windows XP (SP1 and later) and Windows Server 2003
- Windows 2000

Windows XP (Prior to SP1)

Unlike previous Windows versions, Windows XP includes built-in support for IEEE 802.11 wireless LAN networking with the following features:

- Wireless network adapter support
- Roaming
- Wireless Zero Configuration service
- IEEE 802.1X authentication
- Wireless network configuration user interface

Wireless Network Adapter Support

For Windows XP, Microsoft partnered with 802.11 network adapter vendors to improve the configuration and connection experience by automating the process of configuring the network adapter to associate with an available network, which is done by the Wireless Zero Configuration (WZC) service (described in detail later in this chapter). To support the WZC service, wireless network adapter drivers had to be updated for Windows XP.

The wireless network adapter and its Network Driver Interface Specification (NDIS) driver must support additional NDIS facilities that are used to query and set device and driver behavior. The wireless network adapter scans for available wireless networks and passes the network names (also known as Service Set Identifiers [SSIDs]) to the WZC service.

Roaming Support

The media sense feature originally included in Windows 2000 was enhanced in Windows XP to detect when the wireless client moves within range of a new wireless access point (AP). This process forces a new authentication with the new wireless AP. Along with reauthentication, a Windows XP wireless client also performs a DHCP renewal of the IP address configuration for the wireless network adapter. Within the same Extended Service Set (ESS)—a subnet—the IP address configuration does not change. When the Windows XP wireless client crosses an ESS boundary to a new subnet, the DHCP renewal obtains a new IP address and configuration relevant for that subnet.

Through Windows sockets extensions, network-aware applications are notified of changes in network connectivity and can update their behavior based on these changes.

Wireless Zero Configuration Service

The Wireless Zero Configuration (WZC) service dynamically selects the wireless network to which a connection is attempted, based either on configured preferences or default settings. This process includes automatically selecting and connecting to a more preferred wireless network when it becomes available. If none of the preferred wireless networks is found nearby, the WZC service configures the wireless adapter so that there is no accidental connection until the wireless client roams within the range of a preferred network.

You can use the Services snap-in (available in the Administrative Tools folder) to view the current status of (as well as stop, start, and restart) the WZC service. You can also manage the WZC service from the command prompt by using the Net command. For example, to stop the WZC service, type **net stop "Wireless Zero Configuration"** at a command prompt.

Note The WZC service in Windows Server 2003 is named the *Wireless Configuration service*.

How the WZC Service Works

The WZC service minimizes the configuration that is required to access wireless networks and allows you to travel to different wireless networks without reconfiguring the network connection settings on your computer for each location. For the initial scan of available wireless networks, the WZC service performs the following process:

1. The WZC service attempts to connect to the preferred networks that appear in the list of available networks in the preferred networks preference order.

2. If there are no successful connections, the WZC service attempts to connect to the preferred networks that do not appear in the list of available networks in the preferred networks preference order. Thus, it can connect even when the wireless APs are configured to suppress the beaconing of the SSID of the wireless network.

3. If there are no successful connections and there is an ad hoc network in the list of preferred networks that is available, the WZC service tries to connect to it.

4. If there are no successful connections, and there is an ad hoc network in the list of preferred networks that is not available, the WZC service configures the wireless network adapter to act as the first node in the ad hoc network.

5. If there are no successful connections to preferred networks, and there are no ad hoc networks in the list of preferred networks, the WZC service determines the Automatically Connect To Non-Preferred Networks setting (located on the Wireless Networks tab of the wireless network connection).

6. If the Automatically Connect To Non-Preferred Networks setting is disabled, the WZC service creates a random network name and places the wireless network adapter in infrastructure mode.

   This behavior prevents the Windows XP wireless client from accidentally connecting to a wireless network that does not appear in the list of preferred networks. You then see the One Or More Wireless Networks Are Available message in the notification area. The wireless adapter is not connected to any wireless network, but continues to scan for preferred wireless networks every 60 seconds.

7. If the Automatically Connect To Non-Preferred Networks setting is enabled, the WZC service attempts to connect to the available networks in the order in which the wireless adapter sensed them.

   If all connection attempts fail, the WZC service creates a random network name and places the wireless network adapter in infrastructure mode. You then see the One Or More Wireless Networks Are Available message in the notification area.

For subsequent scans, the WZC service determines whether there are any changes in the wireless environment that require switching the connection. If the Windows XP wireless client is already connected to a wireless network and there is no other preferred network higher in the preference list that has not been attempted already, the WZC service maintains the existing connection. If the Windows XP wireless client is already connected to a wireless network, but a more preferred wireless network becomes available, the WZC service disconnects from the currently connected wireless network and attempts to connect to the more preferred wireless network.

The operation of the WZC service provides the following:

- The first time a wireless adapter is added to a computer running Windows XP and a wireless network is available, the WZC service prompts you with the One Or More Wireless Networks Are Available message in the notification area, which leads you to select a wireless network in the Connect To Wireless Network dialog box.

  After you select a wireless network and the connection is successful, the selected network is automatically added as a preferred network, and you are no longer prompted with the One Or More Wireless Networks Are Available message whenever you are within range of it.

  For an organization, this is the typical process for configuring the initial connection to a private wireless network. After the initial configuration, the WZC service connects (and then maintains the connection) to the organization's wireless network.

  When you take your laptop computer to your home wireless network, to an airport, or to another location with public wireless access, the WZC service first attempts to connect to your preferred network. When that connection attempt fails, you are prompted again with the One Or More Wireless Networks Are Available message to connect to your home wireless network or to the public access wireless network.

- If there are two preferred wireless networks, and the most preferred one is not initially available, the WZC service configures a wireless connection to the next most preferred network. When the most preferred network eventually becomes available, the WZC service automatically switches the wireless client connection to it after the next scan.

- If there are no preferred networks in the list of those available, the WZC service attempts to configure connections to the preferred networks in their configured order, in case the wireless APs for the wireless network are configured to prohibit the beaconing of their SSID.

IEEE 802.1X Authentication

Windows XP supports IEEE 802.1X authentication by using the Extensible Authentication Protocol-Transport Level Security (EAP-TLS, enabled by default) or EAP-Message Digest 5-Challenge Handshake Authentication Protocol (EAP-MD5-CHAP) authentication method for all LAN-based network adapters, including Ethernet and wireless.

More Info For more information about 802.1X authentication, see Chapter 2, "Wireless Security." For more information about EAP, see Chapter 5, "EAP."

Wireless Network Configuration User Interface

The wireless network configuration user interface for Windows XP consists of the following, discussed in the following sections:

- Notification area of the desktop
- Connect To Wireless Network dialog box
- Wireless Networks tab from the properties of a wireless connection
- Advanced dialog box from the Wireless Networks tab
- Windows Network Properties dialog box
- Authentication tab from the properties of a wireless connection

Notification Area of the Desktop

If there is a condition that requires either user notification or intervention, the WZC service prompts you with a message in the notification area of your desktop. Typical messages tell you that a wireless network is unavailable, authentication has failed, or you need to select the correct wireless network from a list of wireless networks that were discovered.

Figure 3-1 shows an example of a notification area message to the user.

Figure 3-1. *Example of use of the notification area of the desktop.*

Connect to Wireless Network Dialog Box

When the WZC service determines that you must select from a list of available networks, it prompts you with the One Or More Wireless Networks Are Available message, as shown in Figure 3-1. When you click the message, the Connect To Wireless Network dialog box displays, enabling you to select an available network with which to attempt a connection. When the WZC service successfully connects to the selected network for the first time, it is automatically added to the top of the list of preferred networks, grouped by type of network (infrastructure or ad hoc mode).

You can also access the Connect To Wireless Network dialog box by doing one of the following:

- Right-click the network icon in the notification area that corresponds to the wireless connection and then click View Available Wireless Networks.

- Right-click the wireless connection in Network Connections and then click View Available Wireless Networks.

Figure 3-2 shows the Connect To Wireless Network dialog box. (The settings shown in the following screen shots reflect the default settings unless otherwise noted.)

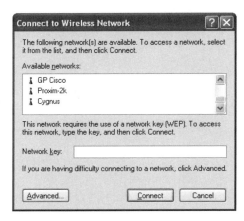

Figure 3-2. *The Connect To Wireless Network dialog box.*

From the Connect To Wireless Network dialog box, you can view and configure the following:

- **Available Networks**   This option allows you to select from a list of available networks discovered in the latest scan of the wireless network adapter.

- **Network Key**   This option allows you to type the Wired Equivalent Privacy (WEP) key used for either shared key authentication or the WEP encryption key. If you are using EAP-TLS authentication, the WEP encryption key is automatically determined. If you type a network key, it is automatically configured in the settings of the wireless network.

More Info   For more information about WEP and shared key authentication, see Chapter 2.

- **Advanced**   This option displays the Wireless Networks tab for the wireless network adapter, from which you can create a customized configuration of wireless networks.

- **Connect**   This option attempts to connect and authenticate to the wireless network selected in Available Networks.

Wireless Networks Tab from the Properties of a Wireless Connection

If the wireless network adapter driver supports the WZC service, there is a Wireless Networks tab from the properties of a connection in the Network Connections folder that corresponds to an installed wireless adapter.

Figure 3-3 shows the Wireless Networks tab.

Figure 3-3. *The Wireless Networks tab.*

On the Wireless Networks tab, you can view and configure the following:

- **Use Windows To Configure My Wireless Network Settings**   This option specifies whether you want to use the WZC service to automatically configure your wireless settings. If you have third-party wireless configuration software that you want to use, clear this check box.

- **Available Networks**   This option displays the list of wireless networks that are within range of your wireless network adapter. To view or change the configuration of a specific wireless network and add it to the list of preferred networks, click it in the list of available networks and then click Configure. To force the wireless adapter to initiate a new scan of wireless networks, click Refresh.

- **Preferred Networks** This option displays the list, by order of preference, of wireless networks with which the wireless client will attempt to connect and authenticate. To add a new wireless network that does not appear in the Available Networks list, click Add. To remove a wireless network, click Remove. To configure the settings of a selected preferred network, click Properties.

- **Advanced** This option configures advanced wireless settings that are independent of the wireless networks to which you are connecting.

Advanced Dialog Box from the Wireless Networks Tab

Figure 3-4 shows the Advanced dialog box.

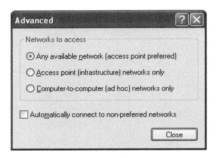

Figure 3-4. *The Advanced dialog box.*

In the Advanced dialog box, you can configure the following:

- **Networks To Access** This option specifies the different types of networks that the Windows XP wireless client accesses. To attempt to connect to wireless LAN networks that are operating in either ad hoc or infrastructure mode (preferring infrastructure mode), select Any Available Network. To limit attempts to connect to wireless LAN networks that are operating only in infrastructure mode, select Access Point. To limit attempts to connect to wireless LAN networks that are operating only in ad hoc mode, select Computer-To-Computer.

- **Automatically Connect To Non-Preferred Networks** This option specifies whether connection attempts are made to any wireless network within range, regardless of whether they are listed in the Preferred Networks list.

Wireless Network Properties Dialog Box

Figure 3-5 shows the Wireless Network Properties dialog box.

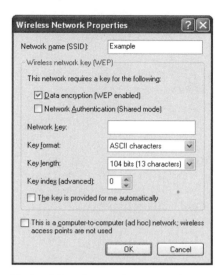

Figure 3-5. *The Wireless Network Properties dialog box.*

In the Wireless Network Properties dialog box, you can view and configure the following:

- **Network Name (SSID)**   This option displays or allows you to type the wireless LAN network name, also known as the SSID. The network name is sent out with beacon frames by wireless APs unless SSID suppression is enabled, and is automatically learned by wireless clients during the wireless client scanning process.

- **Data Encryption (WEP Enabled)**   This option specifies whether WEP is enabled for this wireless LAN network. When you add a new wireless network, this setting is disabled by default.

- **Network Authentication (Shared Mode)**   This option specifies whether IEEE 802.11 shared key authentication is used to authenticate the wireless client. If disabled, open system authentication is used.

Note   This setting does not affect IEEE 802.1X authentication, which is configured on the Authentication tab. For more information about shared key and open system authentication, see Chapter 2.

- **Network Key**   This option provides a space to type a manually configured network key that is used for WEP. Typical implementations use the same key for shared key authentication and for WEP encryption.

- **Key Format**   This option allows you to select the format for the network key (ASCII characters or hexadecimal digits).

- **Key Length** This option allows you to select the size of the network key (40 bits or 104 bits).

- **Key Index (Advanced)** This option allows you to specify the encryption key index values, identifying the location in which the key is stored. Historically, IEEE 802.11 allowed for four different keys to be stored on wireless network adapters and wireless APs. The encryption key index is an offset that is used to specify a single key when four keys are used. You can select values from 0 to 3.

- **The Key Is Provided for Me Automatically** This option specifies whether a WEP key is provided through some means other than manual configuration, such as a key provided on the wireless network adapter or through IEEE 802.1X authentication. If you disable this setting, you cannot perform 802.1X authentication. When you add a new wireless network, this setting is enabled by default.

- **This Is A Computer-To-Computer (Ad Hoc) Network; Wireless Access Points Are Not Used** This option specifies whether this wireless LAN network is operating in ad hoc mode. If enabled, the wireless client first attempts to connect to another wireless client in the ad hoc network. If unsuccessful, the wireless client becomes the first wireless client in the ad hoc network.

Authentication Tab from the Properties of a Wireless Connection

The Authentication tab appears for all LAN-based network adapters.

Figure 3-6 shows the Authentication tab.

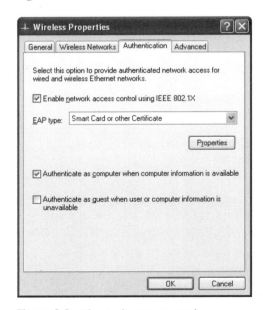

Figure 3-6. *The Authentication tab.*

On the Authentication tab, you can view and configure the following:

- **Enable Network Access Control Using IEEE 802.1X**   This option allows you to use IEEE 802.1X to perform authentication for this connection.

- **EAP Type**   This option lists the EAP types that correspond to EAP DLLs installed on the computer. The default EAP types for Windows XP (prior to SP1) are MD5-Challenge and Smart Card Or Other Certificate. For more information about EAP types, see Chapter 5.

- **Properties**   This button leads to a dialog box in which you can configure the properties of the selected EAP type (not available for the MD5-Challenge EAP type).

- **Authenticate As Computer When Computer Information Is Available**   This option specifies whether the computer will attempt to authenticate using computer credentials (such as a computer certificate) without the user logging on.

- **Authenticate As Guest When User Or Computer Information Is Unavailable**   This option specifies whether the computer will attempt to authenticate as a guest when either user or computer credentials are not available.

Windows XP (SP1 and Later) and Windows Server 2003

Windows XP (SP1 and later) and Windows Server 2003 include all the wireless support provided with Windows XP, with the following enhancements:

- Additional support for Protected EAP (PEAP), with PEAP-Microsoft Challenge Handshake Authentication Protocol version 2 (PEAP-MS-CHAP v2) and PEAP-TLS authentication (for more information, see Chapter 5).

- Improvements for the Smart Card Or Other Certificate dialog box for TLS authentication (for more information, see Chapter 5).

- Additional support for smart cards for EAP-TLS-based wireless authentication.

- Improved user interface for managing wireless networks.

Note   Support for EAP-MD5-CHAP authentication (the MD5-Challenge EAP type) has been removed for wireless networks.

Changes to the Wireless Network Configuration User Interface

The changes to the wireless network configuration user interface include the following, which are described in the following sections:

- Connect to Wireless Networks dialog box

- Properties of a wireless network connection

Connect to Wireless Networks Dialog Box

The dialog box used to connect to an available wireless network has the following changes:

- The title of the dialog box is the name of the wireless connection. For example, if the wireless connection is named Wireless, the dialog box is titled Wireless.

- There is a new Confirm Network Key text box, in which you can retype the manually configured WEP key. The Confirm Network Key text box becomes available only after you type a key in Network Key.

- There is a new Enable 802.1x Authentication For This Network check box.

Figure 3-7 shows the new dialog box to connect to an available network.

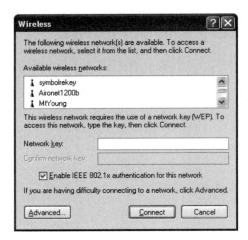

Figure 3-7. *The new dialog box to connect to an available network.*

Properties of a Wireless Network Connection

The most significant changes are for the configuration of the properties of a wireless connection, which include the following:

- The Authentication tab has been removed.

- From the properties of a wireless network on the Wireless Networks tab, there is now an Association tab and an Authentication tab. The Association tab contains the settings that define the properties of the wireless network and how to associate with it. The Association tab is essentially the same as the properties of a wireless network with Windows XP (prior to SP1), with some minor changes. The Authentication tab has been moved from the properties of the wireless network adapter to the properties of each wireless network.

Figure 3-8 shows the new properties for a wireless network connection.

Figure 3-8. *The new properties for a wireless network connection.*

Association Tab   The following are the changes to the settings of a wireless network on the new Association tab:

- There is a new Confirm Network Key text box that provides a space to retype the manually configured WEP key.

- The Key Format and Key Length text boxes have been removed. The key format and length are automatically determined from the typed key.

- The Key Index (Advanced) field has been changed to allow encryption key index values only from 1 to 4. This change was done so that the Windows wireless client encryption key index values match the encryption key index values used by many wireless APs.

Figure 3-9 shows the new Association tab for a wireless network.

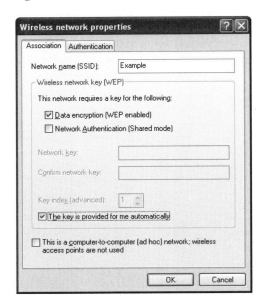

Figure 3-9. *The new Association tab for a wireless network.*

Authentication Tab   The new Authentication tab for a wireless network is functionally the same as the Authentication tab for a wireless network adapter. The only change is in the title of the first check box: Enable Network Access Control Using IEEE 802.1X has been changed to Enable IEEE 802.1x Authentication For This Network. The title change better reflects the change from 802.1X settings for all the wireless networks of the wireless network adapter (as in Windows XP prior to SP1) to 802.1X settings for each individual wireless network of a wireless network adapter.

Figure 3-10 shows the new Authentication tab for a wireless network.

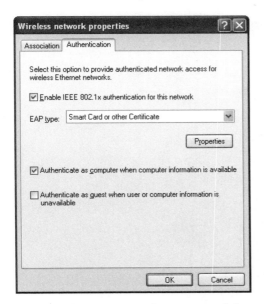

Figure 3-10. *The new Authentication tab for a wireless network.*

Changes to WPA Wireless Security Update

To use the new Wi-Fi Protected Access (WPA) standard for wireless clients running Windows XP (SP1 and later) and Windows Server 2003 that are using a wireless network adapter that supports the WZC service, you must obtain and install the WPA Wireless Security Update in Windows XP—a free download that is available from *http://support.microsoft.com/?kbid=815485*. It updates the wireless network configuration dialog boxes to support new WPA options. WPA is described in the "Wi-Fi Protected Access" section in Chapter 2.

Installing the WPA Wireless Security Update changes the Association tab, as Figure 3-11 shows.

The Wireless Network Key (WEP) section is now named Wireless Network Key, and the Data Encryption (WEP Enabled) and Network Authentication (Shared Mode) check boxes previously described are replaced with drop-down boxes.

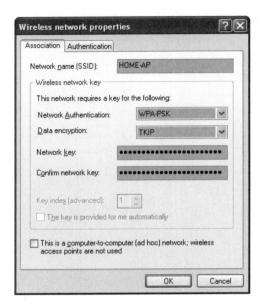

Figure 3-11. *The new Association tab for the WPA Wireless Security Update.*

The Data Encryption (WEP Enabled) check box is replaced with a Data Encryption drop-down box that provides the following selections:

- **Disabled**   Encryption of 802.11 frames is disabled.

- **WEP**   802.11 WEP is used as the encryption algorithm.

- **TKIP**   Temporal Key Integrity Protocol (TKIP) is used as the encryption algorithm.

- **AES**   Advanced Encryption Standard (AES) is used as the encryption algorithm. This selection is available only if the wireless network adapter and its driver support the optional AES encryption algorithm.

Note   If the wireless network adapter and its driver do not support WPA, you do not see the TKIP and AES options.

The Network Authentication (Shared Mode) check box is replaced with a Network Authentication drop-down box that provides the following selections:

- **Open**   The open system authentication method is used.

- **Shared**   The shared key authentication method is used, and the key is typed in Network Key and Confirm Network Key.

- **WPA**   WPA authentication is used with an EAP type configured on the Authentication tab.

- **WPA-PSK**   WPA authentication is used with a pre-shared key, and the key is typed in Network Key and Confirm Network Key.

Note   If the wireless network adapter and its driver do not support WPA, you will not see the WPA and WPA-PSK options.

Windows 2000 Family

The Windows 2000 family of products originally shipped without built-in support for IEEE 802.11 and 802.1X. Additional support for 802.1X authentication for wireless connections for computers running Windows 2000 with SP3 or later is achieved by installing Microsoft 802.1X Authentication Client, a free download available at *http://support.microsoft.com/default.aspx?scid=kb;en-us;313664*, which allows computers running Windows 2000 to use IEEE 802.1X to authenticate network connections (including wireless). Microsoft 802.1X Authentication Client includes support for EAP-TLS, PEAP-MS-CHAP v2, and PEAP-TLS; and for the improved Smart Card Or Other Certificate Properties dialog box described in Chapter 5. However, because Microsoft 802.1X Authentication Client does not include the WZC service, configuration of 802.11 settings for wireless networks must be done using configuration tools provided by the wireless network adapter vendor.

When Microsoft 802.1X Authentication Client is installed, the Wireless Configuration service, which provides IEEE 802.1X support, is configured by default in a disabled state. Use the Services snap-in to set the startup value for the Wireless Configuration service to Automatic and then start the service. After the service is started, an Authentication tab is present on the properties of LAN connections in Dial-up And Network Connections. If the Authentication tab is present but is unavailable, the network adapter driver does not support 802.1X correctly. Contact your wireless network adapter vendor to obtain an updated driver.

The Authentication tab has the same settings as the Authentication tab for Windows XP (prior to SP1), except that Protected EAP (PEAP) is available as an EAP type.

Note   For the Windows 2000 Server family, Microsoft 802.1X Authentication Client also provides support for PEAP authentication (both PEAP-MS-CHAP v2 and PEAP-TLS) for the Internet Authentication Service (IAS)—the Microsoft implementation of a RADIUS server. A computer running a member of the Windows 2000 Server family with SP3 or later, Microsoft 802.1X Authentication Client, and IAS can act as a RADIUS server that performs authentication and authorization for 802.1X-based wireless clients that use EAP-TLS, PEAP-MS-CHAP v2, or PEAP-TLS authentication types.

Figure 3-12 shows the Authentication tab for a wireless network adapter in Windows 2000.

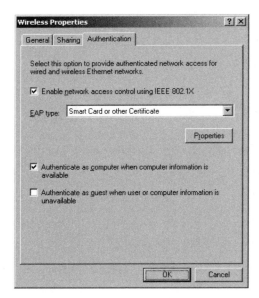

Figure 3-12. *The Authentication tab in Windows 2000.*

To view the authentication status for the wireless connection, position the mouse pointer over the connection icon in the notification area of the desktop.

Microsoft 802.1X Authentication Client supports only one wireless network adapter at a time. Although it is technically possible to have a computer with more than one wireless network adapter installed, Microsoft 802.1X Authentication Client works with only one at a time.

Note At the time of the publication of this book, additional Microsoft 802.1X Authentication Client packages for Windows 98/Windows Millennium Edition and Microsoft Windows NT 4.0 Workstation are available through the Microsoft Premier and Alliance Support organizations only to customers with Premier and Alliance support contracts. For details about obtaining the clients, please contact your Technical Account Manager (TAM). Microsoft 802.1X Authentication Client packages for Windows 98/Windows Millennium Edition and Windows NT 4.0 Workstation are not available for redistribution.

Configuring Windows Wireless Clients

Windows wireless clients can be configured either manually or with Group Policy configuration, as described in the following sections.

Manual Configuration

Manual configuration of Windows wireless clients that support the WZC service—Windows XP and Windows Server 2003 with an appropriate wireless network adapter driver—consists of selecting the correct network in the Connect To Wireless Network dialog box and configuring custom settings on the Wireless Networks tab of the properties of a wireless connection.

For Windows 2000 wireless clients or wireless clients with network adapter drivers that do not support the WZC service, you must configure wireless settings with a configuration tool provided by the wireless network adapter vendor.

Group Policy Configuration

The manual configuration of wireless settings is aided by the WZC service, which provides automatic configuration of wireless settings with three mouse clicks:

1. One click for the One Or More Wireless Networks Are Available message in the notification area.

2. One click to select the wireless network in the Connect To Wireless Network dialog box.

3. One click for the Connect button in the Connect To Wireless Network dialog box.

This is the best-case scenario, in which the default settings for a new preferred wireless network apply, as follows:

- The SSID of the network is determined from the wireless AP beacon.

- WEP encryption is enabled.

- Shared key authentication is disabled.

- The WEP key is determined automatically.

- IEEE 802.1X authentication is enabled using the EAP-TLS authentication method.

If the wireless network does not conform to these settings, the user must manually configure the wireless network settings. Although this might not be a problem in a Small Office/Home Office network with a small number of wireless client computers, leaving the manual configuration of critical wireless settings to the user in a medium to large organization with hundreds or thousands of wireless client computers is a network administration and troubleshooting issue.

To automate the configuration of wireless network settings for Windows XP (SP1 and later) and Windows Server 2003 wireless client computers, Windows Server 2003 Active Directory domains support a new Wireless Network (IEEE 802.11) Policies Group Policy extension that allows you to configure wireless network settings that are part of Computer Configuration Group Policy.

Wireless network settings include the list of preferred networks, WEP settings, and IEEE 802.1X settings. These settings encompass all the items on the Association and Authentication tab of the properties of a wireless network and additional settings. These settings are downloaded to Windows XP (SP1 and later) and Windows Server 2003 wireless client computers that are members of a Windows Server 2003 Active Directory domain, making it much easier to deploy a specific configuration for secure wireless connections. You can configure wireless policies from the Computer Configuration/Windows Settings/Security Settings/Wireless Network (IEEE 802.11) Policies node in the Group Policy snap-in. Figure 3-13 shows the location of the Wireless Network (IEEE 802.11) Policies node.

Figure 3-13. *The location of the Wireless Network (IEEE 802.11) Policies node.*

Note These policy settings do not apply to Windows XP (prior to SP1) or Microsoft 802.1X Authentication Client wireless clients.

By default, there are no Wireless Network (IEEE 802.11) Policies. To create a new policy, right-click Wireless Network (IEEE 802.11) Policies in the console tree of the Group Policy snap-in and then click Create Wireless Network Policy. The Create Wireless Network Policy Wizard is launched. The main page of the wizard, the Wireless Network Policy Name page, allows you to configure a name and description for the new wireless network. You can create only a single wireless network policy for each Group Policy object.

To modify the settings of the wireless network policy, right-click its name in the details pane and then click Properties. The properties of a wireless network policy consist of a General tab and a Preferred Networks tab.

Figure 3-14 shows the General tab for a wireless network policy.

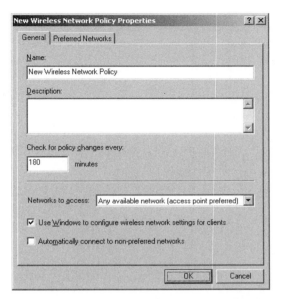

Figure 3-14. *The General tab for a wireless network policy.*

On the General tab, you can view and configure the following:

- **Name**   This option allows you to type a friendly name for the wireless network policy.

- **Description**   This option allows you to type a description for the wireless network policy.

- **Check For Policy Changes Every**   This option allows you to type the interval in minutes after which wireless clients that are Active Directory members check for changes in the wireless network policy.

- **Networks To Access**   This option selects the types of wireless networks with which the wireless client is allowed to create connections:

  - Any Available Network (Access Point Preferred)

  - Access Point (Infrastructure) Networks Only

  - Computer-To-Computer (Ad Hoc) Networks Only

- **Use Windows To Configure Wireless Network Settings for Clients** This option enables the WZC service.

- **Automatically Connect to Non-preferred Networks** This option enables automatic connections to wireless networks that are not configured as preferred networks.

Figure 3-15 shows the Preferred Networks tab for a wireless network policy.

Figure 3-15. *The Preferred Networks tab for a wireless network policy.*

On the Preferred Networks tab, you can view and configure the following:

- **Networks** This option displays the list of preferred wireless networks.

- **Add/Edit/Remove** These buttons create a new preferred wireless network, modify the settings of the selected preferred wireless network, and delete the selected preferred wireless network.

- **Move Up/Move Down** These buttons move the selected preferred wireless network up or down in the Networks list.

The properties of a preferred wireless network consist of a Network Properties tab and an IEEE 802.1x tab.

Figure 3-16 shows the Network Properties tab for a preferred wireless network.

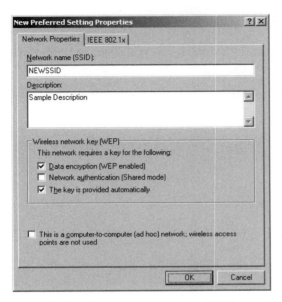

Figure 3-16. *The Network Properties tab for a preferred wireless network.*

On the Network Properties tab, you can view and configure the following settings (which are equivalent to the settings of a wireless network for a Windows wireless client that supports the WZC service):

- Network Name (SSID)

- Data Encryption (WEP Enabled)

- Network Authentication (Shared Mode)

- The Key Is Provided Automatically

- This Is A Computer-to-Computer (Ad Hoc) Network; Wireless Access Points Are Not Used

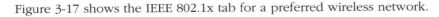

Note   Microsoft is investigating the inclusion of an update to the Network Properties tab in Windows Server 2003 SP1 that includes configuration options for WPA authentication and encryption settings. An example of the final Network Properties tab was not available at the time of the printing of this book. Microsoft is also investigating the inclusion of an update in Windows XP SP2 so that the new WPA encryption and authentication settings in the Wireless Network (IEEE 802.11) Policies Group Policy extension are recognized and configured.

Figure 3-17 shows the IEEE 802.1x tab for a preferred wireless network.

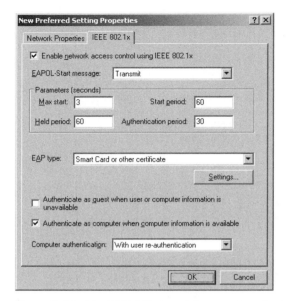

Figure 3-17. *The IEEE 802.1x tab for a preferred wireless network.*

On the IEEE 802.1x tab, you can view and configure the following settings (which are equivalent to the authentication settings of a Windows wireless client):

- Enable Network Access Control Using IEEE 802.1x

- EAP Type and Settings

- Authenticate As Guest When User Or Computer Information Is Unavailable

- Authenticate As Computer When Computer Information Is Available

The following are additional settings on the IEEE 802.1x tab that do not appear on authentication settings of a Windows wireless client:

- **EAPOL-Start Message** This option allows you to specify the transmission behavior of the EAPOL-Start message when authenticating. You can select from the following:

  - Do Not Transmit

  - Transmit

  - Transmit Per 802.1x

- **Max Start** This option allows you to specify the number of successive EAPOL-Start messages that are sent out when no response is received to the initial EAPOL-Start messages.

- **Start Period**   This option allows you to specify the interval, in seconds, between the retransmission of EAPOL-Start messages when no response is received to the previously sent EAPOL-Start message.

- **Held Period**   This option allows you to specify the period, in seconds, for which the authenticating client will not perform any 802.1X authentication activity after it has received an authentication failure indication from the authenticator.

- **Authentication Period**   This option allows you to specify the interval, in seconds, for which the authenticating client will wait before retransmitting any 802.1X requests after end-to-end 802.1X authentication has been initiated.

- **Computer Authentication**   This option allows you to specify how computer authentication works with user authentication. There are three possible settings:

  - **With User Authentication**   When users are not logged on to the computer, authentication is performed using the computer credentials. After a user logs on to the computer, authentication is maintained using the computer credentials. If a user travels to a new wireless access point, authentication is performed using the user credentials.

  - **With User Re-Authentication**   When users are not logged on to the computer, authentication is performed using the computer credentials. After a user logs on to the computer, authentication is performed using the user credentials. When a user logs off of the computer, authentication is performed with the computer credentials. This is the recommended setting because it ensures that the connection to the wireless AP is always using the security credentials of the computer's current security context (computer credentials when no user is logged on and user credentials when a user is logged on).

  - **Computer Only**   Authentication is always performed using the computer credentials. User authentication is never performed.

Summary

Windows XP and Windows Server 2003 include built-in support for the IEEE 802.11 and 802.1X standards. Windows 2000 SP3 and higher support the 802.1X standard with Microsoft 802.1X Authentication Client. With the WZC service, most of the configuration is automatic. Configuration of Windows XP (SP1 and later) and Windows Server 2003 wireless clients can be further automated through the use of the Wireless Network (IEEE 802.11) Policies Group Policy extension.

Chapter 4
RADIUS, IAS, and Active Directory

The authentication infrastructure for wireless connections consists of a set of Remote Authentication Dial-In User Service (RADIUS) components and account databases. In a Microsoft Windows environment, you use Internet Authentication Service (IAS) as a RADIUS server or proxy. IAS uses remote access policies and account properties to determine authorization and connection constraints and connection request policies to determine its role as a RADIUS server or proxy. IAS is integrated with the Active Directory directory service and can leverage Active Directory accounts, domains, and groups.

This chapter provides a detailed discussion of RADIUS, an overview of IAS in Windows 2000 Server and Windows Server 2003 (complete with examples of all configuration dialog boxes), and a brief discussion of Active Directory users and groups.

RADIUS

RADIUS is a widely deployed protocol enabling centralized authentication, authorization, and accounting for network access.

Originally developed for dial-up remote access, RADIUS is now supported by wireless access points (APs), authenticating Ethernet switches, virtual private network (VPN) servers, Digital Subscriber Line (DSL) access servers, and other types of network access servers.

> **More Info** RADIUS is described in RFC 2865, "Remote Authentication Dial-In User Service (RADIUS)," and RFC 2866, "RADIUS Accounting."

Components of a RADIUS Infrastructure

A RADIUS authentication, authorization, and accounting infrastructure consists of the following components:

- Access clients
- Access servers (RADIUS clients)
- RADIUS servers
- User account databases
- RADIUS proxies

These components are shown in Figure 4-1.

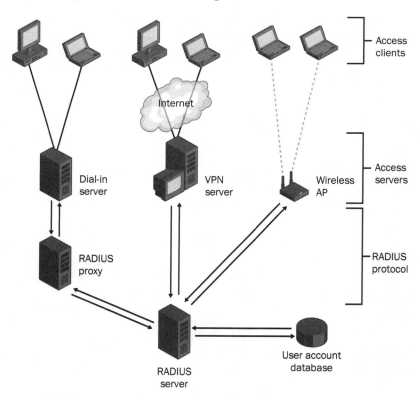

Figure 4-1. *The components of a RADIUS infrastructure.*

These components are described in detail in the following sections.

Access Clients

An *access client* requires access to a network or another part of the network. Examples of access clients are dial-up or VPN remote access clients, wireless clients, or LAN clients connected to a switch.

Access Servers

An *access server* provides access to a network. An access server using a RADIUS infrastructure is also a RADIUS client, sending connection requests and accounting messages to a RADIUS server. Examples of access servers are the following:

- Wireless APs that provide physical layer access to an organization's network by using wireless-based transmission and reception technologies.

- Switches that provide physical layer access to an organization's network by using traditional LAN technologies such as Ethernet.

- Network access servers (NASs) that provide remote access connectivity to an organization's network or the Internet. An example is a computer running Windows Server 2003 or Windows 2000 Server and the Routing and Remote Access service and providing either traditional dial-up or VPN-based remote access to an organization's intranet.

RADIUS Servers

A *RADIUS server* receives and processes connection requests or accounting messages sent by RADIUS clients or RADIUS proxies. During a connection request, the RADIUS server processes the list of RADIUS attributes in the connection request. Based on a set of rules and the information in the user account database, the RADIUS server either authenticates and authorizes the connection and sends back an Access-Accept message or sends back an Access-Reject message. The Access-Accept message can contain connection restrictions that are enforced by the access server for the duration of the connection.

Note   The IAS component of Windows 2000 Server and Windows Server 2003 is an industry standard–compliant RADIUS server.

User Account Databases

A *user account database* is a list of user accounts and their properties that can be checked by a RADIUS server to verify authentication credentials and obtain user account properties containing authorization and connection parameter information.

The user account databases that IAS can use are the local Security Accounts Manager (SAM), a Microsoft Windows NT 4.0 domain, or Active Directory. For Active Directory, IAS can provide authentication and authorization for user or computer accounts in the domain in which the IAS server is a member; two-way trusted domains; and trusted forests with domain controllers running a member of the Windows 2000 Server or Windows Server 2003 families.

If the user accounts for authentication reside in a different type of database, you can use a RADIUS proxy to forward the authentication request to a RADIUS server that does have access to the user account database.

RADIUS Proxies

A *RADIUS proxy* routes RADIUS connection requests and accounting messages between RADIUS clients (and RADIUS proxies) and RADIUS servers (and RADIUS proxies). The RADIUS proxy uses information within the RADIUS message to route the RADIUS message to the appropriate RADIUS client or server.

A RADIUS proxy can be used as a forwarding point for RADIUS messages when the authentication, authorization, and accounting must occur at multiple RADIUS servers in different organizations.

With the RADIUS proxy, the definition of "RADIUS client" and "RADIUS server" becomes blurred. A RADIUS client to a RADIUS proxy can be an access server (that originates connection requests or accounting messages) or another RADIUS proxy (in a chained proxy configuration). There can be multiple RADIUS proxies between the originating RADIUS client and the final RADIUS server using chained RADIUS proxies. In a similar way, a RADIUS server to a RADIUS proxy can be the final RADIUS server (to which the RADIUS message is ultimately destined) or another RADIUS proxy. Therefore, when referring to RADIUS clients and servers from a RADIUS proxy perspective, a RADIUS client is the RADIUS entity from which it receives RADIUS request messages, and a RADIUS server is the RADIUS entity to which it forwards RADIUS request messages.

Note The IAS component of Windows Server 2003 is an industry standard–compliant RADIUS proxy.

RADIUS Messages

RADIUS messages are sent as User Datagram Protocol (UDP) messages. UDP port 1812 is used for RADIUS authentication messages, and UDP port 1813 is used for RADIUS accounting messages. Some older access servers might use UDP port 1645 for RADIUS authentication messages and UDP port 1646 for RADIUS accounting messages. Only one RADIUS message is included in the UDP payload of a RADIUS packet.

A RADIUS message consists of a RADIUS header and RADIUS attributes. Each RADIUS attribute contains a specific item of information about the connection. For example, there are RADIUS attributes for the username, the user password, the type of service requested by the user, and the IP address of the access server.

RADIUS attributes are used to convey information between RADIUS clients, RADIUS proxies, and RADIUS servers. For example, the list of attributes in the Access-Request message includes information about the user credentials and the parameters of the connection attempt. In contrast, the list of attributes in the Access-Accept message includes information about the type of connection that can be made, connection constraints, and any vendor-specific attributes (VSAs).

More Info   RADIUS attributes are described in RFCs 2865, 2866, 2867, 2868, 2869, and 3162. RFCs and Internet drafts for VSAs define additional RADIUS attributes.

RFCs 2865 and 2866 define the following RADIUS message types:

- **Access-Request**   Sent by a RADIUS client to request authentication and authorization for a network access connection attempt.

- **Access-Accept**   Sent by a RADIUS server in response to an Access-Request message. This message informs the RADIUS client that the connection attempt is authenticated and authorized.

- **Access-Reject**   Sent by a RADIUS server in response to an Access-Request message. This message informs the RADIUS client that the connection attempt is rejected. A RADIUS server sends this message if either the credentials are not authentic or the connection attempt is not authorized.

- **Access-Challenge**   Sent by a RADIUS server in response to an Access-Request message. This message is a challenge to the RADIUS client that requires a response. This challenge helps to verify the identity of the client.

- **Accounting-Request**   Sent by a RADIUS client to specify accounting information for a connection that was accepted.

- **Accounting-Response**   Sent by the RADIUS server in response to the Accounting-Request message. This message acknowledges the successful receipt and processing of the Accounting-Request message.

For Point-to-Point Protocol (PPP) authentication protocols such as Password Authentication Protocol (PAP), Challenge Handshake Authentication Protocol (CHAP), Microsoft Challenge Handshake Authentication Protocol (MS-CHAP), and MS-CHAP version 2 (MS-CHAPv2), the results of the authentication negotiation between the access server and the access client are forwarded to the RADIUS server for verification in the Access-Request message.

For Extensible Authentication Protocol (EAP) authentication, the negotiation occurs between the RADIUS server and the access client. The RADIUS server uses Access-Challenge messages to send EAP messages to the access client. The access server forwards EAP messages sent by the access client to the RADIUS server as Access-Request messages. For more information, see Chapter 5, "EAP"

RADIUS Authentication, Authorization, and Accounting Processes

Authentication, authorization, and accounting of network access connections use RADIUS messages in the following way:

1. Access servers, such as dial-up network access servers, VPN servers, and wireless APs, receive connection requests from access clients.

2. The access server, configured to use RADIUS as the authentication, authorization, and accounting protocol, creates an Access-Request message and sends it to the RADIUS server.

3. The RADIUS server evaluates the Access-Request message.

4. If required (for example, when the authentication protocol is EAP), the RADIUS server sends an Access-Challenge message to the access server. The response to the challenge is sent as a new Access-Request to the RADIUS server.

5. The user credentials and the authorization of the connection attempt are verified.

6. If the connection attempt is both authenticated and authorized, the RADIUS server sends an Access-Accept message to the access server.

   If the connection attempt is either not authenticated or not authorized, the RADIUS server sends an Access-Reject message to the access server.

7. Upon receipt of the Access-Accept message, the access server completes the connection process with the access client and sends an Accounting-Request message to the RADIUS server.

8. After the Accounting-Request message is processed, the RADIUS server sends an Accounting-Response message.

More Info   For a detailed description of the RADIUS authentication process for wireless access, see Chapter 5.

Securing RADIUS Traffic

RADIUS traffic, like any other network traffic, is susceptible to interception and analysis. To provide the best security for your RADIUS traffic, you should use the following:

- Strong shared secrets

- Message-Authenticator attribute

- Internet Protocol security (IPSec)

Using Strong Shared Secrets

To provide security for RADIUS messages, the RADIUS client and the RADIUS server are configured with a common shared secret. The shared secret is used to authenticate RADIUS messages (by using the Authenticator field in the RADIUS header of RADIUS response messages) and to encrypt sensitive RADIUS attributes. The shared secret is commonly configured as a text string on both the RADIUS client and server.

In many RADIUS installations, the same shared secret is used to protect many RADIUS client-server pairs, and the RADIUS shared secret does not have sufficient randomness (or *information entropy*) to prevent a successful offline dictionary attack. For a guess of the RADIUS shared secret, the value of the Authenticator field in the RADIUS response message is easily computed. These results are compared to the values contained within a captured Access-Accept, Access-Reject, or Access-Challenge message.

Creating a Strong Shared Secret

A simple RADIUS shared secret can be easily compromised, so it is important to create strong shared secrets. If the shared secret must be a sequence of keyboard characters, it should be at least 22 characters long and consist of a random sequence of upper- and lowercase letters, numbers, and punctuation. If the shared secret can be configured as a sequence of hexadecimal digits, use at least 32 random hexadecimal digits.

RFC 2865 recommends shared secrets be at least 16 characters long, but for a total of 128 bits of information entropy, each character must contain a full 8 bits of information entropy. If the shared secret is limited to keyboard characters (as opposed to hexadecimal digits), each character has only 5.8 bits of information entropy. To provide 128 bits of information entropy, the RADIUS client, server, or proxy should allow the configuration of shared secrets at least 22 keyboard characters long. For example, shared secrets for Windows 2000 Server IAS and Windows Server 2003 IAS can be up to 128 keyboard characters long.

To ensure a random shared secret, use a computer program to generate a random sequence at least 22 characters long and use as many different shared secrets as you can.

Using the Message-Authenticator Attribute

By default, there is no cryptographic verification of the incoming Access-Request message by the RADIUS server. The RADIUS server verifies that the message originated from an Internet Protocol (IP) address for a configured RADIUS client, but source IP addresses for RADIUS messages can be easily spoofed and therefore provide little assurance that the incoming request is genuine or has not been altered.

The solution is for the RADIUS server to require the Message-Authenticator attribute in all Access-Request messages. The Message-Authenticator attribute is the keyed Message Digest 5 (MD5) hash of the entire Access-Request message using the shared secret as the key. The access server must send Access-Request messages with the Message-Authenticator attribute, and the RADIUS server must silently discard the message if the Message-Authenticator attribute is either not present or fails verification. Normally, the Message-Authenticator attribute is required only for EAP over RADIUS messages. Requiring the Message-Authenticator attribute for IAS is configured from the properties of a RADIUS client in the Internet Authentication Service snap-in.

Fortunately, for wireless access, EAP is always used and the Message Authenticator attribute is always present in Access-Request messages.

Using IPSec

To provide data confidentiality for the entire RADIUS message, implement IPSec using Encapsulating Security Payload (ESP) and an encryption algorithm such as Triple Data Encryption Standard (3DES). (This technique is described more fully in RFC 3162.) By encrypting the entire RADIUS message with IPSec, sensitive RADIUS fields (such as the Request Authenticator field in the Access-Request message) and attributes (such as User-Password, Tunnel-Password, and the MPPE-Key attributes) are further protected from compromise while traveling over the network.

An attacker must first decrypt the IPSec-protected RADIUS message before they can analyze the RADIUS message contents. Support for certificate-based IPSec authentication is recommended to prevent an attacker from launching online attacks against a RADIUS server.

IAS

IAS in Windows 2000 Server is the Microsoft implementation of a RADIUS server. IAS in Windows Server 2003 is the Microsoft implementation of a RADIUS server and proxy. IAS performs centralized connection authentication, authorization, and accounting for many types of network access, including wireless, authenticating switch, dial-up, virtual private network (VPN) remote access, and site-to-site connections. IAS supports RFCs 2865 and 2866, as well as additional RFCs and Internet drafts that define RADIUS extensions.

IAS enables the use of a heterogeneous set of wireless, switch, remote access, or VPN equipment, and can be used with the Windows 2000 Server or Windows Server 2003 Routing and Remote Access service.

When an IAS server is a member of an Active Directory–based domain, IAS uses Active Directory as its user account database and is part of a single sign-on solution. The same set of credentials is used for network access control (authenticating and authorizing access to a network), to log on to an Active Directory-based domain, and to access secured resources in the domain.

IAS configurations can be created for the following solutions:

- Wireless access

- Organization dial-up or VPN remote access

- Outsourced dial or wireless access

- Internet access

- Authenticated access to extranet resources for business partners

More Info   For detailed information about how to configure IAS for wireless access, see Chapter 8, "Intranet Wireless Deployment Using EAP-TLS," Chapter 10, "Intranet Wireless Deployment Using PEAP-MS-CHAP v2", and Chapter 11, "Additional Intranet Wireless Deployment Configurations."

The following sections describe the global properties of IAS for Windows 2000 Server and Windows Server 2003, regardless of its role as a RADIUS server or RADIUS proxy.

More Info   For more information about how IAS is used for solutions that do not involve wireless access, see Windows 2000 Server Help or Windows Server 2003 Help and Support.

Installing IAS

IAS is not installed by default in Windows Server 2000 and Windows Server 2003. To install IAS, go to Control Panel, choose Add Or Remove Programs, and then Add/Remove Windows Components. In the list of components, select Networking Services and click Details to list the subcomponents of Networking Services, which includes IAS. After IAS is installed, you configure it by using the Internet Authentication Service snap-in, which is available in the Administrative Tools folder.

IAS Configuration Settings for Windows 2000 Server

The global properties of IAS consist of server properties and remote access logging properties. (The settings shown in the following screen shots reflect the default settings, unless otherwise noted.)

Server Properties

To configure the global properties of an IAS server running Windows 2000 Server in the Internet Authentication Service snap-in, right-click Internet Authentication Service and then click Properties.

Service Tab   Figure 4-2 shows the Service tab for IAS in Windows 2000 Server.

Figure 4-2. *The Service tab for IAS in Windows 2000 Server.*

From the Service tab, you can view and configure the following:

- **Description**   Type the name of the server to distinguish it from other IAS servers.

- **Log Rejected Or Discarded Authentication Requests**   Enable or disable the logging of rejected or discarded authentication requests in the Windows 2000 system event log.

- **Log Successful Authentication Requests** Enable or disable the logging of successful authentication requests in the Windows 2000 system event log.

RADIUS Tab Figure 4-3 shows the RADIUS tab for IAS in Windows 2000 Server.

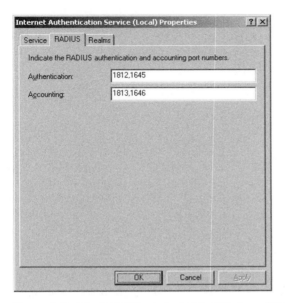

Figure 4-3. *The RADIUS tab for IAS in Windows 2000 Server.*

From the RADIUS tab, you can view and configure the following:

- **Authentication** Enumerate the list of UDP ports over which RADIUS authentication messages are received, separating each port with a comma. By default, IAS uses UDP ports 1812 and 1645. UDP port 1812 is the reserved RADIUS authentication port described in RFC 2865. Earlier RADIUS clients use UDP port 1645.

- **Accounting** Enumerate the list of UDP ports over which RADIUS accounting messages are received, separating each port with a comma. By default, IAS uses UDP ports 1813 and 1646. UDP port 1813 is the reserved RADIUS accounting port described in RFC 2866. Earlier RADIUS clients use UDP port 1646.

Realms Tab   Figure 4-4 shows the Realms tab for IAS in Windows 2000 Server.

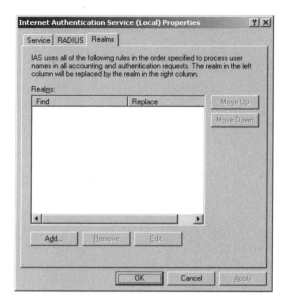

Figure 4-4. *The Realms tab for IAS in Windows 2000 Server.*

You use the Realms tab to configure a prioritized list of find-and-replace rules to manipulate realm names before attempting to resolve the name to an account and perform authentication. The realm is the portion of the username in the authentication credentials that identifies the location of the user account. There are different forms of realm names:

- **The realm name can be a prefix.**   For example, Example\user1, where Example is the name of a Windows NT 4.0 domain.

- **The realm name can be a suffix.**   For example, user1@example.microsoft.com, where example.microsoft.com is either a DNS domain name or the name of an Active Directory domain.

Pattern-matching syntax is used to specify the strings to find and replace. Find-and-replace rules can be added, edited, and removed. The rules are applied to the incoming username in the order in which they are listed. Use the Move Up and Move Down buttons to specify the order.

More Info   For more information about pattern matching syntax, see the topic titled "Pattern Matching Syntax" in Windows 2000 Server Help.

Note   IAS for Windows Server 2003 does not include a Realms tab. Realm name manipulation for Windows Server 2003 IAS is done by using connection request policies.

Remote Access Logging-Local File Properties

Within the Remote Access Logging folder of the Internet Authentication Service snap-in, is the Local File object. This object allows IAS to log connection accounting information to a file. To configure its properties, right-click Local File in the details pane and click Properties.

Settings Tab   Figure 4-5 shows the Settings tab for the Local File object in Windows 2000 Server IAS.

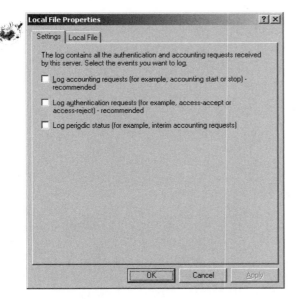

Figure 4-5. *The Settings tab for the Local File object in Windows 2000 Server IAS.*

From the Settings tab, you can view and configure the following:

- **Log Accounting Requests**   Enable or disable the logging of accounting requests in the IAS log file. Accounting requests include Accounting-On, Accounting-Off, Accounting-Start, and Accounting-Stop messages. IAS logs only accounting requests sent by the RADIUS client. If the RADIUS client is not configured for RADIUS accounting, accounting requests for that client are not logged.

- **Log Authentication Requests**   Enable or disable the logging of authentication requests in the IAS log file.

- **Log Periodic Status**   Enable or disable the logging of interim accounting requests in the IAS log file.

Local File Tab Figure 4-6 shows the Local File tab for the Local File object in Windows 2000 Server IAS.

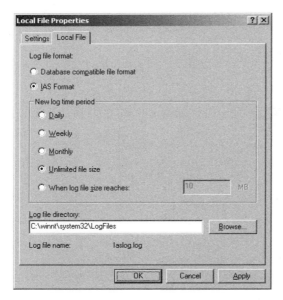

Figure 4-6. *The Local File tab for the Local File object in Windows 2000 Server IAS.*

From the Local File tab, you can view and configure the following:

- **Log File Format** Specify the log file format. The database-compatible format is Open Database Connectivity (ODBC)-compatible and is typically selected when you want to store the log file information in a database. The IAS format is an ID-value paired format that provides information on all RADIUS attributes in the RADIUS message.

- **New Log Time Period** Specify how often a new log file will be created. New log files can be created based on time or log file size.

- **Log File Directory** Specify the location of the IAS log file.

More Info For more information about log file formats, see Windows 2000 Server Help.

IAS Configuration Settings for Windows Server 2003

The IAS global properties consist of server properties and remote access logging properties. (The settings shown in the following screenshots reflect the default settings, unless otherwise noted.)

Server Properties

To configure the global properties of an IAS server running Windows Server 2003 in the Internet Authentication Service snap-in, right-click Internet Authentication Service, and then click Properties.

General Tab   Figure 4-7 shows the General tab for IAS in Windows Server 2003.

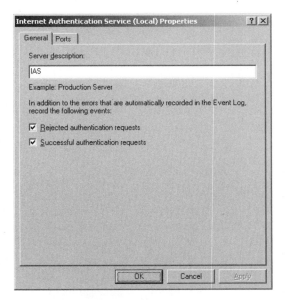

Figure 4-7. *The General tab for IAS in Windows Server 2003.*

From the General tab, you can view and configure the following:

- **Server Description**   Type the name of the server to distinguish it from other IAS servers.

- **Rejected Authentication Requests**   Enable or disable the logging of rejected or discarded authentication requests in the Windows Server 2003 system event log.

- **Successful Authentication Requests**   Enable or disable the logging of successful authentication requests in the Windows Server 2003 system event log.

Ports Tab   Figure 4-8 shows the Ports tab for IAS in Windows Server 2003.

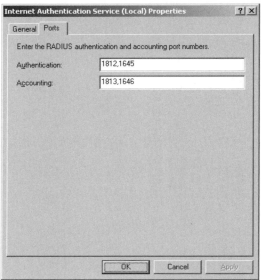

Figure 4-8. *The Ports tab for IAS in Windows Server 2003.*

From the Ports tab, you can view and configure the following:

- **Authentication**   Enumerate the list of UDP ports over which RADIUS authentication messages are received. By default, IAS uses UDP ports 1812 and 1645. UDP port 1812 is the reserved RADIUS authentication port described in RFC 2865. Earlier RADIUS clients use UDP port 1645.

- **Accounting**   Enumerate the list of UDP ports over which RADIUS accounting messages are received. By default, IAS uses UDP ports 1813 and 1646. UDP port 1813 is the reserved RADIUS accounting port described in RFC 2866. Earlier RADIUS clients use UDP port 1646.

Remote Access Logging

The Remote Access Logging folder of the Internet Authentication Service snap-in contains the Local File and SQL Server objects. These objects represent two different ways that IAS can log connection accounting information: to a file and to a structured query language (SQL) server. To configure the Local File or SQL Server object properties, right-click one of them in the details pane of the snap-in and click Properties.

Local File-Settings Tab   Figure 4-9 shows the Settings tab for the Local File object in Windows Server 2003 IAS.

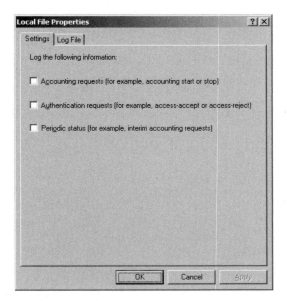

Figure 4-9. *The Settings tab for the Local File object in Windows Server 2003 IAS.*

From the Settings tab, you can view and configure the following:

- **Accounting Requests**   Enable or disable the logging of accounting requests in the IAS log file. Accounting requests include Accounting-On, Accounting-Off, Accounting-Start, and Accounting-Stop messages. IAS logs only accounting requests sent by the RADIUS client. If the RADIUS client is not configured for RADIUS accounting, accounting requests for that client are not logged.

- **Authentication Requests**   Enable or disable the logging of authentication requests in the IAS log file.

- **Periodic Status**   Enable or disable the logging of interim accounting requests in the IAS log file.

Local File-Log File Tab Figure 4-10 shows the Log File tab for the Local File object in Windows Server 2003 IAS.

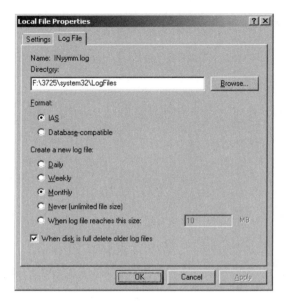

Figure 4-10. *The Log File tab for the Local File object in Windows Server 2003 IAS.*

From the Log File tab, you can view and configure the following:

- **Directory** Specify the location of the IAS log file.

- **Format** Specify the log file format. The IAS format is an ID-value paired format that provides information on all RADIUS attributes in the RADIUS message. The database-compatible format is an ODBC-compatible format that is typically selected when you want to store the log file information in a database.

- **Create A New Log File** Specify how often a new log file will be created. New log files can be created based on time or log file size.

- **When Disk Is Full Delete Other Log Files** Enable the automatic deletion of the oldest log files (as determined by the filename) when the disk becomes full.

More Info For more information about log file formats, see Windows Server 2003 Help and Support.

SQL Server-Settings Tab   Figure 4-11 shows the Settings tab for the SQL Server object in Windows Server 2003 IAS.

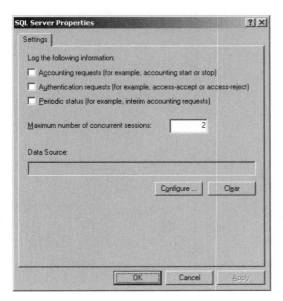

Figure 4-11. *The Settings tab for the SQL Server object in Windows Server 2003 IAS.*

From the Settings tab, you can view and configure the following:

- **Accounting Requests**   Enable or disable the logging of accounting requests in the SQL server database. Accounting requests include Accounting-On, Accounting-Off, Accounting-Start, and Accounting-Stop messages. IAS logs only accounting requests sent by the RADIUS client. If the RADIUS client is not configured for RADIUS accounting, then accounting requests for that client are not logged.

- **Authentication Requests**   Enable or disable the logging of authentication requests in the SQL server database.

- **Periodic Status**   Enable or disable the logging of interim accounting requests in the SQL server database.

- **Maximum Number Of Concurrent Sessions**   Specify the maximum number of sessions that the IAS server can have with the specified SQL server.

- **Data Source**   Specify the SQL server database to which the RADIUS accounting information is sent. Click Configure to specify the database and its data link properties, or click Clear to remove the current data source.

IAS as a RADIUS Server

IAS can be used as a RADIUS server to perform authentication, authorization, and accounting for RADIUS clients. A RADIUS client can be either an access server or a RADIUS proxy. IAS as a RADIUS server is shown in Figure 4-12.

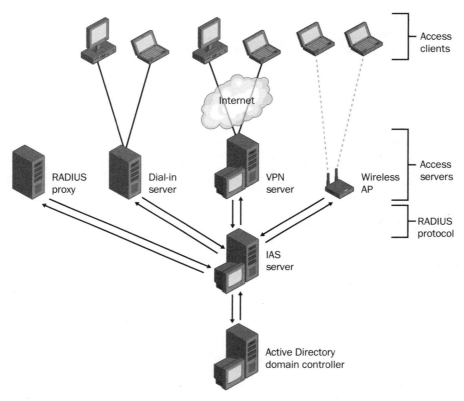

Figure 4-12. *IAS as a RADIUS server.*

Between the access server and IAS server, RADIUS messages are exchanged. Between the IAS server and the Active Directory domain controller, there is a secure communications channel.

When IAS is used as a RADIUS server, it provides the following:

- A central authentication and authorization service for all access requests that are sent by RADIUS clients and RADIUS proxies.

    IAS uses either a Windows NT Server 4.0 domain, an Active Directory–based domain, or the local SAM to authenticate user credentials for a connection attempt. IAS uses the dial-in properties of the user account and remote access policies to authorize a connection and enforce connection constraints.

- A central accounting recording service for all accounting requests that are sent by RADIUS clients.

  For Windows 2000 Server, accounting requests are stored in a local log file for analysis. For Windows Server 2003, accounting requests can either be stored in a local log file or sent to a SQL server database for analysis.

You can use IAS as a RADIUS server in the following circumstances:

- You use a Windows NT Server 4.0 domain, an Active Directory–based domain, or the local SAM as your user account database for access clients.

- You use the Windows 2000 Server or Windows Server 2003 Routing and Remote Access service on multiple dial-up servers, VPN servers, or site-to-site routers; and you want to centralize both the configuration of remote access policies and accounting of connection information.

- You outsource your dial-in, VPN, or wireless access to a service provider. The access servers use RADIUS to authenticate and authorize connections that are made by members of your organization.

- You want to centralize authentication, authorization, and accounting for a heterogeneous set of access servers.

More Info   For more information about using IAS as a RADIUS server, see Windows 2000 Server Help or Windows Server 2003 Help and Support.

Configuring RADIUS Clients

As a RADIUS server, IAS must be configured with RADIUS clients that correspond to either the access servers or RADIUS proxies that will be sending RADIUS request messages. RADIUS clients are added, configured, and removed from the Clients folder in the Internet Authentication Service snap-in for Windows 2000 Server IAS and from the RADIUS Clients folder in the Internet Authentication Service snap-in for Windows Server 2003 IAS.

To add a RADIUS client for Windows 2000 Server IAS, right-click the Clients folder and click New Client. To add a RADIUS client for Windows Server 2003 IAS, right-click the RADIUS Clients folder and click New RADIUS Client. A New RADIUS Client Wizard or a set of dialog boxes guides you through the configuration of a RADIUS client.

Figure 4-13 shows the properties of a RADIUS client in Windows Server 2003 IAS.

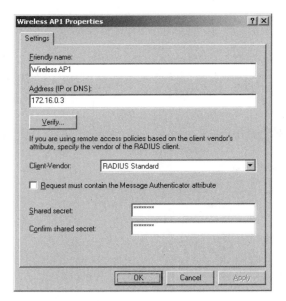

Figure 4-13. *The properties of a RADIUS client in Windows Server 2003 IAS.*

From the Settings tab, you can view and configure the following:

- **Friendly Name** Specify a friendly name for the RADIUS client. This name does not have to correspond to the DNS, NetBIOS, or computer name of the RADIUS client.

- **Address (IP Or DNS)** Specify either the IP address or the DNS name of the RADIUS client. With IAS in Windows Server 2003, Enterprise Edition, and Windows Server 2003, Datacenter Edition, you can configure RADIUS clients by specifying an IP address range.

- **Verify** If you specify a DNS name in the Address (IP Or DNS) text box, you can verify that the name is being resolved to the correct address. If the DNS name is associated with multiple IP addresses, you can choose the address to use.

- **Client-Vendor** Specify the vendor of the RADIUS client. Select RADIUS standard for a vendor-independent client.

- **Request Must Contain The Message Authenticator Attribute** Specify whether the client must always include the RADIUS Message-Authenticator attribute (also known as the Signature attribute) in Access-Request messages for connection requests using the PAP, Shiva Password Authentication Protocol (SPAP), CHAP, MS-CHAP, and MS-CHAP v2 authentication protocols. With EAP, the signature attribute is always included, and this check box does not have to be enabled. If you enable this, you must ensure that the RADIUS client is configured to always send the Message-Authenticator attribute. Otherwise, IAS will discard the Access-Request message upon receipt. For

Windows 2000 Server IAS, this check box is titled Client Must Always Send The Signature Attribute In The Request.

- **Shared Secret**   Specify the shared secret. Both IAS and the RADIUS client must be configured with the same shared secret for successful communication to occur. The shared secret can be up to 128 bytes long, is case-sensitive, and can contain alphanumeric and special characters. To protect your RADIUS traffic from an offline dictionary and shared secret compromise, make the shared secret a long (22 characters or longer) sequence of random letters, numbers, and punctuation.

- **Confirm Shared Secret**   Specify the shared secret again.

Remote Access Policy Overview

For a connection attempt to be accepted, it must be both authenticated and authorized. Authentication is done by verifying the credentials of the access client. Authorization is granted on the basis of user account dial-in properties and remote access policies. *Remote access policies* are an ordered set of rules that define how connections are either authorized or rejected. For each rule, there are one or more conditions, a set of profile settings, and a remote access permission setting.

When a connection is authorized, the remote access policy profile specifies a set of connection restrictions. The dial-in properties of the user account also provide a set of restrictions. Where applicable, user account connection restrictions override the remote access policy profile connection restrictions.

Remote Access Policy Conditions and Restrictions

Before authorizing the connection, remote access policies can validate a number of connection settings, including the following:

- Group membership
- Type of connection
- Time of day
- Authentication method
- Identity of the access server
- Whether unauthenticated access is allowed

After authorizing the connection, remote access policies can specify connection restrictions, including the following:

- Idle timeout time
- Maximum session time
- Encryption strength

- Authentication method

- IP packet filters

For example, you can have policies that specify different maximum session times for different types of connections or groups. Additionally, you can have policies that specify restricted access for business partners or unauthenticated connections.

Remote Access Policy Configuration

A remote access policy is a named rule that consists of the following elements:

- Conditions

- Remote access permission

- Profile

Remote access policies are configured from the Remote Access Policies object in the tree pane of the Internet Authentication Service snap-in. In Windows 2000 Server IAS, the Add Remote Access Policy Wizard guides you through the configuration of the elements of a remote access policy. In Windows Server 2003 IAS, the New Remote Access Policy Wizard greatly simplifies remote access policy creation.

Figure 4-14 shows the properties of a remote access policy named Wireless Access that was created for wireless connections.

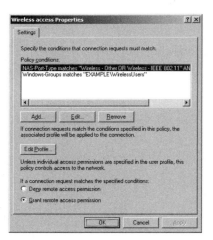

Figure 4-14. *Properties of a remote access policy.*

Remote Access Policy Conditions

Remote access policy conditions are one or more attributes that are compared with the properties of the connection attempt. If there are multiple conditions, all conditions must be met in order for the connection attempt to match the policy.

More Info   For a list of all the conditions and a description of each one, see Windows 2000 Server Help or Windows Server 2003 Help and Support.

Remote Access Permission

If all the conditions of a remote access policy are met, remote access permission is either granted or denied. Use the Grant Remote Access Permission option or the Deny Remote Access Permission option to set remote access permission for a policy.

Remote access permission is also configured on each account. When the remote access permission on the account is set to either Allow Access or Deny Access, the account remote access permission overrides the policy remote access permission. When remote access permission on an account is set to Control Access Through Remote Access Policy, the policy remote access permission determines whether the connection has remote access permission.

Granting access through the Account Remote Access Permission setting or the Policy Remote Access Permission setting is only the first step of accepting a connection. The connection attempt is then subjected to the settings of the account properties and the policy profile properties. If the connection attempt does not match the conditions or constraints of the account properties or the profile properties, the connection attempt is rejected.

Note   By default, the New Remote Access Policy Wizard for Windows Server 2003 configures Grant Remote Access Permission.

Remote Access Policy Profile Settings

The remote access policy profile is a set of properties that is applied to a connection when the connection is granted remote access permission—either through the account remote access permission setting or the policy permission setting. A profile consists of the following groups of properties:

- Dial-In Constraints
- IP
- Multilink
- Authentication
- Encryption
- Advanced

These groups of properties are configured from tabs in the Edit Dial-In Profile dialog box. (The settings shown in the following screen shots reflect the default settings, unless otherwise noted.)

Note Because the remote access policy configuration dialog boxes are so similar between Windows 2000 Server and Windows Server 2003, only the dialog boxes for Windows Server 2003 are shown. Differences between Windows Server 2003 and Windows 2000 Server are noted as needed.

Dial-In Constraints Tab   Figure 4-15 shows the Dial-In Constraints tab for a remote access policy in Windows Server 2003 IAS.

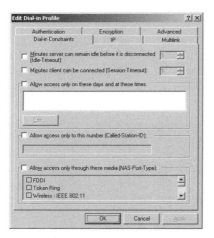

Figure 4-15. *The Dial-In Constraints tab for a remote access policy.*

From the Dial-In Constraints tab, you can view and configure the following:

- **Minutes Server Can Remain Idle Before It Is Disconnected**   The amount of time after which the access server disconnects a connection when there is no activity on the connection. By default, this property is not set, and there is no idle disconnect. This constraint corresponds to the RADIUS Idle-Timeout attribute.

- **Minutes Client Can Be Connected**   The maximum amount of time that a connection can remain connected. The access server disconnects the connection after the maximum session length. By default, this property is not set, and the connection has no maximum session limit. This constraint corresponds to the RADIUS Session-Timeout attribute.

- **Allow Access Only On These Days And At These Times**   The days of the week and hours of each day that a connection is allowed. If the day and time of the connection attempt do not match the configured day and time limits, the connection attempt is rejected. By default, this property is not set, and the access server has no day or time limits. The access server does not disconnect active connections that are connected at a time when connection attempts are not allowed.

- **Allow Access Only To This Number**   The specific phone number that a caller must call for a connection to be allowed. If the dial-in number of the connection attempt does not match the configured dial-in number, the connection attempt is rejected. By default, this property is not set and the remote access server allows all dial-in numbers. This constraint corresponds to the RADIUS Calling-Station-Id attribute.

- **Allow Access Only Through These Media**   The specific types of media—such as wireless, dial-up, or VPN—that a client must use for a connection to be allowed. If the dial-in medium of the connection attempt does not match the configured dial-in media, the connection attempt is rejected. By default, this property is not set and all dial-in media types are allowed. This constraint corresponds to the RADIUS NAS-Port-Type attribute.

IP Tab   Figure 4-16 shows the IP tab for a remote access policy in Windows Server 2003 IAS.

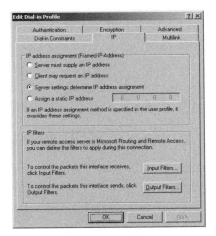

Figure 4-16. *The IP tab for a remote access policy.*

From the IP tab, you can view and configure the following:

- **IP Address Assignment**   You can set IP properties to specify whether the access client can request a specific IP address for a connection. By default, IAS allows the access server to determine the IP address assigned to the access client. This setting corresponds to the Framed-IP-Address RADIUS attribute.

- **IP Filters**   To define the allowed traffic across the connection after the connection has been made, you can configure IP packet filters for remote access policy profiles. You can use profile packet filters to configure IP traffic that the access server allows out of the connection to the access client (Output Filters) or into the connection from the access client (Input Filters) on an exception basis: either all traffic except traffic specified by filters or no traffic except traffic specified by filters. These filters are used by the Routing and Remote Access service for remote access connections. Output Filters correspond to the To Client filters, and Input Filters correspond to the From Client filters in Windows 2000 Server IAS.

Multilink Tab Figure 4-17 shows the Multilink tab for a remote access policy in Windows Server 2003 IAS.

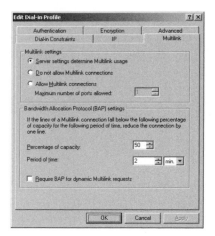

Figure 4-17. *The Multilink tab for a remote access policy.*

From the Multilink tab, you can set properties that enable multilink and determine the maximum number of ports that a multilink connection can use. Additionally, you can set Bandwidth Allocation Protocol (BAP) policies that determine BAP usage and when extra BAP lines are dropped. The multilink and BAP properties are specific to Windows dial-up remote access.

Authentication Tab Figure 4-18 shows the Authentication tab for a remote access policy in Windows Server 2003 IAS.

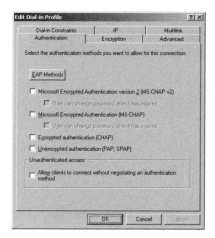

Figure 4-18. *The Authentication tab for a remote access policy.*

From the Authentication tab, you can set properties to enable the types of authentication that are allowed for a connection and specify the list of EAP types and their order of negotiation that must be used. For Windows Server 2003 IAS, the default authentication methods depend on your choices in the New Remote Access Policy Wizard.

For Windows 2000 Server IAS, you can select only a single EAP type for use with EAP-based authentication.

Encryption Tab   Figure 4-19 shows the Encryption tab for a remote access policy in Windows Server 2003 IAS.

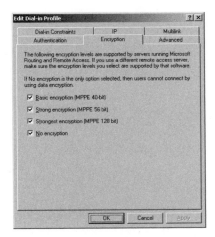

Figure 4-19. *The Encryption tab for a remote access policy.*

From the Encryption tab, you can view and configure the following:

- **Basic Encryption**   For dial-up and PPTP-based VPN connections, Microsoft Point-to-Point Encryption (MPPE) with a 40-bit key is used. For L2TP/IPSec–based VPN connections, 56-bit Data Encryption Standard (DES) encryption is used.

- **Strong Encryption**   For dial-up and PPTP-based VPN connections, MPPE with a 56-bit key is used. For L2TP/IPSec–based VPN connections, 56-bit DES encryption is used.

- **Strongest Encryption**   For dial-up and PPTP-based VPN connections, MPPE with a 128-bit key is used. For L2TP/IPSec–based VPN connections, 3DES encryption is used. For Windows 2000 Server IAS, this option is available only after the Windows 2000 High Encryption Pack or Service Pack 2 or later is installed.

- **No Encryption**   When selected, this option allows a non-encrypted connection. To require encryption, clear the No encryption check box.

These encryption settings correspond to the MS-MPPE-Encryption-Policy and MS-MPPE-Encryption-Types RADIUS attributes (RFC 2548). For Windows Server 2003 IAS, the default encryption strengths depend on your choices in the New Remote Access Policy Wizard.

Advanced Tab Figure 4-20 shows the Advanced tab for a remote access policy in Windows Server 2003 IAS.

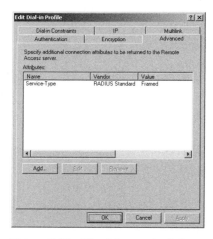

Figure 4-20. *The Advanced tab for a remote access policy.*

From the Advanced tab, you can set properties to specify the series of additional RADIUS attributes that are sent back to the RADIUS client by the IAS server. To add RADIUS attributes, click Add. You can select from the list of RADIUS attributes or select the Vendor-Specific attribute to configure RADIUS VSAs. The VSAs are saved with the profile settings for each policy.

For Windows Server 2003 IAS, the default attributes depend on your choices in the New Remote Access Policy Wizard. For wireless connections, the Service-Type attribute is set to Framed by default.

Authorizing Access with Remote Access Policy

There are two ways to use remote access policies to grant authorization, as described in the following sections.

- By user
- By group

Authorization by User

If you are managing authorization by user, set the remote access permission on the user or computer account to either Grant Access or Deny Access, and (optionally) create different remote access policies based on different types of connections. For example, you might want to have one remote access policy that is used for dial-up connections and a different remote access policy that is used for wireless connections. Managing authorization by user is recommended only when you have a small number of user or computer accounts to manage.

If you are managing authorization by user, the basic process for authorizing a connection attempt occurs as follows:

- If the connection attempt matches all policy conditions, check the remote access permission setting of the account.

- If the remote access permission is set to Grant Access, apply the connection settings of the policy profile and account.

- If the remote access permission is set to Deny Access, reject the connection attempt.

- If the connection attempt does not match all policy conditions, process the next remote access policy.

- If the connection attempt does not match all conditions of any remote access policy, reject the connection attempt.

Authorization by Group

If you are managing authorization by group, set the remote access permission on the user account to Control Access Through Remote Access Policy, and create remote access policies that are based on different types of connections and group membership. For example, you might want to have one remote access policy for dial-up connections for employees (members of the Employees group) and a different remote access policy for dial-up connections for contractors (members of the Contractors group).

If you are managing authorization by group, the basic process for authorizing a connection attempt occurs as follows:

- If the connection attempt matches all policy conditions, check the remote access permission of the remote access policy.

- If the remote access permission is set to Grant Remote Access Permission, apply the connection settings of the policy profile and account.

- If the remote access permission is set to Deny Remote Access Permission, reject the connection attempt.

- If the connection attempt does not match all policy conditions, process the next remote access policy.

- If the connection attempt does not match all conditions of any remote access policy, reject the connection attempt.

Note The Control Access Through Remote Access Policy remote access permission setting is available only on accounts that are members of a Windows 2000 native-mode Active Directory domain or a Windows Server 2003, Windows 2000 native, or Windows Server 2003 functional level domain.

IAS as a RADIUS Proxy

IAS can be used as a RADIUS proxy to provide the routing of RADIUS messages between RADIUS clients (access servers) and RADIUS servers that perform user authentication, authorization, and accounting for the connection attempt. When used as a RADIUS proxy, IAS is a central switching or routing point through which RADIUS access and accounting messages flow. IAS records information in an accounting log about the messages that are forwarded. Figure 4-21 shows IAS as a RADIUS proxy.

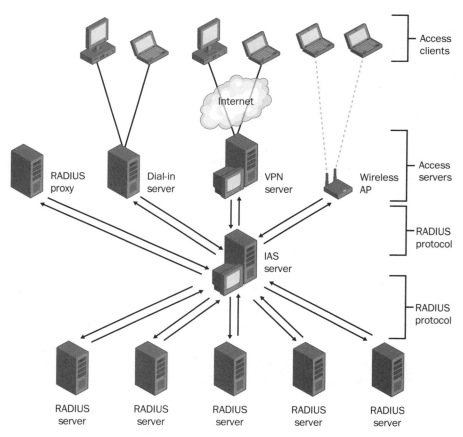

Figure 4-21. *IAS as a RADIUS proxy.*

When IAS is used as a RADIUS proxy between a RADIUS client and a RADIUS server, RADIUS messages for network access connection attempts are forwarded in the following way:

1. Access servers—such as dial-up network access servers, VPN servers, and wireless access points—receive connection requests from access clients.

2. The access server—configured to use RADIUS as the authentication, authorization, and accounting protocol—creates an Access-Request message and sends it to the IAS server that is being used as a RADIUS proxy.

3. The IAS RADIUS proxy receives the Access-Request message and, based on the locally configured connection request policies, determines where to forward the Access-Request message.

4. The IAS RADIUS proxy forwards the Access-Request message to the appropriate RADIUS server.

5. The RADIUS server evaluates the Access-Request message.

6. If required, the RADIUS server sends an Access-Challenge message to the IAS RADIUS proxy, where it is forwarded to the access server.

7. The access server processes the challenge with the access client and sends an updated Access-Request to the IAS RADIUS proxy, where it is forwarded to the RADIUS server.

8. The RADIUS server authenticates and authorizes the connection attempt.

9. If the connection attempt is both authenticated and authorized, the RADIUS server sends an Access-Accept message to the IAS RADIUS proxy, where it is forwarded to the access server.

   If the connection attempt is either not authenticated or not authorized, the RADIUS server sends an Access-Reject message to the IAS RADIUS proxy, where it is forwarded to the access server.

10. The access server completes the connection process with the access client and sends an Accounting-Request message to the IAS RADIUS proxy. The IAS RADIUS proxy logs the accounting data and forwards the message to the RADIUS server.

11. The RADIUS server sends an Accounting-Response to the IAS RADIUS proxy, where it is forwarded to the access server.

You can use IAS as a RADIUS proxy under the following circumstances:

- You are a service provider that offers outsourced dial, VPN, or wireless network access services to multiple customers.

- You want to provide authentication and authorization for accounts that are not members of either the domain in which the IAS server is a member or another domain that has a two-way trust with the domain in which the IAS server is a member.

- You want to perform authentication and authorization by using a database that is not a Windows account database.

- You want to process a large number of connection requests. The IAS RADIUS proxy dynamically balances the load of connection and accounting requests across multiple RADIUS servers and increases the processing of large numbers of RADIUS clients and authentications per second.

- You want to provide RADIUS authentication and authorization for outsourced service providers and minimize intranet firewall configuration.

More Info For more information about using Windows Server 2003 IAS as a RADIUS proxy, see Windows Server 2003 Help and Support.

Connection Request Processing

To determine if a RADIUS client message should be processed locally or forwarded to another RADIUS server, a Windows Server 2003 IAS server uses connection request processing. Connection request processing is a combination of the following:

- **Connection request policies** For any incoming RADIUS request message, connection request policies determine whether the message is processed locally or forwarded to another RADIUS server.

- **Remote RADIUS server groups** When forwarding RADIUS messages, remote RADIUS server groups specify the set of RADIUS servers to which the messages are forwarded.

Connection Request Policies

Connection request policies are rules specifying conditions and profile settings that give you flexibility to configure how the IAS server handles incoming authentication and accounting request messages. With connection request policies, you can create a series of policies so that some RADIUS request messages are processed locally (IAS is being used as a RADIUS server), and other types of messages are forwarded to another RADIUS server (IAS is being used as a RADIUS proxy).

Connection request policies allow you to use IAS as a RADIUS server or as a RADIUS proxy, based on the time of day and day of the week, the realm name in the request, the type of connection being requested, the IP address of the RADIUS client, and so on.

It is important to remember that with connection request policies, a RADIUS request message is processed only if the settings of the incoming RADIUS request message match at least one of the connection request policies. For example, if the attributes of an incoming RADIUS Access-Request message do not match at least one of the connection request policies, an Access-Reject message is sent.

A connection request policy is a combination of the following:

- **Conditions** Connection request policy conditions are one or more RADIUS attributes that are compared to the attributes of the incoming RADIUS request message. If there are multiple conditions, all of the conditions must match the attributes of the incoming RADIUS message in order for the RADIUS request message to match the policy.

- **Profile settings** A connection request policy profile is a set of properties that are applied to an incoming RADIUS message once it has matched all the conditions. A connection request policy profile consists of the following groups of properties:

  - Authentication

  - Accounting

  - Attribute

  - Advanced

Figure 4-22 shows the connection request policy properties for the default policy named Use Windows Authentication For All Users.

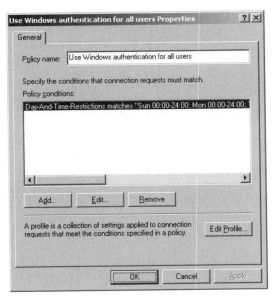

Figure 4-22. *Properties of a connection request policy.*

More Info For a complete list of conditions and their descriptions, see Windows Server 2003 Help and Support.

Authentication Tab Figure 4-23 shows the Authentication tab for a connection request policy in Windows Server 2003 IAS.

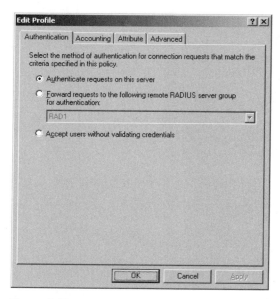

Figure 4-23. *The Authentication tab for a connection request policy.*

From the Authentication tab, you can view and configure the following:

- **Authenticate Requests On This Server** Use a Windows NT 4.0 domain or Active Directory, or the local SAM for both authentication database and the matching remote access policy and account dial-in properties for authorization. In this case, the IAS server is being used as a RADIUS server.

- **Forward Requests To The Following Remote RADIUS Server Group For Authentication** Forward the Access-Request message to another RADIUS server in a specified remote RADIUS server group. In this case, the IAS server is being used as a RADIUS proxy. When you select this option, you must also select a remote RADIUS server group.

- **Accept Users Without Authenticating Credentials** Do not check authentication of the user credentials and authorization of the connection attempt. An Access-Accept message is immediately sent to the RADIUS client.

This authentication option cannot be used when the access client's authentication protocol is MS-CHAP v2 or EAP-Transport Level Security (EAP-TLS), both of which provide mutual authentication. In mutual authentication, the access client proves that it is a valid access client to the authenticating server (the IAS server), and the authenticating server proves that it is a valid authenticating server to the access client. When this authentication option is used, the Access-Accept message is returned. However, the authenticating server does not provide validation to the access client, and mutual authentication fails.

Accounting Tab   Figure 4-24 shows the Accounting tab for a connection request policy in Windows Server 2003 IAS, which determines how IAS handles RADIUS Accounting-Request messages.

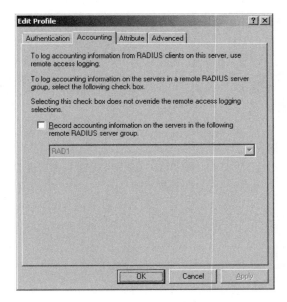

Figure 4-24.   *The Accounting tab for a connection request policy.*

From the Accounting tab, you can specify that RADIUS Accounting-Request messages are forwarded to another RADIUS server in a specified remote RADIUS server group. In this case, the IAS server is acting as a RADIUS proxy. IAS always records the accounting information for Accounting-Request messages based on remote access logging settings.

Attribute Tab Figure 4-25 shows the Attribute tab for a connection request policy in Windows Server 2003 IAS.

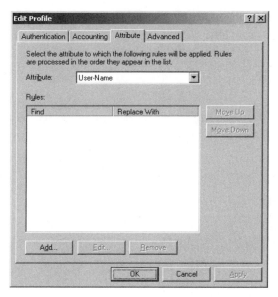

Figure 4-25. *The Attribute tab for a connection request policy.*

From the Attribute tab, you can configure a set of find-and-replace rules that manipulate the text strings of one of the following attributes:

- User-Name
- Called-Station-ID
- Calling-Station-ID

Find-and-replace rule processing occurs for one of the preceding attributes before the RADIUS message is subject to authentication and accounting settings. Configuring attribute manipulation for the User-Name attribute is equivalent to configuring realm replacement rules for Windows 2000 Server IAS.

If you use the MS-CHAP v2 authentication protocol, you cannot manipulate the User-Name attribute if the connection request policy is used to forward the RADIUS message. The only exception occurs when a backslash (\) character is used, and then the manipulation affects only the information to the left of it. A backslash character is typically used to indicate a domain name (the information to the left of the backslash character) and a user account name within the domain (the information to the right of the backslash character). In this case, only attribute manipulation rules that modify or replace the domain name are allowed.

Note   Find-and-replace rules apply only to a single attribute. You cannot configure find-and-replace rules for each attribute, and you cannot add to the list of
attributes available for manipulation.

Advanced Tab   Figure 4-26 shows the Advanced tab for a connection request policy in Windows Server 2003 IAS.

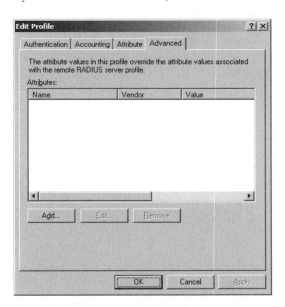

Figure 4-26. *The Advanced tab for a connection request policy.*

From the Advanced tab, you can set properties to specify the series of RADIUS
attributes that are

- Added to the RADIUS response message when the IAS server is being used
  as a RADIUS authentication or accounting server.

  When there are attributes specified on both a remote access policy and the
  connection request policy, the attributes that are sent in the RADIUS
  response message are the combination of the two sets of attributes.

- Added to the RADIUS message when the IAS server is being used as a
  RADIUS authentication or accounting proxy.

  If the attribute already exists in the message that is forwarded, it is replaced
  with the value of the attribute specified in the connection request policy.

Remote RADIUS Server Groups

A remote RADIUS server group is a named group that contains one or more RADIUS servers. When IAS is being used as a RADIUS proxy for RADIUS request messages, a remote RADIUS server group must be specified. This group is used to facilitate the common configuration of both a primary and at least one backup RADIUS server. You can specify various settings to either determine the order in which the servers are used or distribute the RADIUS messages across all servers in the group.

Figure 4-27 shows the properties of a remote RADIUS server group named RAD1.

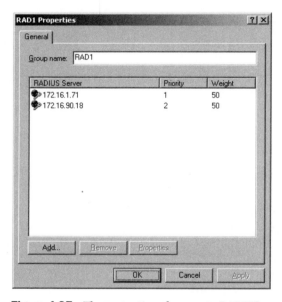

Figure 4-27. *The properties of a remote RADIUS server group.*

After a remote RADIUS server group is configured, it can be specified in the authentication and accounting settings of a connection request policy; so you should configure a remote RADIUS server group first. Next, you can configure the connection request policy to use the newly configured remote RADIUS server group. Alternately, you can use the New Connection Request Policy Wizard to create a new remote RADIUS server group while you are creating the connection request policy.

Note Remote RADIUS server groups are separate from Windows groups.

Each server in a remote RADIUS server group has the following groups of properties:

- Address
- Authentication/Accounting
- Load Balancing

Address Tab   Figure 4-28 shows the Address tab for a RADIUS server in a remote RADIUS server group in Windows Server 2003 IAS.

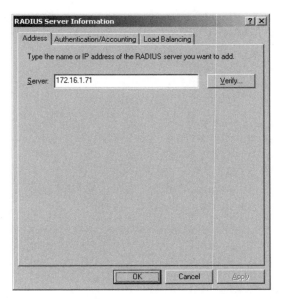

Figure 4-28.   *The Address tab for a RADIUS server in a remote RADIUS server group.*

On the Address tab, you can configure the name or address of the RADIUS server. If you specify a name, you can click Verify to resolve the name and select the correct resolved address.

Authentication/Accounting Tab   Figure 4-29 shows the Authentication/ Accounting tab for a RADIUS server in a remote RADIUS server group in Windows Server 2003 IAS.

From the Authentication/Accounting tab, you can view and configure the following:

- **Authentication Port**   Type the destination UDP port for RADIUS Access-Request messages sent to this RADIUS server. By default, the authentication port is 1812.

- **Shared Secret**   Type the shared secret between the IAS server (acting as a RADIUS proxy) and this RADIUS server for connection request traffic. Within a chain of RADIUS entities, the shared secret between a RADIUS proxy and an access client (or another RADIUS proxy) can and should be different from the shared secret between the RADIUS proxy and the RADIUS server (or another RADIUS proxy). For best protection of your RADIUS traffic, use a shared secret at least 22 characters long and consisting of a random sequence of upper- and lowercase letters, numbers, and punctuation.

- **Confirm Shared Secret** Type the authentication shared secret again.

- **Accounting Port** Type the destination UDP port for Accounting-Request messages sent to this RADIUS server. By default, the accounting port is 1813.

- **Use The Same Shared Secret For Authentication And Accounting** Enable the same shared secret for both authentication (connection requests) and accounting messages. In many cases, including IAS, RADIUS servers provide only the configuration of a single shared secret per RADIUS client that is used for both authentication and accounting messages.

- **Shared Secret** If Use The Same Shared Secret For Authentication And Accounting is disabled, type the shared secret between the IAS server (acting as a RADIUS proxy) and this RADIUS server for accounting traffic; that is, configured separately from the shared secret for authentication traffic.

- **Confirm Shared Secret** If Use The Same Shared Secret For Authentication And Accounting is disabled, type the accounting shared secret again.

- **Forward Network Access Server Start And Stop Notifications To This Server** Enable to forward accounting start and stop messages to this RADIUS server.

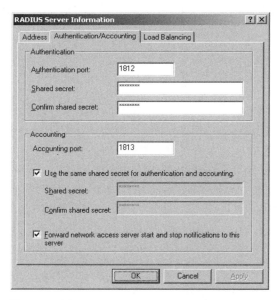

Figure 4-29. *The Authentication/Accounting tab for a RADIUS server in a remote RADIUS server group.*

Load Balancing Tab   Figure 4-30 shows the Load Balancing tab for a RADIUS server in a remote RADIUS server group in Windows Server 2003 IAS.

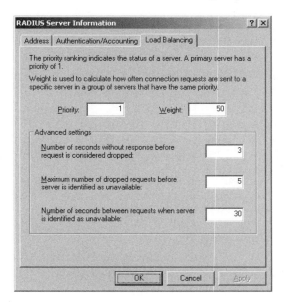

Figure 4-30. *The Load Balancing tab for a RADIUS server in a remote RADIUS server group.*

From the Load Balancing tab, you can view and configure the following:

- **Priority**   Type the priority of this RADIUS server in the remote RADIUS server group. IAS uses the priority value to determine which server in the RADIUS server group is the most favored when forwarding RADIUS messages. The primary RADIUS server has a priority value of 1.

- **Weight**   Type the weight of this RADIUS server in the remote RADIUS server group. For group members that have the same priority, the weight setting is used to calculate how often RADIUS messages are sent to each of them.

- **Number Of Seconds Without Response Before Request Is Considered Dropped**   Type the number of seconds after which a response is not received that IAS can consider the request dropped. This is the response timeout value.

- **Maximum Number Of Dropped Requests Before Server Is Identified As Unavailable**   Type the maximum number of unanswered requests after which the server is considered unavailable.

- **Number Of Seconds Between Requests When Server Is Identified As Unavailable**   Type the number of seconds after which an authentication request is sent when the server is considered unavailable. In order to detect when a RADIUS server has become available again, IAS sends RADIUS messages periodically to attempt to get a response. When a response is received, the server is considered available.

Active Directory

Active Directory can be installed on servers running members of the Windows 2000 Server and Windows Server 2003 families. Active Directory stores information about objects on the network and makes this information easy for administrators and users to find and use. Active Directory uses a structured data store as the basis for a logical, hierarchical organization of directory information.

This data store, or directory, contains information about Active Directory objects. These objects typically include shared resources such as servers, volumes, printers, and the network user and computer accounts.

Security is integrated with Active Directory through logon authentication and access control to objects in the directory. With a single network logon, administrators can manage and organize directory data throughout their network, and authorized users can access resources anywhere on the network. Policy-based administration eases the management of even the most complex network.

Active Directory also includes the following:

- A set of rules (or schema) that defines the classes of objects and attributes contained in the directory, the constraints and limits on instances of these objects, and the format of their names.

- A global catalog that contains information about every object in the directory. This catalog allows users and administrators to find directory information regardless of which domain in the directory actually contains the data.

- A query and index mechanism, so that objects and their properties can be published and found by network users or applications.

- A replication service that distributes directory data across a network. All domain controllers in a domain participate in replication and contain a complete copy of all directory information for their domain. Any change to directory data is replicated to all domain controllers in the domain.

Accounts

Active Directory user accounts and computer accounts represent a physical entity such as a computer or person. User accounts can also be used as dedicated service accounts for some applications.

User accounts and computer accounts (as well as groups) are also referred to as security principals. *Security principals* are directory objects that are automatically assigned security identifiers (SIDs), which can be used to access domain resources. A user or computer account is used to do the following:

- **Authenticate the identity of a user or computer**   A user account in Active Directory enables a user to log on to computers and domains with an identity that can be authenticated by the domain. Each user who logs on to the network should have their own unique user account and password. To maximize security, you should avoid multiple users sharing one account.

- **Authorize or deny access to domain resources**   When the user is authenticated, the user is authorized or denied access to domain resources based on the explicit permissions assigned to that user on the resource.

- **Administer other security principals**   Active Directory creates a foreign security principal object in the local domain to represent each security principal from a trusted external domain.

- **Audit actions performed using the user or computer account**   Auditing can help you monitor account security.

You can manage user accounts with the Active Directory Users and Computers snap-in. Each user account must be unique.

Every computer running Windows NT, Windows 2000, Windows XP, or a server running Windows Server 2003 that joins a domain has a computer account. Similar to user accounts, computer accounts provide a means for authenticating and auditing computer access to the network and to domain resources. Each computer account must be unique.

User and computer accounts can be added, disabled, reset, and deleted using the Active Directory Users and Computers snap-in. A computer account can also be created when you join a computer to a domain.

Dial-In Properties of an Account

In Windows 2000 and Windows Server 2003, user and computer accounts for an Active Directory–based server contain a set of dial-in properties that are used when allowing or denying a connection attempt. On an Active Directory–based domain, you can set the dial-in properties on the Dial-In tab for the user and computer account in the Active Directory Users and Computers snap-in. Figure 4-31 shows the Dial-In tab for a user account in a Windows 2000 native or Windows Server 2003 functional level domain.

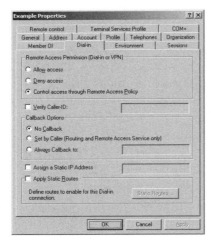

Figure 4-31. *The Dial-In tab of a user account.*

From the Dial-In tab, you can view and configure the following:

- **Remote Access Permission (Dial-In Or VPN)**   You can use this property to set remote access permission to be explicitly allowed, denied, or determined through remote access policies. In all cases, remote access policies are also used to authorize the connection attempt. If access is explicitly allowed, remote access policy conditions, user account properties, or profile properties can still deny the connection attempt. The Control Access Through Remote Access Policy option is available only on user and computer accounts in a Windows 2000 native or Windows Server 2003 functional level domain.

  New accounts that are created for a Windows 2000 native or Windows Server 2003 functional level domain are set to Control Access Through Remote Access Policy. New accounts that are created in a Windows 2000 mixed functional level domain are set to Deny Access.

- **Verify Caller-ID**   If this property is enabled, the access server verifies the caller's phone number. If the caller's phone number does not match the configured phone number, the connection attempt is denied. This setting is designed for dial-in connections.

- **Callback Options**   If this property is enabled, the access server calls the caller back during the connection process. Either the caller or the network administrator sets the phone number that is used by the server. This setting is designed for dial-in connections.

- **Assign A Static IP Address**   You can use this property to assign a specific IP address to a user when a connection is made. This setting is designed for dial-in connections.

- **Apply Static Routes**   You can use this property to define a series of static IP routes that are added to the routing table of the server running the Routing and Remote Access service when a connection is made. This setting is designed for demand-dial routing.

> **Note**   Dial-in properties for computer accounts in Windows 2000 Active Directory domains are available only after Windows 2000 SP3 or later is installed on domain controllers.

Groups

A *group* is a collection of user and computer accounts, contacts, and other groups that can be managed as a single unit. Users and computers that belong to a particular group are referred to as *group members*. Using groups can simplify administration by assigning a common set of permissions and rights to many accounts at once, rather than assigning permissions and rights to each account individually.

Groups can be either directory-based or local to a particular computer. Active Directory provides a set of default groups upon installation, and also allows the option to create groups.

Groups in Active Directory allow you to do the following:

- Simplify administration by assigning permissions on a shared resource to a group, rather than to individual users. This assigns the same access on the resource to all members of that group.

- Delegate administration by assigning user rights once to a group through Group Policy and then adding necessary members to the group that you want to have the same rights as the group.

Groups have a scope and type. *Group scope* determines the extent to which the group is applied within a domain or forest. Active Directory defines universal, global, and domain local scopes for groups. *Group type* determines whether a group can be used to assign permissions from a shared resource (for security groups) or whether a group can be used for e-mail distribution lists only (for distribution groups).

> **More Info**   For more information about the types of groups, group scope, and domain functional levels, see Windows Server 2003 Help and Support or *http://www.microsoft.com/windowsserver2003/technologies/activedirectory/default.mspx.*

Nesting allows you to add a group as a member of another group. You nest groups to consolidate member accounts and reduce replication traffic. Nesting options depend on whether the functionality of your Windows Server 2003 domain is set to the Windows 2000 native or Windows 2000 mixed functional level.

When you have decided how to nest groups based on your domain functional level, organize your wireless access user and computer accounts into the appropriate groups. For a Windows 2000 native or Windows Server 2003 functional level domain, you can use universal and nested global groups. For example, create a universal group named WirelessUsers that contains global groups of wireless user and computer accounts for intranet access. Then you need only to specify that group name when you create your remote access policy with IAS.

Summary

RADIUS is an industry-standard protocol that is used to centralize the authentication, authorization, and accounting of network access connections. IAS is an implementation of a RADIUS server (in Windows 2000 Server and Windows Server 2003) and proxy (in Windows Server 2003). IAS uses connection request processing to determine its role as a RADIUS server or proxy for a given incoming RADIUS request message. As a RADIUS server, IAS uses Windows account databases to verify authentication and the dial-in properties of account and remote access policies to determine authorization. As a RADIUS proxy, IAS uses connection request policies and remote RADIUS server groups to determine the RADIUS server to which the RADIUS request message is forwarded. In an enterprise, IAS uses Active Directory account credentials to perform authentication and Active Directory account properties and groups to perform authorization.

Chapter 5
EAP

The Extensible Authentication Protocol (EAP) was originally created as an extension to the Point-to-Point Protocol (PPP) that allows for development of arbitrary network access authentication methods. With PPP authentication protocols such as Challenge Handshake Authentication Protocol (CHAP), Microsoft Challenge Handshake Authentication Protocol (MS-CHAP), and MS-CHAP version 2 (MS-CHAP v2), a specific authentication mechanism is chosen during the link establishment phase. During the authentication phase, the connection is validated by using the negotiated authentication protocol. The authentication protocol itself is a fixed series of messages sent in a specific order. With EAP, the specific authentication mechanism is not chosen during the link establishment phase of the PPP connection; instead, each PPP peer negotiates to perform EAP during the connection authentication phase. When the connection authentication phase is reached, the peers negotiate the use of a specific EAP authentication scheme known as an *EAP type*. EAP is described in RFC 2284.

After the EAP type is agreed upon, EAP allows for an open-ended exchange of messages between the access client and the authenticating server (for wireless, the RADIUS server) that can vary based on the parameters of the connection. The conversation consists of requests and responses for authentication information. The EAP type determines the length and detail of the authentication conversation.

Architecturally, EAP allows authentication plug-in modules at both the access client and authenticating server ends of a connection. To add support for a new EAP type, install an EAP type library file on both the access client and the authenticating server. This capability to extend EAP provides vendors with the opportunity to create new authentication schemes. EAP provides the highest flexibility to allow for more secure authentication methods.

You can use EAP to support authentication schemes such as Generic Token Card, One Time Password (OTP), Message Digest 5 (MD5)-Challenge, Transport Layer Security (TLS) for smart card and certificate authentication, and future authentication technologies. EAP is a critical technology component for establishing secure connections.

In addition to support within PPP, EAP is supported within the IEEE 802 link layer. IEEE 802.1X defines how EAP is used for authentication by IEEE 802 devices, including IEEE 802.11b, 802.11a, and 802.11g wireless access points (APs) and

Ethernet switches. IEEE 802.1X differs from PPP in that only EAP authentication methods are supported.

EAP Types in Windows

The following EAP types are included with Microsoft Windows XP (Service Pack 1 [SP1] and later), Windows Server 2003, and the Windows 2000 family with Microsoft 802.1X Authentication Client:

- EAP-MD5 CHAP

- EAP-TLS

- Protected EAP (PEAP)

Note Windows XP (prior to SP1) includes only the EAP-MD5 CHAP and EAP-TLS EAP types.

EAP types on the wireless client are configured from the Authentication tab for a network adapter (in Windows XP and Windows 2000 with Microsoft 802.1X Authentication Client) and for a wireless network (in Windows XP SP1 and later and Windows Server 2003). In each case, a single EAP type is selected for authentication.

EAP types on the Internet Authentication Service (IAS) server are configured from the Authentication tab in the profile properties of a remote access policy. For Windows 2000 IAS, a specific EAP type is selected from the Authentication tab, as shown in Figure 5-1.

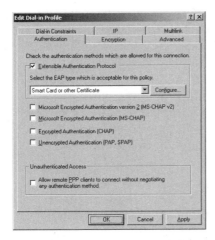

Figure 5-1. *Authentication tab for Windows 2000 IAS.*

For Windows Server 2003 IAS, you can select more than one EAP type and determine the order of negotiation. The Select EAP Providers dialog box is shown in Figure 5-2, in which EAP types are referred to as EAP *providers*.

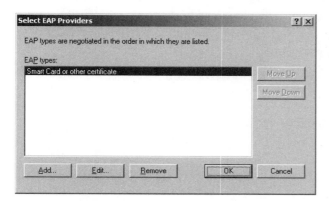

Figure 5-2. *Select EAP Providers dialog box for Windows Server 2003 IAS.*

From the Select EAP Providers dialog box, you can add or remove supported EAP types, configure their properties, and specify the order of their negotiation. You can access this dialog box by clicking the EAP Methods button on the Authentication tab in the profile properties of a remote access policy. The default EAP provider is configured based on options you select in the New Remote Access Policy Wizard.

EAP-MD5 CHAP

EAP-Message Digest 5 Challenge Handshake Authentication Protocol (EAP-MD5 CHAP) is an EAP type that uses the same challenge handshake protocol as PPP-based CHAP, but the challenges and responses are sent as EAP messages. EAP-MD5 CHAP is described in RFC 2284.

You can use EAP-MD5 CHAP to authenticate the credentials of remote access clients by using username and password security systems and to test EAP interoperability.

EAP-MD5 CHAP is not a suitable authentication method for Windows-based wireless connections for the following reasons:

- CHAP requires the availability of a reversibly encrypted form of the account password to verify the CHAP challenge response. This property of accounts is not enabled for local computer or domain accounts by default.

- CHAP authentication for wireless connectivity results in multiple user logons: one to obtain wireless connectivity and another to log on to a domain.

- CHAP is a password-based authentication method in which the user chooses passwords that could result in a relatively weak authentication scheme.

- CHAP is susceptible to offline dictionary attacks in which a malicious user captures the CHAP exchange and then attempts to determine the password.

- CHAP authentication does not result in mutually determined keying material for data encryption and data signing.

There are no configuration properties for EAP-MD5 CHAP on either the wireless client or IAS. Windows XP (SP1 and later), Windows 2000 with Microsoft 802.1X Authentication Client, and Windows Server 2003 no longer allow the use of EAP-MD5 CHAP as a wireless authentication method.

EAP-TLS

EAP-Transport Layer Security (EAP-TLS) is an EAP type that is used in certificate-based security environments and provides the strongest authentication method. If you use smart cards for remote access authentication, you must use the EAP-TLS authentication method. The EAP-TLS exchange of messages provides mutual authentication, integrity-protected cipher suite negotiation, and encryption key determination. These parameters are negotiated between the access client and the authenticating server and are described in RFC 2716.

EAP-TLS using user and computer certificates is the preferred authentication method for Windows-based wireless connectivity for the following reasons:

- EAP-TLS does not require any dependencies on the user account's password.

- EAP-TLS authentication occurs automatically, usually with no intervention by the user.

- EAP-TLS uses certificates, which provide a relatively strong authentication scheme.

- EAP-TLS exchange is protected with public key cryptography and is not susceptible to offline dictionary attacks.

- EAP-TLS authentication results in mutually determined keying material for data encryption and signing.

Note EAP-TLS authentication with smart cards is supported for wireless connections with Windows XP (SP1 and later), Microsoft 802.1X Authentication Client, and Windows Server 2003. Windows XP (prior to SP1) does not support the use of smart cards for wireless authentication.

The EAP-TLS type authentication for wireless connections in Windows has client-side and server-side configuration requirements. The client-side configuration is done on the wireless client; the server-side configuration is done on the IAS server.

Configuring EAP-TLS on the Wireless Client

Figure 5-3 shows the client-side Smart Card Or Other Certificate Properties dialog box for Windows XP (prior to SP1). This dialog box can be accessed from the Authentication tab on the properties of a wireless network adapter.

Figure 5-3. *Client-side Smart Card Or Other Certificate Properties dialog box.*

From the Smart Card Or Other Certificate Properties dialog box, you can view and configure the following:

- **When Connecting**   To use a certificate in the Current User or Local Computer certificate stores for authentication, select Use A Certificate On This Computer, which is the default. When there are multiple user certificates installed, you are prompted to select a specific user certificate for the first association. Its use is cached for reassociations until the Windows user session is ended. To use the certificate on a smart card, select Use My Smart Card.

- **Validate Server Certificate**   This option, which is enabled by default, allows you to validate the computer certificate of the authenticating server (typically a RADIUS server for wireless clients).

- **Connect Only If Server Name Ends With**   This option, which is disabled by default, determines whether you want to specify a string that must match the last part of the name in the authenticating server's computer certificate. If you enable this option and type the wrong string, the authentication fails. For example, if you want to connect only if the fully qualified domain names in the Subject field of the server certificates end in "corpnet.example.com", type **corpnet.example.com**.

- **Trusted Root Certificate Authority** This option allows you to select the specific root certification authority (CA) of the RADIUS server's computer certificate. (By default, there is no specific trusted root CA selected.) If you select the wrong trusted root CA, you are asked during authentication whether you want to accept the connection using the root CA of the RADIUS server's certificate. If you click OK, your selection of the trusted root CA is automatically set to the root CA of the RADIUS server certificate.

- **Use A Different User Name For The Connection** This option, which is disabled by default, specifies whether you want to use a username for authentication that is different from the username in the certificate. If enabled, you are prompted to select a user certificate, even if only one user certificate is installed. The selected certificate is used until the user session is ended.

For Windows XP (SP1 and later), Windows 2000 with Microsoft 802.1X Authentication Client, and Windows Server 2003, the properties of the Smart Card Or Other Certificate dialog box have changed. Figure 5-4 shows the new Smart Card Or Other Certificate Properties dialog box, which you can access from the Authentication tab on the properties of a wireless network or wireless network adapter.

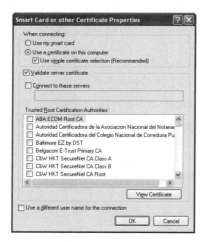

Figure 5-4. *The new client-side Smart Card Or Other Certificate Properties dialog box.*

The new Smart Card Or Other Certificate Properties dialog box contains the following new configuration items:

- **Use Simple Certificate Selection** This option enables and disables simple certificate selection. When enabled, Windows attempts to simplify the list of certificates with which the user is prompted for selection. The certificates that are usable for EAP-TLS authentication are grouped by the entity that was issued the certificate, based on the Subject Alternative Name and Subject fields of the certificates. The most recently issued certificate from each group is used to create the list that is presented to the user. Simple certificate selection is used only when Use A Certificate On This Computer is selected (the option is enabled by default).

To determine the certificates that are usable for EAP-TLS authentication, the certificates in the Current User or Local Computer certificates stores are filtered. This filtering, which occurs whether simple certificate selection is enabled or not, eliminates certificates that have expired, those that do not have the Client Authentication enhanced key usage, those that do not have an associated private key, and those whose private key is not available without requiring user interaction (for example, prompting the user for a personal identifier [PIN] to unlock the private key corresponding to the certificate).

- **Connect To These Servers**   This option allows you to specify RADIUS servers providing authentication and authorization for the connection by name. The server names must exactly match those in the Subject field of the RADIUS server's certificate. Use semicolons to specify multiple RADIUS server names. (By default, there are no server names listed.)

- **Trusted Root Certification Authorities**   This option allows you to select multiple trusted root CAs when authenticating the certificate of the RADIUS server.

- **View Certificate**   This button allows you to view the properties of the root certificate currently selected in the Trusted Root Certification Authorities list.

Configuring EAP-TLS on the IAS Server

Figure 5-5 shows the server-side Smart Card Or Other Certificate Properties dialog box for Windows 2000 Server and Windows Server 2003 IAS. This dialog box can be accessed from the Authentication tab of the profile properties of a remote access policy.

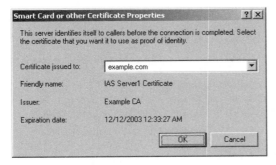

Figure 5-5. *Certificate selection in Windows 2000 Server and Windows Server 2003 IAS.*

The server-side Smart Card Or Other Certificate Properties dialog box contains the following elements:

- **Certificate Issued To**   This option allows you to select the computer certificate to send to the wireless client during EAP-TLS authentication. The certificates in this list correspond to the list of certificates in the Local Computer certificate store. If a certificate is installed on the computer in the Local Computer certificate store but does not appear in this list, the certificate does not support the SChannel cryptographic provider and therefore cannot be used for EAP-TLS authentication.

- **Friendly Name**   This field displays the friendly name for the certificate (it might not be configured by default). You can configure a friendly name for the certificate from the properties of the certificate by using the Certificates snap-in. Locate the computer certificates in Certificates (Local Computer)\Personal\Certificates. Right-click the certificate and select Properties. On the General tab, type a friendly name in the Friendly Name text box.

- **Issuer**   This field displays the name of the CA that issued the certificate.

- **Expiration Date**   This field displays the expiration date and time for the certificate.

To view all the fields of the certificate, use the Certificates snap-in.

Protected EAP (PEAP)

Windows XP (SP1 and later), Windows Server 2003, and Microsoft 802.1X Authentication Client support Protected EAP (PEAP) as a new EAP type. For more information, see the section on PEAP later in this chapter.

Note   The Security Dynamics' ACE/Agent for Windows 2000 is an additional EAP type for Security Dynamics-based authentication methods for hard tokens, soft tokens, and smart cards. It is included on the Windows 2000 Server product CD-ROM in the Valueadd\3rdparty\Security\Sdti folder. This EAP type is not supported for wireless connections.

EAP over RADIUS

EAP over RADIUS is not an EAP type; it is the passing of EAP messages of any EAP type by the access server to a RADIUS server for authentication. An EAP message sent between the access client and access server is formatted as the EAP-Message RADIUS attribute (RFC 2869, section 5.13) and sent in a RADIUS message between the access server and the RADIUS server. The access server becomes a pass-through device, passing EAP messages between the access client and the RADIUS server. EAP message processing occurs at the access client and the RADIUS server, not at the access server. This relationship is shown in Figure 5-6.

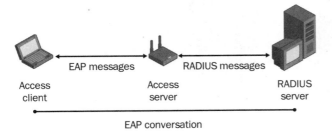

Figure 5-6. *EAP over RADIUS.*

EAP over RADIUS is used in environments where RADIUS is the authentication provider. An advantage of using EAP over RADIUS is that EAP types do not need to be installed at each access server, only at the RADIUS server. However, the access server must support the negotiation of EAP as an authentication protocol and the passing of EAP messages to a RADIUS server.

In a typical use of EAP over RADIUS, the access server is configured to use EAP and to use RADIUS as its authentication provider. Because EAP is part of the IEEE 802.1X standard, you must enable IEEE 802.1X authentication to enable a wireless AP to use EAP.

When a connection attempt is made, the access client negotiates the use of EAP with the access server. When the client sends an EAP message to the access server, the access server encapsulates the EAP message as the EAP-Message attribute of a RADIUS Access-Request message and sends it to its configured RADIUS server. The RADIUS server processes the EAP message in the EAP-Message attribute and sends an EAP response message as a RADIUS Access-Challenge message with the EAP-Message attribute to the access server. The access server then forwards the EAP message to the access client.

EAP-TLS and the IEEE 802.1X Authentication Process

The following is the EAP-TLS authentication process for a wireless client authenticating to a wireless AP configured to use a RADIUS server as its authentication server:

1. Association and request for identity.

   If the wireless AP observes a new wireless client associating with it, the wireless AP transmits an EAP-Request/Identity message to the wireless client. Alternately, when a wireless client associates with a new wireless AP, it transmits an EAP-Start message. If the IEEE 802.1X process on the wireless AP receives an EAP-Start message from a wireless client, it transmits an EAP-Request/Identity message to the wireless client.

2. EAP-Response/Identity response.

If there is no user logged on to the wireless client, it transmits an EAP-Response/Identity containing the computer name. For Windows wireless clients, the FQDN of the computer account is sent. If there is a user logged on to the wireless client, it transmits an EAP-Response/Identity containing the username. For Windows wireless clients, the user principal name (UPN) of the user account is sent. The wireless AP forwards the EAP-Response/Identity message to the RADIUS server in the form of a RADIUS Access-Request message.

3. EAP-Request from RADIUS server (Start TLS).

The RADIUS server sends a RADIUS Access-Challenge message containing an EAP-Request message with the EAP-Type set to EAP-TLS, requesting a start to the TLS authentication process. The wireless AP forwards the EAP message to the wireless client.

4. EAP-Response from the wireless client (TLS Client Hello).

The wireless client sends an EAP-Response message with the EAP-Type set to EAP-TLS, indicating the TLS client hello. The wireless AP forwards the EAP message to the RADIUS server in the form of a RADIUS Access-Request message.

5. EAP Request from RADIUS server (RADIUS Server's Certificate).

The RADIUS server sends a RADIUS Access-Challenge message containing an EAP-Request message with the EAP-Type set to EAP-TLS and includes the RADIUS server's certificate chain. The wireless AP forwards the EAP message to the wireless client.

6. EAP-Response from the wireless client (Wireless Client's Certificate).

The wireless client sends an EAP-Response message with the EAP-Type set to EAP-TLS and includes the wireless client's certificate chain. The wireless AP forwards the EAP message to the RADIUS server in the form of a RADIUS Access-Request message.

7. EAP-Request from RADIUS server (Cipher suite, TLS complete).

The RADIUS server sends a RADIUS Access-Challenge message containing an EAP-Request message with the EAP-Type set to EAP-TLS, which includes the cipher suite and an indication that TLS authentication message exchanges are complete. The wireless AP forwards the EAP message to the wireless client.

8. EAP-Response from the wireless client.

The wireless client sends an EAP-Response message with the EAP-Type set to EAP-TLS. The wireless AP forwards the EAP message to the RADIUS server in the form of a RADIUS Access-Request message.

9. EAP-Success from RADIUS server.

The RADIUS server derives the per-client unicast session key and the signing key from the keying material that is a result of the EAP-TLS authentication process. Next, the RADIUS server sends a RADIUS Access-Accept message containing an EAP-Success message and the MPPE-Send-Key and MPPE-Recv-Key attributes to the wireless AP.

The wireless AP uses the key encrypted in the MS-MPPE-Send-Key attribute as the per-client unicast session key for data transmissions to the wireless client (truncated to the appropriate WEP key length). The wireless AP uses the key encrypted in the MS-MPPE-Recv-Key attribute as a signing key for data transmissions to the wireless client that require signing (truncated to the appropriate WEP key length).

The wireless client derives the per-client unicast session key (the same value as the decrypted MS-MPPE-Send-Key attribute in the RADIUS message sent to the wireless AP) and the signing key (the same value as the decrypted MS-MPPE-Recv-Key attribute in the RADIUS message sent to the wireless AP) from the keying material that is a result of the EAP-TLS authentication process. Therefore, the wireless AP and the wireless client are using the same keys for both the encryption and signing of unicast data.

After receiving the RADIUS server message, the wireless AP forwards the EAP-Success message to the wireless client. The EAP-Success message does not contain the per-station unicast session or signing keys.

10. Multicast/global encryption key to the wireless client.

The wireless AP sends an EAP over LAN (EAPOL)-Key message to the wireless client containing the multicast/global key that is encrypted using the per-client unicast session key.

The Key field of the IEEE 802.1X EAPOL-Key message is RC4-encrypted by using the per-client unicast session key, and portions of the message are signed with HMAC-MD5 by using the per-client unicast signing key.

After receiving the EAPOL-Key message, the wireless client uses the per-client unicast session and signing keys to verify the signed portions of the EAPOL-Key message and decrypt the multicast/global key. Next, the wireless LAN network adapter driver indicates the per-client unicast session key, the per-client unicast signing key, and the multicast/global key to the wireless LAN network adapter. After the keys are indicated, the wireless client begins the protocol configuration by using the wireless adapter (such as using Dynamic Host Configuration Protocol [DHCP] to obtain an IP address configuration).

When the wireless AP changes the multicast/global key, it generates and sends EAPOL-Key messages to its connected wireless clients. Each EAPOL-Key message contains the new multicast/global key encrypted with the particular wireless client's per-client unicast session key.

This process is summarized in Figure 5-7.

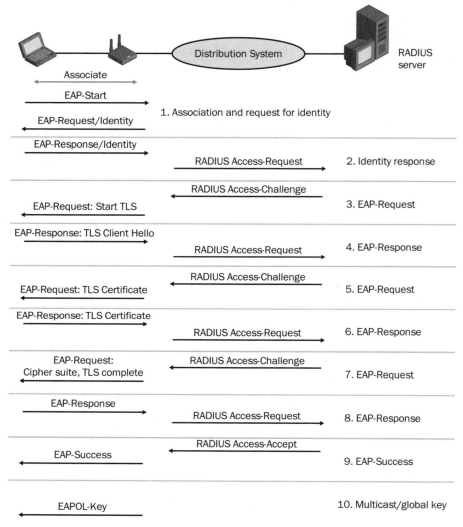

Figure 5-7. *EAP-TLS and the IEEE 802.1X authentication process.*

PEAP

Although EAP provides authentication flexibility through the use of EAP types, the entire EAP conversation might be sent as clear text (unencrypted). A malicious user with access to the media can inject packets into the conversation or capture the EAP messages from a successful authentication for offline analysis. This security breach is especially problematic for wireless connections, in which the malicious user can be located outside of your business. EAP occurs during the IEEE 802.1X authentication process, before wireless frames are encrypted with Wired Equivalent Privacy (WEP).

PEAP is an EAP type that addresses this security issue by first creating a secure channel that is both encrypted and integrity-protected with TLS. Then, a new EAP negotiation with another EAP type occurs, authenticating the network access attempt of the client. Because the TLS channel protects EAP negotiation and authentication for the network access attempt, password-based authentication protocols that are normally susceptible to an offline dictionary attack can be used for authentication in wireless environments.

Like EAP-TLS, PEAP has a client-side and server-side configuration.

Configuring PEAP on the Wireless Client

Figure 5-8 shows the client-side Protected EAP Properties dialog box for Windows XP (SP 1 and later), Windows 2000 with Microsoft 802.1X Authentication Client, and Windows Server 2003. This dialog box can be accessed from the Authentication tab on the properties of a wireless network or wireless network adapter.

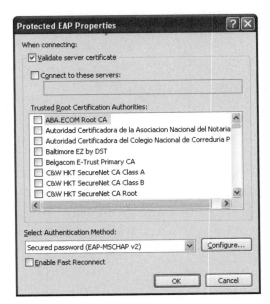

Figure 5-8. *Client-side Protected EAP Properties dialog box.*

From the Protected EAP Properties dialog box, you can view and configure the following:

- **Validate Server Certificate**   This option, which is enabled by default, allows you to validate the computer certificate of the RADIUS server.

- **Connect To These Servers** This option allows you to specify by name the RADIUS servers that provide authentication and authorization for the connection. If you specify a server name, it must exactly match the server name in the Subject field of the RADIUS server's certificate. Use semicolons to specify multiple RADIUS server names.

- **Trusted Root Certification Authorities** This option allows you to select multiple trusted root CAs that the wireless client will accept to verify the certificate of the RADIUS server.

- **Select Authentication Method** This option allows you to select the specific PEAP type to use for authentication. Only Secured Password (EAP-MSCHAP v2) and Smart Card Or Other Certificate are selectable by default.

- **Enable Fast Reconnect** This option, which is disabled by default, specifies whether you want to enable or disable fast reconnect to reduce reauthentication times. For more information, see the "PEAP Fast Reconnect" section later in this chapter.

Configuring PEAP on the IAS Server

Figure 5-9 shows the server-side Protected EAP Properties dialog box for Windows 2000 with Microsoft 802.1X Authentication Client and Windows Server 2003 IAS. This dialog box can be accessed from the Authentication tab of the profile properties of a remote access policy.

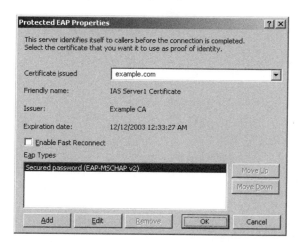

Figure 5-9. *Server-side Protected EAP Properties dialog box.*

From the server-side Protected EAP Properties dialog box, you can view and configure the following:

- **Certificate Issued**   This option allows you to select the computer certificate to send to the wireless client during the initial PEAP authentication. The certificates in this list correspond to the list of certificates in the Local Computer certificate store. If a certificate in the Local Computer certificate store does not appear in this list, the certificate does not support the SChannel cryptographic provider, so it cannot be used for authentication by the client.

- **Friendly Name**   This field displays the friendly name for the certificate, which might not be configured by default. To configure a friendly name, obtain properties of the certificate by using the Certificates snap-in configured for the computer account (for the Local Computer certificate store). From the Details tab, click Edit Properties. On the General tab, type a friendly name in the Friendly Name text box.

- **Issuer**   This field displays the name of the CA that issued the selected certificate.

- **Expiration Date**   This field displays the expiration date and time for the selected certificate.

- **Enable Fast Reconnect**   This option, which is disabled by default, specifies whether you want to use fast reconnect to reduce reauthentication times. For more information, see the "PEAP Fast Reconnect" section later in this chapter.

- **EAP Types**   This option lists the EAP types selected for use with PEAP. No EAP types are listed by default, unless automatically configured using the Windows Server 2003 New Remote Access Policy Wizard. To add a PEAP EAP type, click Add. To configure the properties of a PEAP EAP type, select the EAP type and click Edit. To remove a PEAP EAP type, select the EAP type and click Remove.

PEAP-MS-CHAP v2 and PEAP-TLS are provided with Windows XP (SP1 and later) and Windows Server 2003 as part of enhanced EAP and IEEE 802.1X support.

Microsoft 802.1X Authentication Client provides client-side PEAP-MS-CHAP v2 and PEAP-TLS support for computers running Windows 2000. Microsoft 802.1X Authentication Client also updates IAS on Windows 2000 Server to support PEAP-MS-CHAP v2 and PEAP-TLS, allowing an IAS server to authenticate wireless clients running Windows XP (SP1 or later), Windows Server 2003, and Microsoft 802.1X Authentication Client.

PEAP-MS-CHAP v2

MS-CHAP v2 is a password-based, challenge-response, mutual authentication protocol that uses the industry-standard Message Digest 4 (MD4) and Data Encryption Standard (DES) algorithms to encrypt responses. The authenticating server challenges the access client, and the access client challenges the authenticating server. If either challenge is not correctly answered, the connection is rejected. Microsoft originally designed MS-CHAP v2 as a PPP authentication protocol to provide better protection for dial-up and VPN connections.

Although MS-CHAP v2 provides better protection than previous PPP-based challenge-response authentication protocols, it is still susceptible to an offline dictionary attack. A malicious user can capture a successful MS-CHAP v2 exchange and methodically guess passwords until the correct one is determined. Using the combination of PEAP with MS-CHAP v2, the MS-CHAP v2 exchange is protected with the strong security of the TLS channel.

Like EAP-TLS, PEAP-MS-CHAP v2 has a client-side and server-side configuration.

Configuring PEAP-MS-CHAP v2 on the Wireless Client

Figure 5-10 shows the client-side EAP MSCHAPv2 Properties dialog box for Windows XP (SP 1 and later), Windows 2000 with Microsoft 802.1X Authentication Client, and Windows Server 2003. This dialog box can be accessed from the Authentication tab on the properties of a wireless network or wireless network adapter.

Figure 5-10. *Client-side EAP MSCHAPv2 Properties dialog box.*

From the EAP MSCHAPv2 Properties dialog box, you can configure the Automatically Use My Windows Logon Name And Password (And Domain If Any) check box. When enabled (which is the default), the current user-based Windows logon name and password is used for the MS-CHAP v2 authentication credentials.

Configuring PEAP-MS-CHAP v2 on the IAS Server

Figure 5-11 shows the server-side EAP MSCHAPv2 Properties dialog box for Windows 2000 with Microsoft 802.1X Authentication Client and Windows Server 2003 IAS. This dialog box can be accessed from the Authentication tab of the profile properties of a remote access policy. To view this dialog box, click EAP Methods, add the Protected EAP (PEAP) EAP provider (if needed), and then edit the Protected EAP (PEAP) EAP providers. From the Protected EAP Properties dialog box, click the Secured Password (EAP-MS-CHAP v2) EAP type and then click Edit.

Figure 5-11. *Server-side EAP MSCHAPv2 Properties dialog box.*

From the EAP MSCHAPv2 Properties dialog box, you can view and configure the following:

- **Number Of Authentication Retries** This option specifies the number of times that an PEAP-MS-CHAP v2-based authentication can be retried before rejecting the connection. The default is two retries.

- **Allow Client To Change Password After It Has Expired** This option, which is enabled by default, enables or disables the ability of the user at the wireless client to change their password using MS-CHAP v2 after the password has expired.

PEAP with MS-CHAP v2 Operation

The PEAP authentication process occurs in two parts: the first part uses EAP and the PEAP EAP type to create an encrypted TLS channel; the second part uses EAP and a different EAP type to authenticate network access. This section examines the PEAP with MS-CHAP v2 operation, using a wireless client that attempts to authenticate to a wireless AP that uses a RADIUS server for authentication and authorization.

The following steps are used to create the PEAP-TLS channel:

▶ **PEAP Part 1: Creating the TLS Channel**

1. After creating the logical link, the wireless AP sends an EAP-Request/Identity message to the wireless client.

2. The wireless client responds with an EAP-Response/Identity message that contains the identity (username or computer name) of the wireless client.

3. The EAP-Response/Identity message is sent by the wireless AP to the RADIUS server. From this point on, the logical communication occurs between the RADIUS server and the wireless client by using the wireless AP as a pass-through device.

4. The RADIUS server sends an EAP-Request/Start PEAP message to the wireless client.

5. The wireless client and the RADIUS server exchange a series of TLS messages through which the cipher suite for the TLS channel is negotiated, and the RADIUS server sends a certificate chain to the wireless client for authentication.

At the end of the PEAP negotiation, the RADIUS server has authenticated itself to the wireless client. Both nodes have determined mutual encryption keys for the TLS channel by using public key cryptography, not passwords. All subsequent EAP messages sent between the wireless client and the RADIUS server are encrypted.

After the PEAP-TLS channel is created, the following steps are used to authenticate the wireless client credentials with MS-CHAP v2:

▶ **PEAP Part 2: Authenticating with MS-CHAP v2**

1. The RADIUS server sends an EAP-Request/Identity message.

2. The wireless client responds with an EAP-Response/Identity message that contains the identity (user or computer name) of the wireless client.

3. The RADIUS server sends an EAP-Request/EAP-MS-CHAP v2 Challenge message that contains a challenge string.

4. The wireless client responds with an EAP-Response/EAP-MS-CHAP v2 Response message that contains both the response to the RADIUS server challenge string and a challenge string for the RADIUS server.

5. The RADIUS server sends an EAP-Request/EAP-MS-CHAP v2 Success message, indicating that the wireless client response is correct and contains the response to the wireless client challenge string.

6. The wireless client responds with an EAP-Response/EAP-MS-CHAP v2 Ack message, indicating that the RADIUS server response is correct.

7. The RADIUS server sends an EAP-Success message.

At the end of this mutual authentication exchange:

• The wireless client has provided proof of knowledge of the correct password (the response to the RADIUS server challenge string).

• The RADIUS server has provided proof of knowledge of the correct password (the response to the wireless client challenge string).

• The entire exchange has been encrypted through the TLS channel created in the first part of the PEAP authentication.

PEAP-MS-CHAP v2 requires a certificate on each RADIUS server, but not on the wireless clients. IAS servers must have a certificate installed in their Local Computer certificate store. Instead of deploying a PKI, you can purchase individual certificates from a third-party CA to install on your IAS servers. To ensure that wireless clients can validate the IAS server certificate chain, the root CA certificate of the CA that issued the IAS server certificates must be installed on each wireless client.

Windows 2000, Windows XP, and Windows Server 2003 include the root CA certificates of many third-party CAs. If you purchase your IAS server certificates from a third-party CA that corresponds to an included root CA certificate, no additional wireless client configuration is required. If you purchase your IAS server certificates from a third-party CA for which your Windows clients do not include a corresponding root CA certificate, you must install the root CA certificate on each wireless client.

PEAP-TLS

PEAP-TLS is the EAP-TLS authentication method used after PEAP has created a secure channel. PEAP-TLS is slightly more secure than EAP-TLS alone because the entire EAP-TLS authentication exchange is protected with the PEAP secure channel.

You should not use both EAP-TLS and PEAP-TLS for the same kind of network access. Allowing both protected (PEAP) and unprotected (EAP) authentication traffic for the same type of network connection renders the protected authentication traffic susceptible to spoofing attacks. Therefore, do not allow EAP-TLS and PEAP-TLS authentication at the same time for the same type of network access (for example, for wireless). This is not an issue with MS-CHAP v2, which is available only as PEAP-MS-CHAP v2.

The configuration of PEAP-TLS for both the client and server side is the same as that for EAP-TLS.

PEAP with TLS Operation

This section examines PEAP with TLS operation by using a wireless client that attempts to authenticate to a wireless AP that uses a RADIUS server for authentication and authorization.

▶ **PEAP Part 1: Creating the TLS Channel**

- PEAP Part 1 occurs in the same way as previously described for PEAP-MS-CHAP v2.

After the PEAP-TLS channel is created, the following steps are used to authenticate the wireless client credentials with TLS:

▶ **PEAP Part 2: Authenticating with TLS**

1. The RADIUS server sends an EAP-Request/Identity message.

2. The wireless client responds with an EAP-Response/Identity message that contains the identity (username or computer name) of the wireless client.

3. The RADIUS server sends an EAP-Request/Start TLS message.

4. The wireless client responds with an EAP-Response/TLS Client Hello message.

5. The RADIUS server sends an EAP-Request/TLS message that includes the RADIUS server's certificate chain.

6. The wireless client responds with an EAP-Response/TLS message that includes the wireless client's certificate chain.

7. The RADIUS server sends an EAP-Request/TLS message that includes the cipher suite and an indication that TLS authentication message exchanges are complete.

8. The wireless client responds with an EAP-Response/TLS message.

9. The RADIUS server sends an EAP-Success message.

At the end of this mutual authentication exchange:

- The wireless client has provided proof of knowledge of the private key corresponding to its sent certificate and validated the RADIUS server's certificate.

- The RADIUS server has provided proof of knowledge of the private key corresponding to its sent certificate and validated the wireless client's certificate.

PEAP Fast Reconnect

You can also use PEAP to quickly resume a TLS session. If PEAP Part 2 is successful, the RADIUS server can cache the TLS session created during PEAP Part 1. Because the cache entry was created through a successful PEAP Part 2 authentication process, the session can be resumed without having to fully perform PEAP Part 1 or Part 2. In this case, an EAP-Success message is sent almost immediately for a reauthentication attempt. This process, which is known as *fast reconnect*, minimizes the connection delay in wireless environments when a wireless client roams from one wireless AP to another.

Fast reconnect in Windows is enabled from the Protected EAP Properties dialog box, which can be accessed from the following locations:

- For Windows XP (SP1 and later) wireless clients, from the Authentication tab for the settings of a wireless network.

- For Microsoft 802.1X Authentication Client wireless clients, from the Authentication tab for the settings of a wireless network adapter.

- For Windows Server 2003 IAS, from the Authentication tab in the profile settings of a remote access policy.

Fast reconnect is disabled by default. You can enable fast reconnect for multiple wireless clients by using the Wireless Network (IEEE 802.11b) Policies computer configuration Group Policy setting, as described in Chapter 3, "Windows Wireless Client Support."

Windows 2000 IAS with Microsoft 802.1X Authentication Client installed does not support fast reconnect.

Summary

EAP allows for arbitrary methods to authenticate network access. EAP and EAP types are required for IEEE 802.1X–based wireless authentication. Secure wireless access is obtained by using certificates with either EAP-TLS or PEAP-TLS, or passwords with PEAP-MS-CHAP v2. Windows 2000 (with Microsoft 802.1X Authentication Client), Windows XP (SP1 and later), Windows Server 2003 wireless clients, and IAS for Windows 2000 (with Microsoft 802.1X Authentication Client) and Windows Server 2003 support EAP-TLS, PEAP-TLS, and PEAP-MS-CHAP v2.

Chapter 6
Certificates and Public Key Infrastructure

To provide security for the authentication of 802.1X-based wireless connections that use either Extensible Authentication Protocol-Transport Layer Security (EAP-TLS) or Protected EAP-Microsoft Challenge Handshake Authentication Protocol version 2 (PEAP-MS-CHAP v2), certificates are used. For EAP-TLS-based wireless authentication, the wireless client and authenticating server (a RADIUS server) exchange certificates. For PEAP-MS-CHAP v2 authentication, the Remote Authentication Dial-In User Service (RADIUS) server sends the wireless client a certificate. This chapter provides an overview of the elements of certificates and public key infrastructure (PKI) for wireless authentication.

More Info For more information about certificates and security, see the Microsoft Windows 2000 Security Services Web site at *http://www.microsoft.com /windows2000/technologies/security/default.asp* and the Windows Server 2003 Security Services Web site at *http://www.microsoft.com/windowsserver2003 /technologies/security/default.mspx*.

Certificates

Symmetric encryption (also known as *private key encryption* or *conventional encryption*) is based on a secret key that is shared by both communicating parties. The sending party uses the secret key as part of the mathematical operation to encrypt plaintext to ciphertext. The receiving party uses the same secret key to decrypt the ciphertext to plaintext. An example of a symmetric encryption algorithm is Data Encryption Standard (DES), which is used for Internet Protocol security (IPSec) encryption.

Asymmetric encryption, or *public key encryption*, uses two different keys for each communicating party: One is a private key known only to each individual communicating party; the other is a corresponding public key, which is accessible to anyone. The private and public keys are mathematically related by the encryption algorithm. One key is used for encryption, and the other key is used for decryption. When sending an encrypted message, the sender uses the recipient's public key to encrypt the message, and the receiver uses the corresponding private key to decrypt the message.

Public key encryption technologies also allow digital signatures to be placed on messages. To create a digital signature, the sender first calculates a hash of the message. A *hash* is a number that represents a mathematical summary of the message. The sender then encrypts the hash using the private key. The encrypted hash is the digital signature that is sent along with the message. When the message and its digital signature are received, the receiver calculates their own value of the hash for the message. The receiver then uses the sender's corresponding public key to decrypt the hash in the digital signature and verify that the calculated hash equals the decrypted hash. If they are the same, the message was not modified in transit and must have been sent by the sender.

With symmetric encryption, both sender and receiver have a shared secret key. The distribution of the secret key must occur (with adequate protection) prior to any encrypted communication. However, with asymmetric encryption, the sender uses one key to encrypt or digitally sign messages, whereas the receiver uses the other corresponding key for decryption of the message or digital signature verification. The public key can be freely distributed to anyone who needs to encrypt messages or verify the digital signature of messages. The sender needs to carefully protect the private key only.

To secure the integrity of the public key, the public key is published as part of a certificate. A *certificate*, also known as a *digital certificate* or *public key certificate*, is a data structure that contains a digital signature of a certification authority (CA)—an entity that users of the certificate can trust. A certificate is a digitally signed statement that binds the value of a public key to the identity of the person, device, or service that holds the corresponding private key.

Certificate Fields

A certificate is composed of a series of fields that contain the information needed to identify the subject of the certificate and the corresponding public key, to identify the issuer of the certificate, and to verify that the certificate is sound.

The certificates used by Windows components are compliant with the X.509 certificate standard, which defines the following fields for certificates (among others):

- **Subject** The identification of the entity being issued the certificate. In Windows, the entity is a user, a computer, or a service.

- **Subject Public Key** The subject's public key.

- **Subject Identifier Information** Additional information about the subject, such as a directory name or an e-mail address.

- **Validity Period** A certificate is valid for only a specified period of time. Every certificate contains Valid From and Valid To dates, which are the boundaries of the validity period. When a certificate's validity period has passed, the subject must request a new certificate.

- **Issuer Identifier Information**   The identification of the issuer and signer of the certificate (the issuing CA).

- **Certificate Signature**   Contains the digital signature of the certificate as computed by the issuing CA. The certificate signature provides proof of the validity of the binding between the subject public key and the subject identifier information.

A subject's certificate is either published or sent during a negotiation for secure communications. Upon retrieval or receipt of an X.509 certificate, the receiver has the public key of the sender and a means to verify that it belongs to them. To verify the certificate's signature, the receiver does the following:

1. Calculates its own hash of the certificate (using the same hash algorithm of the sender).

2. Obtains the issuing CA's X.509 certificate.

3. Uses the public key contained within the issuing CA's X.509 certificate to decrypt the certificate's signature.

4. Compares the decrypted hash value with the calculated value. If they are the same, the issuing CA issued the sender's certificate. If they are not, the sender's certificate is considered invalid.

For Windows, the fields of a certificate are visible from the Details tab when viewing the properties of a certificate. One way to view the properties of a certificate is through the Certificates snap-in. Figure 6-1 shows an example.

Figure 6-1. *The Details tab when viewing the properties of a certificate.*

Public Key Infrastructure

A public key infrastructure (PKI) is a system of digital certificates and CAs that verifies and authenticates the validity of each entity that is participating in secure communications through the use of public key cryptography.

Certification Authorities

When a certificate is presented to an entity as a means of identifying the certificate holder (the subject of the certificate), it is useful only if the entity being presented the certificate trusts the issuing CA. When you trust an issuing CA, it means you have confidence that the CA has the proper policies in place when evaluating certificate requests and will deny certificates to any entity that does not meet those policies. In addition, you trust that the issuing CA will revoke certificates that should no longer be considered valid by publishing an up-to-date certificate revocation list (CRL). For more information about CRLs, see the "Certificate Revocation" section of this chapter.

For Windows users, computers, and services, trust in a CA is established when you have a copy of the self-signed certificate of the root CA of the issuing CA locally installed, as well as having a valid certification path—meaning that none of the certificates in the certification path has been revoked or has had its validity period expire. The certification path includes every certificate issued to each CA in the certification hierarchy from a subordinate CA to the root CA. For example, for a root CA, the certification path is one certificate: its own self-signed certificate. For a subordinate CA, just below the root CA in the hierarchy, its certification path is two certificates: its own certificate and the root CA certificate.

If your organization is using the Active Directory directory service, trust in your organization's certification authorities will typically be established automatically, based on decisions and settings made by the system administrator.

Certification Hierarchies

A certification hierarchy provides scalability, ease of administration, and consistency with a growing number of commercial and other CA products. In its simplest form, a certification hierarchy consists of a single CA. However, in general, a hierarchy will contain multiple CAs with clearly defined parent-child relationships. In this model, the subordinate certification authorities are certified by their parent CA-issued certificates, which bind a CA's public key to its identity. The CA at the top of a hierarchy is referred to as the root authority, or root CA. The child CAs of the root CAs are called subordinate CAs.

In Windows 2000 Server, Windows XP, and Windows Server 2003, if you trust a root CA (by having its certificate in your Trusted Root Certification Authorities certificate store), you trust every subordinate CA in the hierarchy, unless a subordinate CA has had its certificate revoked by the issuing CA or has an expired certificate. Thus, any root CA is a very important point of trust in an organization and should be secured and maintained accordingly.

Verification of certificates thus requires trust in only a small number of root CAs. At the same time, it provides flexibility in the number of certificate-issuing subordinate CAs. There are several practical reasons for supporting multiple subordinate CAs, including the following:

- **Usage**   Certificates may be issued for a number of purposes, such as secure e-mail and network authentication. The issuing policy for these uses may be distinct, and separation provides a basis for administering these policies.

- **Organizational divisions**   There may be different policies for issuing certificates, depending upon an entity's role in the organization. You can create subordinate CAs to separate and administer these policies.

- **Geographic divisions**   Organizations may have entities at multiple physical sites. Network connectivity between these sites may dictate a requirement for multiple subordinate CAs to meet usability requirements.

- **Load balancing**   If your PKI will support the issuing of a large number of certificates, having only one CA issue and manage all these certificates can result in considerable network load for that single CA. Using multiple subordinate certification authorities to issue the same kind of certificates divides the network load between certification authorities.

- **Backup and fault tolerance**   Multiple certification authorities increase the possibility that your network will always have operational certification authorities available to service users.

Such a certificate hierarchy also provides administrative benefits, including the following:

- Flexible configuration of the CA security environment to tailor the balance between security and usability, such as key strength, physical protection, and protection against network attacks.

    For example, you might choose to employ special-purpose cryptographic hardware on a root CA, operate it in a physically secure area, or operate it offline. These security measures may be unacceptable for subordinate CAs because of cost or usability considerations.

- The ability to "turn off" a specific portion of the CA hierarchy without affecting the established trust relationships.

    For example, you can easily shut down and revoke an issuing CA certificate that is associated with a specific geographic site without affecting other parts of the organization.

The certification path for a certificate can be viewed from the Certification Path tab of the properties of a certificate, as shown in Figure 6-2.

Figure 6-2. *The Certification Path tab when viewing the properties of a certificate.*

For a small business environment, a certificate hierarchy consisting of a single root CA that is also the issuing CA is adequate. For a medium-sized organization, a single root CA with a single level of issuing CAs is adequate. For an enterprise network, you should deploy at least a three-level CA hierarchy, consisting of the following:

- A root CA that is offline (not available on the network)

- A layer of intermediate CAs that are offline

- A layer of issuing CAs that are online

This CA hierarchy provides flexibility and insulates the root CA from attempts to compromise its private key by malicious users. The offline root and intermediate CAs do not have to be Windows Server 2003 or Windows 2000 Server CAs. Issuing CAs can be subordinates of a third-party intermediate CA. This hierarchy is shown in Figure 6-3.

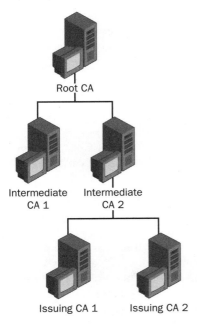

Figure 6-3. *Recommended certificate hierarchy for enterprise networks.*

Certificate Revocation

Revocation of a certificate invalidates a certificate as a trusted security credential prior to the natural expiration of its validity period. There are a number of reasons why a certificate, as a security credential, could become untrustworthy prior to its expiration, including the following:

- Compromise, or suspected compromise, of the certificate subject's private key.

- Compromise, or suspected compromise, of a CA's private key.

- Discovery that a certificate was obtained fraudulently.

- Change in the status of the certificate subject as a trusted entity.

- Change in the name of the certificate subject.

A PKI depends on distributed verification of credentials in which there is no need for direct communication with the central trusted entity that vouches for the credentials. This creates a need to distribute certificate revocation information to individuals, computers, and applications attempting to verify the validity of certificates. The need for revocation information and its timeliness will vary, according to the application and its implementation of certificate revocation checking.

To effectively support certificate revocation, the validating entity must determine whether the certificate is valid or has been revoked. Windows supports industry-standard methods of certificate revocation, including publication of CRLs and delta CRLs in several locations for clients to access in Active Directory and on Web servers and network file shares.

CRLs are digitally-signed lists of unexpired certificates that have been revoked. Clients retrieve this list and can then cache it (based on the configured lifetime of the CRL) and use it to verify certificates presented for use. Because CRLs can get large, depending on the size of the CA, delta CRLs can also be published. Delta CRLs contain only the certificates revoked since the last base CRL was published, which allows clients to retrieve the smaller delta CRL and quickly build a complete list of revoked certificates. The use of delta CRLs also allows more frequent publishing because the size of the delta CRL usually does not require as much overhead as a full CRL.

Note Windows Server 2003 CAs support delta CRLs. Delta CRLs are not supported by Windows 2000 Server CAs.

Certificate Revocation and IAS

By default, the Internet Authentication Service (IAS) server acting as a RADIUS server checks for certificate revocation for all the certificates in the certificate chain sent by the wireless client during the EAP-TLS authentication process. If certificate revocation fails for any of the certificates in the chain, the connection attempt is rejected. The certificate revocation check for a certificate can fail because of the following:

- **The certificate has been revoked** The issuer of the certificate has explicitly revoked the certificate.

- **The CRL for the certificate is not reachable or available** CAs maintain CRLs and publish them to specific CRL distribution points. The CRL distribution points are included in the CRL Distribution Points field of the certificate, which is shown in the following graphic.

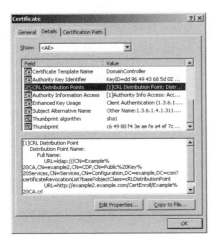

If the CRL distribution points cannot be contacted to check for certificate revocation, the certificate revocation check fails.

Additionally, if there are no CRL distribution points in the certificate, the IAS server cannot verify that the certificate has not been revoked, and the certificate revocation check fails.

- **The publisher of the CRL did not issue the certificate**   Included in the CRL is the publishing CA. If the publishing CA of the CRL does not match the issuing CA for the certificate for which certificate revocation is being checked, the certificate revocation check fails.

- **The CRL is not current**   Each published CRL has a range of valid dates. If the CRL Next Update date has passed, the CRL is considered invalid, and the certificate revocation check fails. New CRLs should be published before the expiration date of the last published CRL.

Certificate revocation checking behavior for IAS can be modified with registry settings. For more information, see Chapter 16, "Troubleshooting the Authentication Infrastructure."

Because certificate revocation checking can prevent wireless access due to the unavailability or expiration of CRLs for each certificate in the certificate chain, you should design your PKI for high availability of CRLs. For instance, configure multiple CRL distribution points for each CA in the certificate hierarchy and configure publication schedules that ensure that the most current CRL is always available.

Certificate revocation checking is only as accurate as the last published CRL. For example, if a certificate is revoked, by default the new CRL containing the newly revoked certificate is not automatically published. CRLs are typically published based on a configurable schedule. This means that the revoked certificate can still be used for authentication because the published CRL is not current; it does not contain the revoked certificate and can therefore still be used to create wireless connections. To prevent this from occurring, the network administrator must manually publish the new CRL with the newly revoked certificate.

By default, the IAS server uses the CRL distribution points in the certificates. However, it is also possible to store a local copy of the CRL on the IAS server. In this case, the local CRL is used during certificate revocation checking. If a new CRL is manually published to the Active Directory, the local CRL on the IAS server is not updated. The local CRL is updated when it expires, which can create a situation wherein a certificate is revoked and the CRL is manually published, but the IAS server still allows the connection because the local CRL has not yet been updated.

Certificate Validation

The certificates that are offered during the negotiation for secure communication must be validated before secure communication can begin. For secure wireless authentication using EAP-TLS, the IAS server must validate the certificate offered by the Windows wireless client. For secure wireless authentication using either EAP-TLS or PEAP-MS-CHAP v2, the Windows wireless client must validate the certificate offered by the IAS server.

Certificate Validation by the IAS Server

In order for the IAS server to validate the certificate of the wireless client, the following must be true for each certificate in the certification path (also known as a certificate chain) sent by the wireless client:

- **The current date is within the validity dates of the certificate** When certificates are issued, they are issued with a range of valid dates, before which they cannot be used and after which they are considered expired.

- **The certificate has not been revoked** By default, the IAS server checks all the certificates in the wireless client's certificate chain (the series of certificates from the wireless client certificate to the root CA) for revocation. If any of the certificates in the chain have been revoked, certificate validation fails. This behavior can be modified with registry settings described in Chapter 16.

  The certificate revocation validation works only as well as the CRL publishing and distribution system. If the CRL in a certificate is not updated often, a certificate that has been revoked can still be used and considered valid because the published CRL that the IAS server is checking is out-of-date.

- **The certificate has a valid digital signature** CAs digitally sign certificates they issue. The IAS server verifies the digital signature of each certificate in the chain, with the exception of the root CA certificate, by obtaining the public key from the certificate's issuing CA and mathematically validating the digital signature.

The wireless client certificate must also have the Client Authentication Enhanced Key Usage (EKU), using the object identifier (OID) of 1.3.6.1.5.5.7.3.2, and must either contain a user principal name (UPN) of a valid user account or fully qualified domain name (FQDN) of a valid computer account for the Subject Alternative Name field of the certificate.

To view the EKU for a certificate, obtain properties of the certificate, click the Details tab, and then click the Enhanced Key Usage field. The Enhanced Key Usage field of a computer certificate is shown in Figure 6-4.

Figure 6-4. *The Enhanced Key Usage field for a computer certificate.*

To view the Subject Alternative Name field for a certificate, obtain properties of the certificate, click the Details tab and then click the Subject Alternative Name field. The Subject Alternative Name field of a computer certificate is shown in Figure 6-5.

Figure 6-5. *The Subject Alternative Name field for a computer certificate.*

Finally, to trust the certificate chain offered by the wireless client, the IAS server must have the root CA certificate of the issuing CA of the wireless client certificate installed in its Trusted Root Certification Authorities Local Computer store.

Certificate Validation by the Windows Wireless Client

In order for the wireless client to validate the certificate of the IAS server for either EAP-TLS or PEAP-MS-CHAP v2 authentication, the following must be true for each certificate in the certificate chain sent by the IAS server:

- The current date must be within the validity dates of the certificate.

- The certificate must have a valid digital signature.

  The wireless client verifies the digital signature of each certificate in the chain, with the exception of the root CA certificate, by obtaining the public key from the certificate's issuing CA and mathematically validating the digital signature.

Additionally, the IAS server computer certificate must have the Server Authentication EKU (OID 1.3.6.1.5.5.7.3.1).

Finally, to trust the certificate chain offered by the IAS server, the wireless client must have the root CA certificate of the issuing CA of the IAS server certificate installed in its Trusted Root Certification Authorities Local Computer store.

Notice that the wireless client does not perform certificate revocation checking for the certificates in the certificate chain of the IAS server's computer certificate. The assumption is that the wireless client does not yet have a physical connection to the network, and therefore it cannot access a Web page or other resource in order to check for certificate revocation.

Windows Certificate Support

Windows has built-in support for certificates in the following ways:

- Every computer running Windows 2000, Windows XP, or Windows Server 2003 has the ability to store computer and user certificates and manage them using the Certificates snap-in, subject to Windows security and permissions.

- Windows 2000 Server and Windows Server 2003 include Certificate Services, which allows a Windows server computer to act as a CA.

Managing Certificates with the Certificates Snap-In

To manage the set of certificates for users, computers, or services installed on a Windows computer, you use the Certificates snap-in. Users and administrators can use the Certificates snap-in to request new certificates from enterprise CAs. In addition, users can find, view, import, and export certificates from within certificate stores. In most cases, users do not have to personally manage their certificates and their certificate stores. Administrators, policy settings, and programs that use certificates typically manage certificates.

Administrators are the primary users of the Certificates snap-in, and as such they are able to perform a wide variety of certificate management tasks in their personal certificate store as well as the certificate stores for any computer or service that they have the right to administer.

There is no prebuilt console file for the Certificates snap-in that is available in the Administrative Tools folder. You must manually build a console that contains the Certificates snap-in and then save the console configuration as a console file for future use.

> **More Info**   For more information about managing consoles and console files in Windows, see Windows help for the Microsoft Management Console (MMC).

▶ **To manage certificates for your user account**

1. Click Start, click Run, type **mmc**, and then click OK.

2. On the Console menu, click File, click Add/Remove Snap-In, and then click Add.

3. Under Snap-In in the Add Standalone Snap-In window, double-click Certificates, and then

   * If you are logged on as an administrator, click My User Account, and then click Finish.

   * If you are logged on as a user, Certificates automatically loads.

4. Click Close.

   Certificates – Current User appears on the list of selected snap-ins for the new console.

5. If you have no more snap-ins to add to the console, click OK.

6. To save this console, click File on the Console menu and then click Save.

7. In the Save As window, type the filename for the console file and click Save.

Figure 6-6 shows the Certificates snap-in for a user account.

Figure 6-6. *The Certificates snap-in for a user account.*

▶ To manage certificates for a computer

1. Log on to the computer using an account that has administrator privileges for that computer.

2. Click Start, click Run, type **mmc**, and then click OK.

3. On the Console menu, click File, click Add/Remove Snap-In, and then click Add.

4. Under Snap-In in the Add Standalone Snap-In window, double-click Certificates, click Computer Account in the Certificates Snap-In window, and then click Next.

5. Do one of the following:

   • To manage certificates for the local computer, click Local Computer and then click Finish.

   • To manage certificates for a remote computer, click Another Computer and type the name of the computer, or click Browse to select the computer name and then click Finish.

6. Click Close.

   Certificates (Local Computer) or Certificate (*ComputerName*) appears on the list of selected snap-ins for the new console.

7. If you have no more snap-ins to add to the console, click OK.

8. To save this console, on the Console menu, click File and then click Save.

9. In the Save As window, type the filename for the console file and click Save.

Figure 6-7 shows the Certificates snap-in for a computer.

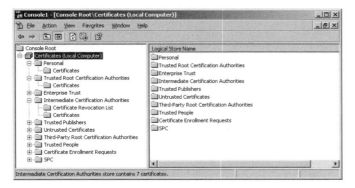

Figure 6-7. *The Certificates snap-in for a computer.*

Windows stores a certificate locally on the computer or device that requested it or, in the case of a user, on the computer or device that the user used to request it. The storage location, which is called the certificate store, often has numerous certificates, possibly issued from a number of different CAs.

Using the Certificates snap-in, you can display the certificate store for a user, a computer, or a service according to the purpose for which the certificates were issued or by using their logical storage categories. When you display certificates according to their storage categories, you can also choose to display the physical stores, showing the certificate storage hierarchy.

If you have the user rights to do so, you can import or export certificates from any of the folders in the certificate store.

Certificate Store Inheritance

If you place a root CA certificate into the computer's trusted root certification authorities store or enterprise trust store, any user of the computer will see that certificate in their own user trusted root certification authorities store or enterprise trust store, even though the root certificate is actually in the computer's store. Essentially, users will trust any CA that their computer trusts.

Certificate store inheritance does not work the other way around: certificates in the user's trusted root certification authorities store and enterprise trust store are not inherited by the computer.

Certificate Services

Certificate Services provides customizable services for issuing and managing certificates used in software security systems employing public key technologies. You can use Certificate Services in Windows 2000 Server and Windows Server 2003 to create a CA that will receive certificate requests, verify the information in the request and the identity of the requester, issue certificates, revoke certificates, and publish CRLs.

Certificate Services can also be used to do the following:

- Enroll users for certificates from the CA using the Web or the Certificates snap-in, or transparently through autoenrollment.

- Use certificate templates to help simplify the choices a certificate requester has to make when requesting a certificate, depending upon the policy used by the CA.

- Take advantage of Active Directory for publishing trusted root certificates, publishing issued certificates, and publishing CRLs.

- Implement the ability to log on to a Windows operating system domain using a smart card.

If your organization is using Certificate Services, the CA is one of two types:

- **Enterprise CA**   An enterprise CA depends upon Active Directory being present. An enterprise CA offers different types of certificates to a requester based on the certificates it is configured to issue as well as the security permissions of the requester. An enterprise CA uses information available in Active Directory to help verify the requester's identity. An enterprise CA publishes its CRL to Active Directory as well as to a shared directory. You can use the Certificate Request wizard within the Certificates snap-in, CA Web pages (Web enrollment), and autoenrollment to request certificates from an enterprise CA.

- **Standalone CA**   A standalone CA is less automated for a user than an enterprise CA because it does not require or depend on the use of Active Directory. Standalone certification authorities that do not use Active Directory generally have to request that the certificate requester provide more complete identifying information. A standalone CA makes its CRL available from a shared folder, or from Active Directory if it is available. By default, users can request certificates from a standalone CA only through Web enrollment.

Obtaining a Certificate for IEEE 802.1X Authentication

The following methods can be used to obtain certificates for Windows wireless clients and IAS server computers:

- Autoenrollment

- Request a certificate via the Web

- Request a certificate using the Certificates snap-in

- Import a certificate using the Certificates snap-in

- Create a program or script using CAPICOM

Autoenrollment

Autoenrollment is the automatic requesting and issuing of certificates based on Group Policy settings. There are two types of autoenrollment:

- **Autoenrollment of computer certificates**   Supported by Windows 2000 and Windows Server 2003 CAs and Windows XP, Windows Server 2003, and wireless clients running Windows 2000 and Microsoft 802.1X Authentication Client.

- **Autoenrollment of user certificates**   Supported by both Windows Server 2003, Enterprise Edition and Windows Server 2003, Datacenter Edition CAs and Windows XP and Windows Server 2003 wireless clients.

Autoenrollment requires an enterprise CA.

Autoenrollment of Computer Certificates

Autoenrollment of computer certificates is done through Computer Configuration Group Policy. By configuring the Automatic Certificate Request Settings Group Policy setting, you can have the computers that are members of the domain system containers to which the Group Policy object applies automatically request a certificate of specified types when Computer Configuration Group Policy settings are refreshed. The Automatic Certificate Request Settings Group Policy setting is found in the Group Policy Editor snap-in of the Management Console under Computer Configuration\Windows Settings\Security Settings\Public Key Policies in the Group Policy snap-in, as shown in Figure 6-8.

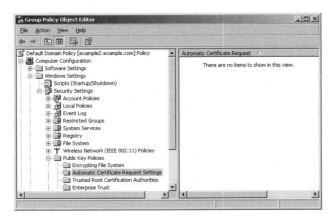

Figure 6-8. *The Group Policy location for autoenrollment of computer certificates.*

For wireless client access and for the IAS server, configure the Automatic Certificate Request Settings Group Policy setting to automatically request the Computer certificate. The Computer certificate (as named in the Certificate Template dialog box of the Automatic Certificate Request Setup Wizard) is stored in the Local Computer certificate store of the member computer; it contains both the User Authentication and Server Authentication EKUs. The OID for the Server Authentication EKU is 1.3.6.1.5.5.7.3.1, and the OID for Client Authentication EKU is 1.3.6.1.5.5.7.3.2.

EAP-TLS in Windows requires that the certificate offered for validation by the authenticating client contain the Client Authentication EKU and that the certificate offered for validation by the authenticating server contain the Server Authentication EKU. If both of these conditions are not met, the authentication fails.

Because the autoenrolled "Computer" certificate contains both the Client Authentication and Server Authentication EKUs, it can be used by both a Windows wireless client to perform computer authentication and by the IAS server as the authenticating server.

Autoenrollment of User Certificates

Autoenrollment of user certificates is done through User Configuration Group Policy. By configuring a certificate template to issue user certificates and the Autoenrollment Settings Group Policy setting, you can have the users who are members of the domain system container to which the Group Policy object applies automatically request a user certificate when User Configuration Group Policy settings are refreshed. The Autoenrollment Settings Group Policy setting is found in the Group Policy snap-in under User Configuration\Windows Settings\Security Settings\Public Key Policies, as shown in Figure 6-9.

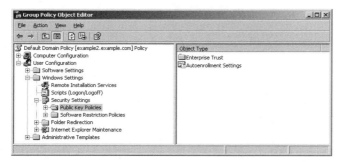

Figure 6-9. *The location of the Autoenrollment Settings Group Policy setting.*

For wireless client access, configure the Autoenrollment Settings Group Policy setting to automatically request a user certificate template that is created using the Certificate Templates snap-in. To modify template properties, you must use a CA that is running Windows Server 2003, Enterprise Edition or Windows Server 2003, Datacenter Edition.

For more information about configuring the certificate template and configuring autoenrollment of user certificates for a Windows Server 2003, Enterprise Edition CA, see Chapter 8, "Intranet Wireless Deployment Using EAP-TLS."

Requesting a Certificate via the Web

Requesting a certificate via the Web, also known as Web enrollment, is done with Microsoft Internet Explorer. For the address, type **http://*servername*/certsrv**, where *servername* is the computer name of the Windows 2000 Server or Windows Server 2003 CA that is also running Internet Information Services (IIS). A Web-based wizard takes you through the steps of requesting a certificate. The location where the certificate is stored (whether it is the Current User store or the Local Computer store) is determined by the Use Local Machine Store check box when performing an advanced certificate request. By default, this option is disabled, and certificates are stored in the Current User store. You must have local administrator privileges to store a certificate in the Local Computer store.

You can use Web enrollment with either an enterprise or standalone CA.

Requesting a Certificate Using the Certificates Snap-in

Another way to request a certificate is by using the Certificates snap-in.

▶ **To request a certificate to store in the current user store**

1. Open the Certificates-Current User\Personal folder.

2. Right-click the Personal folder, point to All tasks, and then click Request New Certificate.

A Certificate Request Wizard guides you through the steps of requesting a certificate. For wireless access, the certificate requested for the Current User store must have the Client Authentication EKU.

▶ **To request a certificate to store in the local computer store**

1. Open the Certificates (Local Computer)\Personal folder.

2. Right-click the Personal folder, point to All tasks, and then click Request New Certificate.

A Certificate Request Wizard guides you through the steps of requesting a certificate. For wireless access, the certificate requested for the Local Computer store must have the Client Authentication EKU. For the certificate installed on the IAS server, the certificate requested for the Local Computer store must have the Server Authentication EKU.

To request a certificate using the Certificates snap-in, you must use an enterprise CA.

Importing a Certificate Using the Certificates Snap-In

All the preceding ways of requesting a certificate assume that network connectivity already exists, such as using the Ethernet port on a laptop. For those configurations in which the only network connectivity is wireless, which cannot be obtained without certificates, you can also import a certificate file from a floppy disk, CD-ROM, or other recordable media using the Certificates snap-in.

▶ **To import a certificate to store in the current user store**

1. Open the Certificates-Current User\Personal folder.

2. Right-click the Personal folder, point to All Tasks, and then click Import.

A Certificate Import Wizard guides you through the steps of importing a certificate from a certificate file. For wireless access, the certificate imported into the Current User store must have the Client Authentication EKU.

▶ **To import a certificate to store in the local computer store**

1. Open the Certificates (Local Computer)\Personal folder.

2. Right-click the Personal folder, point to All tasks, and then click Import.

A Certificate Import Wizard guides you through the steps of importing a certificate from a certificate file. For a Windows wireless client, the certificate imported into the Local Computer store must have the Client Authentication EKU. For the certificate installed on the IAS server, the certificate imported into the Local Computer store must have the Server Authentication EKU.

Best Practices   It is also possible to import a certificate by double-clicking a certificate file that is stored in a folder or sent in an e-mail message. Although this works for certificates created with Windows CAs, this method does not work for third-party CAs. The recommended method of importing certificates is to use the Certificates snap-in.

If you use PEAP-MS-CHAP v2, you might have to install the root CA certificate of the issuing CA of the computer certificates that are installed on your IAS servers. To obtain the root CA certificate, first export the root CA certificate to a file (*.P7B) from the Certificates (Local Computer)\Trusted Root Certification Authorities\Certificates folder on the IAS server. For an individual wireless client computer, import the root CA certificate file into the Certificates (Local Computer)\Trusted Root Certification Authorities\Certificates folder on the wireless client. To distribute the root CA certificate to all wireless client computers in an Active Directory environment, see "Configuring Wireless Client Computers" in Chapter 10, "Intranet Wireless Deployment Using PEAP-MS-CHAP v2."

Creating a Program or Script Using CAPICOM

Requesting a certificate using Web enrollment or the Certificates snap-in requires user intervention. To automate the certificate distribution process, a network administrator can write an executable program or script using CAPICOM. CAPICOM is a Component Object Model (COM) client, supporting automation, which performs cryptographic functions (the CryptoAPI) using Microsoft ActiveX and COM objects.

The CAPICOM interface can be used to perform fundamental cryptographic tasks including signing data, verifying signatures, decrypting enveloped messages, encrypting data, decrypting data, and checking the validity of digital certificates. CAPICOM can be used via Visual Basic, Visual Basic Scripting Edition, and C++.

To perform an enterprise deployment of user and computer certificates, a CAPICOM program or script can be distributed through e-mail for execution, or users can be directed to a Web site containing a link to a CAPICOM program or script. Alternately, the CAPICOM program or script can be placed in the user's logon script file for automatic execution. The storage location of the user or computer certificate can be specified using the CAPICOM application programming interfaces (APIs).

More Info   For information about CAPICOM, search for CAPICOM at *http://msdn.microsoft.com/*.

Computer Authentication and User Authentication

EAP-TLS and PEAP-MS-CHAP v2 support both computer authentication and user authentication. Computer authentication is the authentication of the computer for wireless access. User authentication is the authentication of the user using the computer for wireless access. Computer authentication is needed so the computer can obtain access to the network attached to the wireless network to obtain an IP address configuration, locate Active Directory domain controllers, run logon scripts, download the latest Computer Configuration Group Policy settings, and perform other computer startup processes. If a user successfully logs on to the computer that is already connected to the wireless network via computer authentication, a user authentication process occurs to ensure that the user using the computer can remain connected to the wireless network.

Computer and User Authentication with EAP-TLS

To successfully authenticate a Windows wireless computer with a wireless access point (AP) and EAP-TLS, you must have a computer certificate, a user certificate, or both installed. Wireless clients running Windows XP, Windows Server 2003, and Windows 2000 can use EAP-TLS to authenticate the computer or the user logged on to the computer.

To authenticate the computer, the Windows wireless computer submits a computer certificate (along with its chain) stored in the Local Computer certificate store during EAP-TLS authentication. The Local Computer certificate store is always available, regardless of whether a user has logged on to the computer or who is logged on to the computer. More importantly, the Local Computer certificate store is available during the computer's startup process.

To authenticate the user logged on to the computer, the Windows wireless computer submits a user certificate stored in the Current User certificate store or on a smart card during EAP-TLS authentication. The user's certificate store is available only after the user has successfully logged on to the computer using the proper credentials. Each individual user that logs on to the computer has a separate user certificate store. The user certificate is not available during the startup process.

Without an installed computer certificate, a Windows wireless client computer that starts up within range of a wireless AP associates with it but authentication fails. A user can log on to a computer that does not have wireless LAN network connectivity using cached credentials. Once successfully logged on, the user's certificate store becomes available, and the subsequent authentication with the wireless AP succeeds using the installed user certificate.

Computer and User Authentication with PEAP-MS-CHAP v2

Computer authentication with PEAP-MS-CHAP v2 is done using the account name and password associated with the computer account for the computer, which is automatically assigned when the computer account is created. The credentials for computer authentication are always available and are used during the computer startup process to obtain access to the wireless network.

User authentication with PEAP-MS-CHAP v2 is done using an account name and password associated with the user of the computer. By default, the user's logon credentials (username and password) are automatically used to perform user authentication after the client successfully logs on to the computer. The automatic use of the user logon credentials can be configured from the properties of the MS-CHAP v2 PEAP type.

Controlling Computer and User Authentication with the AuthMode Registry Setting

The following registry setting controls the computer and user authentication behavior of Windows XP and Windows Server 2003:

```
AuthMode
Key: HKEY_LOCAL_MACHINE\Software\Microsoft\EAPOL\Parameters\General\Global
Value Type: REG_DWORD
Valid Range: 0-2
Default value: 0
Present by default: No
```

AuthMode has the following values:

- **0–Computer authentication mode**   If computer authentication is successful, no user authentication is attempted. If the user logon is successful before computer authentication, user authentication is performed. This is the default setting for Windows XP (prior to SP1).

- **1–Computer authentication with re-authentication**   If computer authentication completes successfully, a subsequent user logon results in a re-authentication with user credentials. The user logon has to complete in 60 seconds or the existing network connectivity is terminated. The user credentials are used for subsequent authentication or re-authentication. Computer authentication is not attempted again until the user logs off the computer. This is the default setting for Windows XP (SP1 and later) and Windows Server 2003.

- **2–Computer authentication only**   When a user logs on, it has no effect on the connection. Only computer authentication is performed.

The exception to this behavior is when you have a successful user logon and roam between wireless APs; then, user authentication is performed.

For changes to this setting to take effect, restart the Wireless Zero Configuration (WZC) service (for Windows XP) or the Wireless Configuration service (for Windows Server 2003).

Note   The AuthMode registry setting can be set in an Active Directory environment through the Computer Authentication setting on the IEEE 802.1x tab for a preferred wireless network within the Wireless Network (IEEE 802.11) Policies Group Policy extension. For more information, see Chapter 3, "Windows Wireless Client Support."

Group Policy and IEEE 802.1X Authentication

Group Policy settings define the various components of the user's desktop environment that a system administrator needs to manage; for example, the programs that are available to users, the programs that appear on the user's desktop, and Start menu options. Group Policy settings you specify are contained in a Group Policy object, which is in turn associated with selected Active Directory container objects: sites, domains, or organizational units. Group Policy includes settings for User Configuration, which affect users, and Computer Configuration, which affect computers.

EAP-TLS and Computer Configuration Group Policy

Updates to Computer Configuration Group Policy occur when the computer starts, achieves network connectivity, and locates a domain controller. The computer attempts to download the latest Computer Configuration Group Policy based on the computer's membership in a domain system container.

If a Windows wireless client configured to use EAP-TLS authentication does not have a computer certificate installed, it cannot authenticate to a wireless AP to obtain wireless LAN network connectivity. Therefore, the attempt to locate a domain controller and download the latest Computer Configuration Group Policy fails. This event is recorded in the event log.

The solution to this problem is to install a computer certificate on the Windows wireless client so that wireless LAN network connectivity is present during the location of the domain controller and the download of the Computer Configuration Group Policy.

EAP-TLS and User Configuration Group Policy

Updates to User Configuration Group Policy occur when a user supplies correct credentials and logs on to the domain. If a computer certificate is not installed (and the computer has not authenticated itself against the wireless AP), the logon uses cached credentials. After the user certificate in the user's certificate store becomes available, the Windows wireless client configured to use EAP-TLS authentication attempts to authenticate against the wireless AP. Depending on how long the wireless authentication takes, the download of the User Configuration Group Policy might also fail. This event is recorded in the event log.

The solution to this problem is to install a computer certificate on the Windows wireless client. With an installed computer certificate, the Windows wireless client has wireless LAN network connectivity during the entire logon process, and therefore should always be able to download the latest User Configuration Group Policy.

Best Practices If you are using EAP-TLS for authentication, use both computer and user certificates.

Using Third-Party CAs for Wireless Authentication

You can use third-party CAs to issue certificates for wireless access as long as the certificates installed can be validated and have the appropriate properties.

Certificates on IAS Servers

For the computer certificates installed on the IAS servers, the following must be true:

- They must be installed in the Local Computer certificate store.

- They must have a corresponding private key. When you view the properties of the certificate, you should see the text You Have a Private Key That Corresponds To This Certificate on the General tab.

- The cryptographic service provider for the certificates must support SChannel (Secure Channel). If not, the IAS server cannot use the certificate and it is not selectable from the properties of the Smart Card Or Other Certificate EAP type from the Authentication tab on the properties of a profile for a remote access policy.

- They must contain the Server Authentication EKU. The OID for Server Authentication is 1.3.6.1.5.5.7.3.1.

- They must contain the FQDN of the computer account of the IAS server computer in the Subject Alternative Name field.

Additionally, the root CA certificates for the issuing CAs of the wireless client computer and user certificates must be installed in the Certificates (Local Computer)\Trusted Root Certification Authorities\Certificates folder.

Certificates on Wireless Client Computers

For the user and computer certificates installed on wireless client computers, the following must be true:

- They must have a corresponding private key.

- They must contain the Client Authentication EKU (OID 1.3.6.1.5.5.7.3.2).

- Computer certificates must be installed in the Local Computer certificate store.

- Computer certificates must contain the FQDN of the wireless client computer account in the Subject Alternative Name field.

- User certificates must be installed in the Current User certificate store.

- User certificates must contain the UPN of the user account in the Subject Alternative Name field.

Additionally, the root CA certificates of the issuing CAs of the IAS server computer certificates must be installed in the Certificates (Local Computer)\Trusted Root Certification Authorities\Certificates folder.

Summary

Certificates use public key cryptography to bind the value of a public key to the identity of the person, device, or service that holds the corresponding private key. A PKI is a system of certificates and CAs that issue and verify the validity certificates. Windows supports certificates and PKI by allowing the secure storage of certificates and by acting as a CA, using Certificate Services. Windows computers can obtain certificates through autoenrollment, Web enrollment, by requesting or importing a certificate using the Certificates snap-in, or by running a CAPICOM script or program. Windows wireless clients can authenticate as a computer or as a user. For EAP-TLS authentication, it is recommended to install both computer and user certificates.

You can use third-party CAs for the certificates on wireless client computers or IAS servers as long as they have the correct set of properties.

Part II
Wireless Network Deployment

Chapter 7
Wireless AP Placement

An important and time-consuming task in deploying a wireless LAN is determining where to place the wireless access points (APs) in your organization or home. Wireless APs must be placed to provide seamless coverage across the floor, building, campus, or home. With seamless coverage, wireless users can roam from one location to another without experiencing an interruption in network connectivity. Determining where to place your wireless APs is not as simple as installing them and turning them on. Wireless LAN technologies are based on propagation of a radio signal, which can be obstructed, reflected, shielded, and interfered with.

This chapter explores the various design points to consider before deploying wireless APs and then describes, step-by-step, the process of determining the optimal location for wireless APs.

Wireless LAN Design Considerations

When planning the deployment of wireless APs in an organization, public place, or Small Office/Home Office (SOHO), you should take the following design elements into consideration (as described in the following sections):

- Wireless AP requirements
- Channel separation
- Signal propagation modifiers
- Sources of interference
- Number of wireless APs

Wireless AP Requirements

You must identify the requirements for your wireless APs, which might include the following features:

- **802.1X and RADIUS**   For secure wireless communication for private organizations and public wireless service providers, the wireless AP must support the IEEE 802.1X standard for authentication of wireless connections and authentication, authorization, and accounting using Remote Authentication Dial-In User Service (RADIUS) servers. For a wireless AP in a SOHO, 802.1X and RADIUS support is not required.

- **WPA**   For the additional security provided by replacing Wired Equivalent Privacy (WEP) encryption and data integrity with Wi-Fi Protected Access (WPA), the wireless APs must support the new WPA standard. For the SOHO, WPA also provides a more secure authentication method (WPA with preshared key), which does not require a RADIUS infrastructure.

- **802.11a, b, g**   Depending on your budget and bandwidth requirements, you might need wireless APs that support 802.11b (maximum of 11 Mbps in the S-Band Industrial, Scientific, and Medical [ISM] frequency band), 802.11a (maximum of 54 Mbps in the C-Band ISM), 802.11g (maximum of 54 Mbps in the S-Band ISM), or a combination of technologies.

- **Plenum rating**   The plenum area (the space between the suspended ceiling and the ceiling) is regulated by fire codes. Therefore, for plenum placement of APs, you must purchase wireless APs that are fire-rated. If you place your wireless APs in the plenum area, you must determine the best method for powering the wireless APs. Consult with the wireless AP manufacturer to determine how to meet the power requirements for the wireless APs. Some wireless APs can receive electrical power through the Ethernet cable that connects them to the wired network.

- **Preconfiguration and remote configuration**   Preconfiguring the wireless APs before installing them on location can speed up the deployment process and can save labor costs because less-skilled workers can perform the physical installation. You can preconfigure wireless APs by using the console port (serial port), Telnet, or a Web server that is integrated with the wireless AP. Regardless of whether you decide to preconfigure the wireless APs, make sure that you can access them remotely, configure the wireless APs remotely through a vendor-supplied configuration tool, or upgrade the wireless APs by using scripts.

- **Antenna types**   Verify that the wireless AP supports different types of antennas. For example, in a building with multiple floors, an omnidirectional antenna—which propagates the signal equally in all directions except vertically—might work best.

 More Info   For information about which type of antenna will work best for your wireless LAN (WLAN) deployment, see the documentation for your wireless APs.

Channel Separation

Direct communication between an 802.11b wireless network adapter and a wireless AP occurs over a common channel, which corresponds to a frequency range in the S-Band ISM. You configure the wireless AP for a specific channel, and the wireless network adapter automatically configures itself to the channel of the wireless AP with the strongest signal.

To reduce interference between 802.11b wireless APs, ensure that wireless APs with overlapping coverage volumes use unique channels. The 802.11b standard reserves 14 frequency channels for use with wireless APs. Within the United States, the Federal Communications Commission (FCC) allows channels 1 through 11. In most of Europe, you can use channels 1 through 13. In Japan, you have only one choice: channel 14.

To prevent the signals from adjacent wireless APs from interfering with one another, you must set their channel numbers so that they are at least five channels apart. To get the most usable channels in the United States, you can set your wireless APs to use one of three channels: 1, 6, or 11. If you need fewer than three usable channels, ensure that the channels you choose maintain the five-channel separation.

Figure 7-1 shows an example of a set of wireless APs deployed in multiple floors of a building so that overlapping signals from adjacent wireless APs use different usable channel numbers.

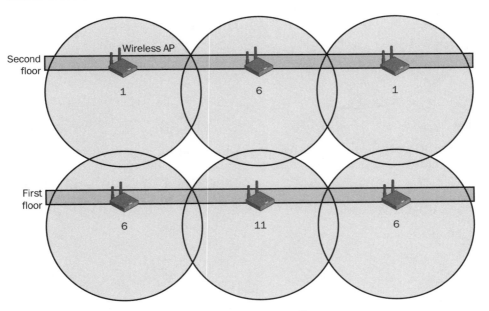

Figure 7-1. *Example of assigning 802.11b channel numbers.*

Signal Propagation Modifiers

The wireless AP is a radio transmitter and receiver that has a limited range. The volume around the wireless AP for which you can send and receive wireless data for any of the supported bit rates is known as the *coverage volume*. (Many wireless references use the term *coverage area*; however, wireless signals propagate in three dimensions.) The shape of the coverage volume depends on the type of antenna used by the wireless AP and the presence of signal propagation modifiers and other interference sources.

With an idealized omnidirectional antenna, the coverage volume is a series of concentric spherical shells of signal strengths corresponding to the different supported bit rates. For example, for 802.11b and an omnidirectional antenna, the idealized coverage volume is shown in Figure 7-2.

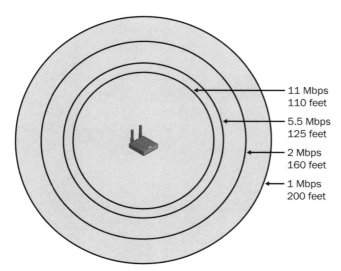

Figure 7-2. *Idealized coverage volume.*

Signal propagation modifiers change the shape of the ideal coverage volume through radio frequency (RF) *attenuation* (the reduction of signal strength), shielding, and reflection, which can affect how you deploy your wireless APs. Metal objects within a building, or used in the construction of a building, can affect the wireless signal. For example:

- Support girders
- Elevator shafts
- Rebar reinforcement in concrete
- Heating and air-conditioning ventilation ducts
- Wire mesh that reinforces plaster or stucco in walls
- Walls that contain metal, cinder blocks, and concrete
- Cabinets, metal desks, or other types of large metal equipment

Sources of Interference

Any device that operates on the same frequencies as your wireless devices (in the S-Band ISM, which operates in the frequency range of 2.4 GHz to 2.5 GHz, or the C-Band ISM, which operates in the frequency range of 5.725 GHz to 5.875 GHz) might interfere with the wireless signals. Sources of interference also change the shape of a wireless AP's ideal coverage volume.

Devices that operate in the S-Band ISM include the following:

- Bluetooth-enabled devices

- Microwave ovens

- 2.4 GHz cordless phones

- Wireless video cameras

- Medical equipment

- Elevator motors

Number of Wireless APs

To determine how many wireless APs to deploy, follow these guidelines:

- Include enough wireless APs to ensure that wireless users have sufficient signal strength from anywhere in the coverage volume.

  Typical wireless APs use omnidirectional antennas, which produce a vertically flattened sphere of signal that propagates between floors of a building. Wireless APs typically have an indoor range within a 200-foot radius. Include enough wireless APs to ensure signal overlap between the wireless APs.

- Determine the maximum number of simultaneous wireless users per coverage area.

- Estimate the data throughput that the average wireless user requires. If needed, add more wireless APs, which will:

  - Improve wireless client network bandwidth capacity.

  - Increase the number of wireless users supported within a coverage area.

    Based on the total data throughput of all users, determine the number of users that you can connect to a wireless AP. Obtain a clear picture of throughput before deploying the network or making changes. Some wireless vendors provide an 802.11 simulation tool, which you can use to model traffic in a network and view throughput levels under various conditions.

  - Ensure redundancy, in the event that a wireless AP fails.

Deploying Your Wireless APs

It is important to locate the wireless APs close enough together to provide ample wireless coverage, but also far enough apart to not interfere with each other. The actual distance needed between any two APs depends on the combination of the type of wireless AP, the type of wireless AP antenna, and the construction of the building; as well as sources of signal degradation, shielding, and reflection.

More Info   For specifications and guidelines for placing wireless APs, see the manufacturer's documentation for the wireless APs and the antennas used with them.

You should strive to maintain the best average ratio of wireless clients to wireless APs. The greater the average number of wireless clients that are associated with a wireless AP, the lower the effective data transmission rate. Too many wireless clients attempting to use the same wireless AP degrade the effective throughput or available bandwidth for each wireless client. By adding wireless APs, you can increase throughput. To increase the number of wireless APs per wireless client, you must increase the number of wireless APs in a given coverage volume. You can move wireless APs closer together up to a point before they start to interfere with each other.

To deploy your wireless APs, do the following:

1. Perform an analysis of wireless AP locations based on plans of floors and buildings.

2. Temporarily install your wireless APs.

3. Perform a site survey analyzing signal strength in all areas.

4. Relocate wireless APs or sources of RF attenuation or interference.

5. Verify the coverage volume.

6. Update the architectural drawings to reflect the final number and placement of the wireless APs.

These steps are discussed in more detail in the following sections.

Perform an Analysis of Wireless AP Locations

Obtain or create scaled architectural drawings of each floor for each building for which wireless access is being planned. On the drawing for each floor, identify the offices, conferences rooms, lobbies, or other areas where you want to provide wireless coverage.

It might be useful to enable wireless coverage for a building in its entirety rather than for specific locations within the building. This type of coverage can prevent connectivity problems that might result from undocking a laptop from an office for use in a different part of your building.

On the plans, indicate the devices that interfere with the wireless signals, and mark the building construction materials or objects that might attenuate, reflect, or shield wireless signals. Then indicate the locations of wireless APs so that each wireless AP is no further than 200 feet from an adjacent wireless AP.

After you have determined the initial locations of the wireless APs, you must determine their channels and then assign those channel numbers to each wireless AP.

▶ **To select the channels for the wireless APs**

1. Identify the wireless networks owned by other organizations in the same building. Find out the placement of their wireless APs and the assigned channel.

   Wireless network signal waves travel through floors and ceilings, so wireless APs located near each other on different floors need to be set to nonoverlapping channels. If another organization located on a floor adjacent to your organization's offices has a wireless network, the wireless APs for that organization might interfere with the wireless APs in your network. Contact the other organization to determine the placement and channel numbers of their wireless APs to ensure that your own wireless APs that provide overlapping coverage use a different channel number.

2. Identify overlapping wireless signals on adjacent floors within your own organization.

3. After identifying overlapping coverage volumes outside and within your organization, assign channel numbers to your wireless APs.

▶ **To assign the channel numbers to the wireless APs**

1. Assign channel 1 to the first wireless AP.

2. Assign channels 6 and 11 to the wireless APs that overlap coverage volumes with the first wireless AP, ensuring that those wireless APs do not also interfere with other coverage volumes with the same channel.

3. Continue assigning channel numbers to the wireless APs, ensuring that any two wireless APs with overlapping coverage are assigned different channel numbers.

Temporarily Install Your Wireless APs

Based on the locations and channel configurations indicated in your plans-based analysis of wireless AP locations, temporarily install your wireless APs.

Perform a Site Survey

Perform a site survey by walking around the building and its floors with a laptop computer equipped with an 802.11 wireless adapter and site survey software (site survey software ships with most wireless adapters and wireless APs). Determine the signal strength and bit rate for the coverage volume for each installed wireless AP.

Relocate Wireless APs or Sources of RF Attenuation or Interference

In locations where signal strength is low, you can make any of the following adjustments to improve the signal:

- Reposition the temporarily installed wireless APs to increase the signal strength for that coverage volume.

- Reposition or eliminate devices that interfere with signal strength (such as Bluetooth devices or microwave ovens).

- Reposition or eliminate metal obstructions that interfere with signal propagation (such as filing cabinets and appliances).

- Add more wireless APs to compensate for the weak signal strength.

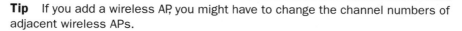

Tip If you add a wireless AP, you might have to change the channel numbers of adjacent wireless APs.

- Purchase antennas to meet the requirements of your building infrastructure.

  For example, to eliminate interference between wireless APs located on adjoining floors in your building, you can purchase directional antennas that flatten the signal (forming a donut-shaped coverage volume) to increase the horizontal range and further decrease the vertical range.

Verify Coverage Volume

Perform another site survey to verify that the changes made to the configuration or placement of the wireless APs eliminated the locations with low signal strength.

Update Your Plans

Update the architectural drawings to reflect the final number and placement of the wireless APs. Indicate the boundaries of the coverage volume and where the data rate changes for each wireless AP.

Summary

Before you deploy your wireless APs, consider your wireless AP requirements; the channel separation; the presence of signal propagation modifiers and sources of interference; and the number of wireless APs needed to meet your wireless coverage, bandwidth, and redundancy requirements.

To deploy your wireless APs, estimate wireless AP locations using building plans and knowledge of signal propagation modifiers and interference sources. Install your wireless APs in their temporary locations and perform a site survey, noting the areas with inadequate coverage. Change the locations of your wireless APs, signal propagation modifiers, or sources of interference and verify coverage by performing an additional site survey. After your final wireless AP locations are determined, update your building plans with their locations and note remaining areas of decreased bandwidth or signal strength.

Chapter 8
Intranet Wireless Deployment Using EAP-TLS

Extensible Authentication Protocol-Transport Layer Security (EAP-TLS) is used for certificate-based wireless authentication when a public key infrastructure (PKI) is available to issue computer and user certificates to all the wireless clients. This chapter describes the steps needed to deploy secure wireless using EAP-TLS authentication.

Required Components

The following components are required for an intranet wireless deployment using EAP-TLS:

- **Wireless client computers running Windows.** Wireless client computers must be running Microsoft Windows XP, Windows Server 2003, or Windows 2000 with Microsoft 802.1X Authentication Client.

- **At least two Internet Authentication Service (IAS) servers.** At least two IAS servers (one primary and one secondary) are recommended to provide fault tolerance for Remote Authentication Dial-In User Service (RADIUS)–based authentication. If only one RADIUS server is configured and it becomes unavailable, wireless access clients cannot connect. By using two IAS servers and configuring all wireless access points (APs) to use both the primary and secondary IAS servers, the wireless APs can detect when the primary RADIUS server is unavailable and automatically fail over to the secondary IAS server.

  You can use either Windows Server 2003 or Windows 2000 Server IAS. IAS servers running Windows 2000 must have Service Pack 3 (SP3) or later installed. (IAS is not included with Windows Server 2003, Web Edition.)

- **Active Directory directory service domains.** Active Directory domains contain the user accounts, computer accounts, and dial-in properties that each IAS server requires to authenticate credentials and evaluate authorization. Although not a requirement, IAS should be installed on Active Directory domain controllers to optimize IAS authentication and authorization response times and to minimize network traffic.

  You can use either Windows Server 2003 or Windows 2000 Server domain controllers. Windows 2000 domain controllers must have SP3 or later installed.

- **Computer certificates installed on the IAS servers.** To authenticate the IAS server to the wireless client during EAP-TLS authentication, a computer certificate must be installed on the IAS server computers.

- **Computer and user certificates installed on the wireless clients.** To authenticate the wireless client computer or user during EAP-TLS authentication, a computer or user certificate must be installed on the wireless client computers.

- **Wireless remote access policy.** A remote access policy is configured for wireless connections so that wireless users and their computers can access the organization's intranet.

- **Multiple wireless APs.** Multiple third-party wireless APs provide wireless access in different coverage areas of an organization. The wireless APs must support IEEE 802.1X, Wired Equivalent Privacy (WEP), RADIUS, and, optionally, Wi-Fi Protected Access (WPA).

Figure 8-1 shows the components of EAP-TLS authentication.

Caution If you use EAP-TLS authentication, do not also use Protected EAP-TLS (PEAP-TLS) for wireless connections. Allowing both protected and unprotected authentication traffic for the same type of network connection renders the protected authentication traffic susceptible to spoofing attacks.

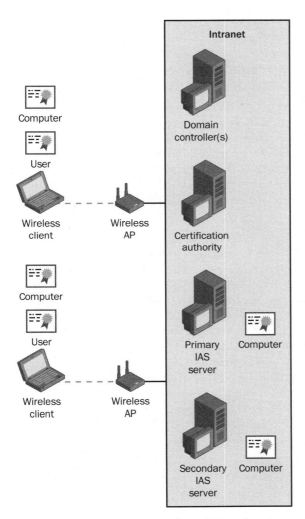

Figure 8-1. *The components of EAP-TLS authentication.*

Configuring the Certificate Infrastructure

For computer authentication with EAP-TLS, you must install a *computer certificate*, also known as a *machine certificate*, on the wireless client computer. A computer certificate is used to authenticate the wireless client computer so that the computer can obtain network connectivity to the enterprise intranet and receive computer configuration through Group Policy updates prior to user login. For user authentication with EAP-TLS, you must use a user certificate stored on a smart card or stored on the wireless client computer. A user certificate is used to authenticate the user of the wireless client computer after a successful login.

A computer certificate is installed on the IAS server computer so that the IAS server has a certificate to send to the wireless client computer for mutual authentication during EAP-TLS authentication, regardless of whether the wireless client computer authenticates with a computer certificate or a user certificate. The computer and user certificates submitted by the wireless client and IAS server during EAP-TLS authentication must conform to the requirements specified in the "Using Third-Party CAs for Wireless Authentication" section of Chapter 6, "Certificates and Public Key Infrastructure."

In a typical enterprise deployment, the PKI consists of a single root certification authority (CA) in a three-level hierarchy consisting of root CA/intermediate CAs/issuing CAs. Issuing CAs are configured to issue computer certificates and user certificates. When the computer or user certificate is installed on the wireless client, the issuing CA certificate, intermediate CA certificates, and root CA certificate are also installed. When the computer certificate is installed on the IAS server computer, the issuing CA certificate, intermediate CA certificates, and root CA certificate are also installed. The issuing CA for the IAS server certificate can be different from the issuing CA for the wireless client certificates. In this case, both the wireless client and the IAS server computer must have all the required certificates needed to perform certificate validation for EAP-TLS authentication.

Best Practices If you use EAP-TLS authentication, install both user and computer certificates on wireless client computers.

If you already have a certificate infrastructure for EAP-TLS authentication and use RADIUS for dial-up or virtual private network (VPN) remote access connections, you can skip some of the certificate infrastructure steps. You can use the same certificate infrastructure for wireless connections. However, you must ensure that computer certificates are installed for computer authentication. Although smart cards are recommended for EAP-TLS-based remote access connections, you must use user certificates stored on the computer for user authentication of wireless connections (rather than using smart cards) for computers running Windows XP (prior to SP1). For computers running Windows Server 2003, Windows XP (SP1 or later), or Windows 2000, you can use either user certificates stored on the computer or a smart card for user authentication.

Tip   Certificates obtained from issuing CAs that are from the same root CA hierarchy chain up to the same root CA certificate. In Windows Server 2003, Windows XP, and Windows 2000, you can view the certificate chain from the Certification Path tab in the properties of a certificate in the Certificates snap-in. You can view the installed root CA certificates in the Trusted Root Certification Authorities\Certificates folder, and you can view the intermediate CA certificates in the Intermediate Certification Authorities\Certificates folder.

Installing a Certificate Infrastructure

When installing a certificate infrastructure, use the following best practices:

- Plan your public key infrastructure (PKI) before deploying CAs.

- The root CA should be offline, and its signing key should be secured by a Hardware Security Module (HSM) and kept in a vault to minimize potential for key compromise.

- Enterprise organizations should not issue certificates to users or computers directly from the root CA, but rather should deploy the following:

  - An offline root CA

  - Offline intermediate CAs

  - Online issuing CAs (using Windows Server 2003 or Windows 2000 Certificate Services as an enterprise CA)

This CA hierarchy provides flexibility and insulates the root CA from attempts to compromise its private key by malicious users. The offline root and intermediate CAs do not have to be Windows Server 2003 or Windows 2000 CAs. Issuing CAs can be subordinates of a third-party CA.

- Backing up the CA database, the CA certificate, and the CA keys is essential to protect against the loss of critical data. The CA should be backed up on a regular basis (daily, weekly, or monthly), based on the number of certificates issued over the same interval. The more certificates issued, the more frequently you should back up the CA.

- You should review the concepts of security permissions and access control in Windows because enterprise CAs issue certificates based on the security permissions of the certificate requester.

Additionally, if you want to take advantage of autoenrollment for computer certificates, use Windows 2000 or Windows Server 2003 Certificate Services and then create an enterprise CA as the issuing CA. If you want to take advantage of autoenrollment for user certificates, use Windows Server 2003, Enterprise Edition or Windows Server 2003, Datacenter Edition, Certificate Services and then create an enterprise CA as the issuing CA.

More Info For more information about single- or multi-level certificate infrastructures, see Chapter 6, "Certificates and Public Key infrastructure." For additional information about PKI and the Windows 2000 Certificate Services including deployment instructions and best practices, see the Windows 2000 Security Services Web site at *http://www.microsoft.com/windows2000/technologies/security/default.asp*. For additional information about Windows Server 2003 security services, see the Windows Server 2003 Security Services Web site at *http://www.microsoft.com/windowsserver2003/technologies/security/default.mspx*.

Configuring Autoenrollment for Computer Certificates

If you use a Windows Server 2003 or Windows 2000 Certificate Services enterprise CA as an issuing CA, you can install a computer certificate on IAS servers and wireless client computers by configuring Group Policy for the autoenrollment of computer certificates for members of an Active Directory system container.

To configure computer certificate enrollment for an enterprise CA, do the following:

1. Open the Active Directory Users And Computers snap-in.

2. In the console tree, double-click Active Directory Users And Computers, right-click the appropriate Active Directory system container, and then click Properties.

3. On the Group Policy tab, click the appropriate Group Policy object (the default object is Default Domain Policy) and then click Edit.

4. In the console tree, open Computer Configuration; then Windows Settings; then Security Settings; then Public Key Policies; then Automatic Certificate Request Settings.

5. Right-click Automatic Certificate Request Settings, point to New, and then click Automatic Certificate Request. The Automatic Certificate Request Wizard appears.

6. Click Next.

7. In Certificate Templates, click Computer and then click Next.

8. If you have more than one enterprise-issuing CA, click the correct enterprise CA, click Next, and then click Finish.

After the domain is configured for autoenrollment of computer certificates, each computer that is a member of the domain system container requests a computer certificate when the computer configuration Group Policy is refreshed. By default, the Winlogon service polls for changes in Group Policy every 90 minutes. To force a refresh of computer Group Policy, restart the computer or type **secedit / refreshpolicy machine_policy** (for a computer running Windows 2000) or **gpupdate /target:computer** (for a computer running Windows XP or Windows Server 2003) at a command prompt.

Perform this procedure for each domain system container as appropriate.

Best Practices   If you use a Windows Server 2003 or Windows 2000 enterprise CA as an issuing CA, configure autoenrollment of computer certificates to install computer certificates on all computers. Ensure that all appropriate domain system containers are configured for autoenrollment of computer certificates, either through inheriting Group Policy settings of a parent system container or explicit configuration.

Configuring Autoenrollment for User Certificates

If you use a Windows Server 2003, Enterprise Edition or a Windows Server 2003, Datacenter Edition enterprise CA as an issuing CA, you can install user certificates through autoenrollment. However, only Windows XP and Windows Server 2003 wireless clients support user certificate autoenrollment.

To configure user certificate enrollment for an enterprise CA, do the following:

1. Click Start, click Run, type **mmc**, and then click OK.

2. On the File menu, click Add/Remove Snap-In and then click Add.

3. Under Snap-In, double-click Certificate Templates, click Close, and then click OK.

4. In the console tree, click Certificate Templates. All certificate templates are displayed in the details pane.

5. In the details pane, click the User template.

6. On the Action menu, click Duplicate Template.

7. In the Display Name field, type the name of the new user certificate template (for example, **WirelessAccess**).

8. Make sure that the Publish Certificate In Active Directory check box is selected.

9. Click the Security tab.

10. In the Group Or User Names field, click Domain Users.

11. In the Permissions For Domain Users list, select the Read, Enroll, and Autoenroll permission check boxes and then click OK. The following figure shows the resulting configuration.

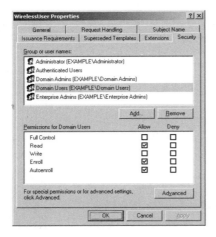

12. Open the Certification Authority snap-in.

13. In the console tree, open Certification Authority; then your CA name; then Certificate Templates.

14. On the Action menu, point to New and then click Certificate To Issue.

15. Click the name of the newly created user certificate template (for example, WirelessAccess) and then click OK.

16. Open the Active Directory Users And Computers snap-in.

17. In the console tree, double-click Active Directory Users And Computers, right-click the appropriate Active Directory system container, and then click Properties.

18. On the Group Policy tab, click the appropriate Group Policy object (the default object is Default Domain Policy) and then click Edit.

19. In the console tree, open User Configuration; then Windows Settings; then Security Settings; then Public Key Policies.

20. In the details pane, double-click Autoenrollment Settings.

21. Click Enroll Certificates Automatically.

22. Select the Renew Expired Certificates, Update Pending Certificates, And Remove Revoked Certificates check box.

23. Select the Update Certificates That Use Certificate Templates check box. The following figure shows the resulting configuration.

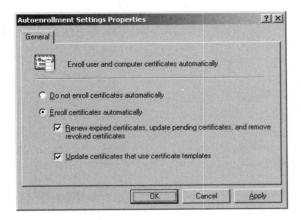

24. Click OK.

Perform this procedure for each domain system container, as appropriate.

Best Practices   If you use a Windows Server 2003, Enterprise Edition or Windows Server 2003, Datacenter Edition enterprise CA as an issuing CA, configure autoenrollment of user certificates to install user certificates on all computers running Windows XP or Windows Server 2003. Ensure that all appropriate domain system containers are configured for autoenrollment of user certificates, either through the inheriting of Group Policy settings of a parent system container or by explicit configuration.

Configuring Active Directory for Accounts and Groups for Wireless Access

To configure Active Directory user and computer accounts and groups for wireless access, do the following:

1. If you use Windows 2000 domain controllers, install Windows 2000 SP3 or later on all domain controllers.

2. Ensure that all users that are making wireless connections have a corresponding user account.

3. Ensure that all computers that are making wireless connections have a corresponding computer account.

4. Set the remote access permission on user and computer accounts to the appropriate setting: either Allow Access or Control Access Through Remote Access Policy. (The remote access permission setting is on the Dial-In tab in the properties dialog box of a user or computer account in the Active Directory Users And Computers snap-in.)

5. Organize your wireless access user and computer accounts into the appropriate groups. For a native-mode domain, you can use universal and nested global groups. For example, create a universal group named WirelessUsers that contains global groups of wireless user and computer accounts for intranet access.

Best Practices Use a native-mode domain and universal and global groups to organize your wireless accounts into a single nested group.

Configuring the IAS Servers

To configure the IAS servers for EAP-TLS authentication, you must do the following (discussed in more detail in the following sections):

- Configure the primary IAS server.

- Configure a remote access policy for wireless access.

- Configure the secondary IAS server.

Configuring the Primary IAS Server

To configure the primary IAS server on a computer, complete these steps as discussed in the following sections:

- Obtain and install a computer certificate.

- Install IAS and configure IAS server properties.

- Configure IAS with RADIUS clients.

Obtaining and Installing a Computer Certificate

If you use computer certificate autoenrollment and Windows 2000 IAS, force a refresh of computer configuration Group Policy by typing **secedit /refreshpolicy machine_policy** from a command prompt. If you use computer certificate autoenrollment and Windows Server 2003 IAS, force a refresh of computer configuration Group Policy by typing **gpupdate /target:computer** from a command prompt.

If you use a Windows 2000 or Windows Server 2003 enterprise CA and you are not using autoenrollment for computer certificates, you can request one, as described in the following procedure.

► **To request a computer certificate**

1. Click Start, click Run, type **mmc**, and then click OK.

2. On the File menu, click Add/Remove Snap-In and then click Add.

3. Under Snap-In, double-click Certificates, click Computer Account, and then click Next.

4. Do one of the following:

   - To manage certificates for the local computer, click Local Computer and then click Finish.

   - To manage certificates for a remote computer, click Another Computer and type the name of the computer, or click Browse to select the computer name and click Finish.

5. Click Close. Certificates (Local Computer or *Computer Name*) appears on the list of selected snap-ins for the new console.

6. Click OK.

7. In the console tree, open Certificates (Local Computer or *Computer Name*) and then click Personal.

8. On the Action menu, point to All Tasks and then click Request New Certificate to start the Certificate Request Wizard.

9. On the Welcome to the Certificate Request Wizard page, click Next.

10. On the Certificate Template page, click Computer and then click Next.

11. On the Certificate Friendly Name and Description page, type a name in Friendly Name and a description in Description and then click Next. (The configuration of a friendly name and description for the certificate is optional.)

12. Click Next.

13. On the Completing the Certificate Request Wizard page, click Finish.

If your PKI does not support autoenrollment of computer certificates, obtain the computer certificate as a saved file and use the following procedure to import the computer certificate on the primary IAS server.

Note   To perform the next procedure, you must be a member of the Administrators group on the local computer, or you must have been delegated the appropriate authority.

▶ **To import the computer certificate on the primary IAS server**

1. Click Start, click Run, type **mmc**, and then click OK.

2. On the File menu, click Add/Remove Snap-In and then click Add.

3. Under Snap-In, double-click Certificates, click Computer Account, and then click Next.

4. Do one of the following:

   • If you logged on to the IAS server, click Local Computer and then click Finish.

   • If you are configuring the IAS server from a remote computer, click Another Computer and type the name of the computer, or click Browse to select the computer name and then click Finish.

5. Click Close.

   Certificates (Local Computer or *Computer Name*) appears on the list of selected snap-ins for the new console.

6. In the console tree, double-click Certificates (Local Computer or *Computer Name*).

7. Right-click Personal, point to All Tasks, and then click Import.

8. On the Welcome To The Certificate Import Wizard page, click Next.

9. On the File To Import page, type the filename of the certificate file provided by the commercial CA in File Name, or click Browse and use the Browse dialog box to locate it.

10. Click Next. On the Certificate Store page, click Place All Certificates In The Following Store. By default, the Personal folder should display as the import location.

11. Click Next.

12. Click Finish on the Completing The Certificate Import Wizard page.

Best Practices   It is also possible to import a certificate by double-clicking a certificate file that is stored in a folder or sent in an email message. Although this works for certificates created with Windows CAs, this method might not work for third-party CAs. The recommended method of importing certificates is to use the Certificates snap-in.

Installing IAS and Configuring IAS Server Properties

To install IAS, do the following:

1. Open Add Or Remove Programs in Control Panel.

2. Click Add/Remove Windows Components.

3. In the Windows Components Wizard dialog box, double-click Networking Services under Components.

4. In the Networking Services dialog box, select Internet Authentication Service. The Networking Services dialog box is shown in the following figure.

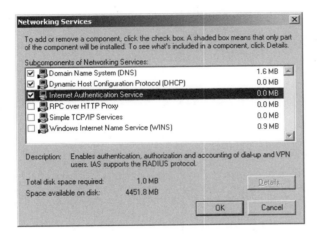

5. Click OK and then click Next.

6. If prompted, insert your Windows product compact disc.

7. After IAS is installed, click Finish and then click Close.

This procedure is the same for Windows 2000 Server IAS and Windows Server 2003 IAS.

Note   If you use Windows 2000 IAS, you must install Windows 2000 SP3 or later. You can obtain Windows 2000 SP3 or later from *http://www.microsoft.com /windows2000/downloads/servicepacks/*.

The primary IAS server computer must be able to access account properties in the appropriate domains. If IAS is being installed on a domain controller, no additional configuration is required in order for IAS to access account properties in the domain to which it belongs. If IAS is not installed on a domain controller, you must configure the primary IAS server computer to read the properties of user accounts in the domain, as described in the following procedure.

▶ **To configure the primary IAS server computer to read the properties of user accounts in the domain**

1. Click Start, point to Programs, point to Administrative Tools, and then click Internet Authentication Service.

2. In the console tree, right-click Internet Authentication Service (Local) and then click Register Server in Active Directory.

   A Register Internet Authentication Server In Active Directory dialog box appears.

3. Click OK.

Alternately, you can do one of the following:

• Use the **netsh ras add registeredserver** command.

Or

• Add the computer account of the IAS server to the RAS and IAS servers security group with the Active Directory Users And Computers snap-in.

If the IAS server authenticates and authorizes wireless connection attempts for user accounts in other domains, verify that the other domains have a two-way trust with the domain in which the IAS server computer is a member. Next, configure the IAS server computer to read the properties of user accounts in other domains by using the **netsh ras add registeredserver** command or the Active Directory Users And Computers snap-in.

If there are accounts in other domains, and the domains do not have a two-way trust with the domain in which the IAS server computer is a member, you must configure a RADIUS proxy between the two untrusted domains. If there are accounts in other untrusted Active Directory forests, you must configure a RADIUS proxy between the forests. For more information, see Chapter 11, "Additional Intranet Wireless Deployment Configurations."

If you want to store authentication and accounting information for connection analysis and security investigation purposes, enable logging for accounting and authentication events. Windows 2000 IAS can log information to a local file; Windows Server 2003 IAS can log information to a local file and to a Structured Query Language (SQL) Server database.

▶ **To enable and configure logging for Windows 2000 IAS**

1. In the console tree of the Internet Authentication snap-in, click Remote Access Logging.

2. In the details pane, double-click Local File.

3. On the Settings tab, select one or more check boxes for recording authentication and accounting requests in the IAS log files:

   - To capture accounting requests and responses, select the Log Accounting Requests check box.

   - To capture authentication requests, access-accept packets, and access-reject packets, select the Log Authentication Requests check box.

   - To capture periodic status updates, such as interim accounting packets, select the Log Periodic Status check box.

4. On the Local File tab, select the log file format and new log time period, and type the log file directory as needed.

▶ **To enable and configure local file logging for Windows Server 2003 IAS**

1. In the console tree of the Internet Authentication snap-in, click Remote Access Logging.

2. In the details pane, double-click Local File.

3. On the Settings tab, select one or more check boxes for recording authentication and accounting requests in the IAS log files:

   - To capture accounting requests and responses, select the Accounting Requests check box.

   - To capture authentication requests, access-accept packets, and access-reject packets, select the Authentication Requests check box.

   - To capture periodic status updates, such as interim accounting packets, select the Periodic Status check box.

4. On the Log File tab, type the log file directory as needed and select the log file format and new log time period.

▶ **To enable and configure SQL Server database logging for Windows Server 2003 IAS**

1. In the console tree of the Internet Authentication snap-in, click Remote Access Logging.

2. In the details pane, double-click SQL Server.

3. On the Settings tab, select one or more check boxes for recording authentication and accounting requests in the IAS log files:

   - To capture accounting requests and responses, select the Accounting Requests check box.

- To capture authentication requests, access-accept packets, and access-reject packets, select the Authentication Requests check box.

- To capture periodic status updates, such as interim accounting packets, select the Periodic Status check box.

4. In Maximum Number of Connections, type the maximum number of simultaneous sessions that IAS can create with the SQL Server.

5. To configure a SQL data source, click Configure.

6. On the Data Link Properties dialog box, configure the appropriate settings for the SQL Server database.

If needed, configure additional User Datagram Protocol (UDP) ports for authentication and accounting messages that are sent by RADIUS clients (the wireless APs). By default, IAS uses UDP ports 1812 and 1645 for authentication messages and UDP ports 1813 and 1646 for accounting messages.

▶ To configure Windows 2000 IAS for different UDP ports

1. In the console tree of the Internet Authentication snap-in, right-click Internet Authentication Service and then click Properties.

2. Click the RADIUS tab; configure the UDP port numbers for your RADIUS authentication traffic in Authentication and the UDP port numbers for your RADIUS accounting traffic in Accounting.

▶ To configure Windows Server 2003 IAS for different UDP ports

1. In the console tree of the Internet Authentication snap-in, right-click Internet Authentication Service and then click Properties.

2. Click the Ports tab; configure the UDP port numbers for your RADIUS authentication traffic in Authentication and the UDP port numbers for your RADIUS accounting traffic in Accounting.

To use multiple port settings for authentication or accounting traffic, separate the port numbers with commas. You can also specify an IP address to which the RADIUS messages must be sent with the following syntax: *IPAddress:UDPPort*. For example, if you have multiple network adapters and you want to receive RADIUS authentication messages sent only to the IP address of 10.0.0.99 and UDP port 1812, type **10.0.0.99:1812** in Authentication. However, if you specify IP addresses and copy the configuration of the primary IAS server to the secondary IAS server, you must modify the ports on the secondary IAS server to either remove the IP address of the primary IAS server or change the IP address to that of the secondary IAS server.

Configuring IAS with RADIUS Clients

You must configure the primary IAS server with the wireless APs as RADIUS clients.

▶ **To add a RADIUS client corresponding to a wireless AP for Windows 2000 IAS**

1. In the console tree of the Internet Authentication snap-in, right-click Clients and then click New Client.

2. In the Add Client dialog box, type a name for the wireless AP in Friendly Name.

3. Click Next. In the Add RADIUS Client dialog box, type the IP address or DNS name of the wireless AP in Client Address (IP Or DNS). If you type a DNS domain name, click Verify to resolve the name to the correct IP address for the wireless AP. Type the RADIUS shared secret for this combination of IAS server and wireless AP in Shared Secret and then type it again in Confirm Shared Secret.

4. Click Finish.

▶ **To add a RADIUS client for Windows Server 2003 IAS**

1. Right-click RADIUS Clients and then click New RADIUS Client.

2. On the Name and Address page, type a name for the wireless AP in Friendly Name. In Client Address (IP Or DNS), type the IP address or DNS domain name. If you type a DNS domain name, click Verify to resolve the name to the correct IP address for the wireless AP.

3. Click Next.

4. On the Additional Information page, type the shared secret for this combination of IAS server and wireless AP in Shared Secret and then type it again in Confirm Shared Secret.

5. Click Finish.

If you use IAS on a computer running Windows Server 2003, Enterprise Edition, or Windows Server 2003, Datacenter Edition, and you have multiple wireless APs on a single subnet (for example, in an Extended Service Set [ESS] configuration), you can simplify RADIUS client administration by specifying an address range instead of specifying the IP address or DNS name of a single RADIUS client. All the RADIUS clients in the range must be configured to use the same RADIUS server and shared secret. The address range for RADIUS clients is expressed in the network prefix length notation $w.x.y.z/p$, where $w.x.y.z$ is the dotted decimal notation of the address prefix and p is the prefix length (the number of high-order bits that define the network prefix). This is also known as *Classless Inter-Domain Routing (CIDR) notation*. An example is 192.168.21.0/24, which indicates all addresses from 192.168.21.1 to 192.168.21.255. To convert from subnet mask notation to network prefix length notation, p is the number of high-order bits set to one in the subnet mask. If you are not using this feature, use a different shared secret for each wireless AP.

Best Practices Use as many RADIUS shared secrets as you can. Each shared secret should be a random sequence of upper- and lowercase letters, numbers, and punctuation that is at least 22 characters long. To ensure randomness, use a random character-generation program to determine shared secrets.

Using IPSec to Secure RADIUS Traffic

To ensure the maximum security for RADIUS messages, it is recommended that you use Internet Protocol security (IPSec) with certificate authentication and Encapsulating Security Payload (ESP) to provide data confidentiality, data integrity, and data origin authentication for RADIUS traffic sent between the IAS servers and the wireless APs. Windows 2000 and Windows Server 2003 support IPSec. To secure RADIUS traffic sent from wireless APs, the wireless APs must also support IPSec.

Configuring a Wireless Remote Access Policy

The procedure for configuring a wireless remote access policy is different for Windows 2000 IAS and Windows Server 2003 IAS.

Configuring Windows 2000 IAS

To create a new remote access policy for wireless intranet access for Windows 2000 IAS, do the following:

1. In the console tree of the Internet Authentication snap-in, right-click Remote Access Policies and then click New Remote Access Policy.

2. On the Policy Name page, type the name of the policy in Policy Friendly Name.

3. On the Conditions page, click Add.

4. On the Select Attribute dialog box, double-click NAS-Port-Type.

5. In the Available Types list, add Wireless-IEEE 802.11 and Wireless-Other to the list of Selected Types and then click OK.

   If SP3 or later is not installed on the IAS server, you do not see the Wireless-IEEE 802.11 and Wireless-Other NAS port types.

6. In the Select Attribute dialog box, double-click Windows-Groups.

7. In the Groups dialog box, click Add.

8. In the Select Groups dialog box, click the names of your wireless groups and click Add.

9. Click OK to close the Select Groups dialog box.

10. Click OK to close the Groups dialog box. An example of the resulting Conditions page is shown in the following figure.

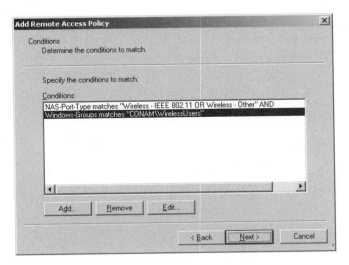

11. Click Next.

12. On the Permissions page, click Grant Remote Access Permission.

13. Click Next.

14. On the User Profile page, click Edit Profile.

15. On the Authentication tab, select the Extensible Authentication Protocol check box and click the Smart Card Or Other Certificate EAP type.

16. Click Configure. In the Smart Card Or Other Certificate Properties dialog box, ensure that the name of the computer certificate installed on the IAS server is visible in Certificate Issued. If there are multiple computer certificates installed on the IAS server, select the correct one in Certificate Issued.

   If you cannot select the certificate, the cryptographic service provider for the certificate does not support SChannel. SChannel support is required for IAS to use the certificate for EAP-TLS authentication.

17. Click OK.

18. Clear the Microsoft Encrypted Authentication Version 2 (MS-CHAP v2) and Microsoft Encrypted Authentication (MS-CHAP) check boxes. The resulting configuration is shown in the following figure.

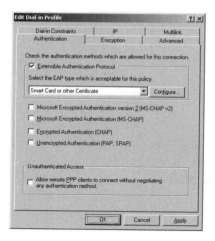

19. On the Encryption tab, clear the No Encryption check box.

20. Click OK.

21. When prompted with a Dial-In Settings message box, click No.

22. On the User Profile page, click Finish.

By default, adding a new remote access policy for Windows 2000 IAS places the new remote access policy at the bottom of the list of existing remote access policies. Therefore, to ensure that the new wireless remote access policy is used, move the new wireless remote access policy so that it is the first in the list (by using the up arrow in the toolbar).

Configuring Windows Server 2003 IAS

To create a remote access policy for wireless access for Windows Server 2003 IAS, do the following:

1. From the console tree of the Internet Authentication Service snap-in, right-click Remote Access Policies and then click New Remote Access Policy.

2. On the Welcome To The New Remote Access Policy Wizard page, click Next.

3. On the Policy Configuration Method page, type the name of the policy in Policy Name.

4. Click Next.

5. On the Access Method page, select Wireless.

6. Click Next.

7. On the User Or Group Access page, select Group.

8. Click Add.

9. In the Select Groups dialog box, type the names of your universal or global wireless groups in Enter The Object Names To Select.

10. Click OK. Your wireless groups are added to the list of groups on the User or Group Access page.

11. Click Next. On the Authentication Methods page, click the Smart Card Or Other Certificate EAP Type.

12. In the Smart Card Or Other Certificate Properties dialog box, ensure that the name of the computer certificate installed on the IAS server is visible in Certificate Issued. If there are multiple computer certificates installed on the IAS server, select the correct one in Certificate Issued.

    If you cannot select the certificate, the cryptographic service provider for the certificate does not support SChannel. SChannel support is required for IAS to use the certificate for EAP-TLS authentication.

13. Click OK.

14. Click Next.

15. On the Completing The New Remote Access Policy page, click Finish.

If the wireless APs require vendor-specific attributes (VSAs), you must add the VSAs to the remote access policy.

▶ **To add a VSA to the wireless remote access policy**

1. In the console tree of the Internet Authentication Service snap-in, click Remote Access Policies.

2. Double-click the wireless remote access policy.

3. Click Edit Profile, click the Advanced tab and then click Add. A list of predefined attributes displays in the Add Attribute dialog box.

4. Look at the list of available RADIUS attributes to determine whether your vendor-specific attribute is already present. If it is, double-click it and configure it as specified in your wireless AP documentation.

5. If the vendor-specific attribute is not in the list of available RADIUS attributes, double-click Vendor-Specific. The Multivalued Attribute Information dialog box displays.

6. Click Add. The Vendor-Specific Attribute Information dialog box displays.

7. To specify the network access server vendor for your wireless AP from the list, click Select From List and then select the wireless AP vendor for which you are configuring the VSA.

8. If the vendor is not listed, click Enter Vendor Code and then type the vendor code in the space provided.

> **More Info** If you do not know the vendor code for your wireless AP, see RFC 1007 for a list of SMI Network Management Private Enterprise Codes.

9. Specify whether the attribute conforms to the RFC 2865 VSA specification. If you are not sure, see your wireless AP documentation. If your attribute conforms, click Yes. It Conforms and then click Configure Attribute. The Configure VSA (RFC-Compliant) dialog box displays.

10. In Vendor-Assigned Attribute Number, type the number that is assigned to the attribute (the numbers available are 0 through 255). In Attribute Format, specify the format for the attribute; in Attribute Value, type the value that you are assigning to the attribute.

11. If the attribute does not conform, click No. It Does Not Conform and then click Configure Attribute. The Configure VSA (Non-RFC-Compliant) dialog box displays.

12. In Hexadecimal Attribute Value, type the value for the attribute.

This procedure is the same for Windows 2000 IAS and Windows Server 2003 IAS.

> **Best Practices** If you manage the remote access permission of user and computer accounts on a per-account basis, use remote access policies that specify a connection type. If you manage the remote access permission through the remote access policy (the recommended method), use remote access policies that specify a connection type and group.

Configuring the Secondary IAS Server

To configure the secondary IAS server on a computer, do the following (described in the following sections):

1. Obtain and install a computer certificate.

2. Copy the configuration of the primary IAS server to the secondary IAS server.

Obtaining and Installing a Computer Certificate

If you use computer certificate autoenrollment and Windows 2000 IAS, force a refresh of computer Group Policy by typing **secedit /refreshpolicy machine_policy** from a command prompt. If you use computer certificate autoenrollment and Windows Server 2003 IAS, force a refresh of computer Group Policy by typing **gpupdate /target:computer** from a command prompt.

If you use a commercial CA or your PKI does not support autoenrollment of computer certificates, obtain the computer certificate and use the certificate import procedure (described in the "Configuring the Primary IAS Server" section of this chapter) to install the computer certificate on the secondary IAS server.

Note   Refer to the "Configuring the Primary IAS Server" section of this chapter for a description of how to install IAS.

If you use Windows 2000 IAS, you must also install Windows 2000 SP3 or later, which you can download from *http://www.microsoft.com/windows2000/downloads /servicepacks/*.

The secondary IAS server computer must be able to access account properties in the appropriate domains. If IAS is being installed on a domain controller, no additional configuration is required in order for IAS to access account properties in the domain of the IAS server. If IAS is not installed on a domain controller, you must configure the secondary IAS server computer to read the properties of user accounts in the domain.

▶ **To configure the secondary IAS server computer to read the properties of user accounts in the domain**

1. Click Start, point to Programs, point to Administrative Tools, and then click Internet Authentication Service.

2. In the console tree, right-click Internet Authentication Service (Local) and then click Register Server In Active Directory. When the Register Internet Authentication Server In Active Directory dialog box appears, click OK.

Alternately, you can do one of the following:

- Use the **netsh ras add registeredserver** command.

Or

- Add the computer account of the IAS server to the RAS and IAS servers security group with the Active Directory Users And Computers snap-in.

If the IAS server authenticates and authorizes wireless connection attempts for user accounts in other domains, verify that the other domains have a two-way trust with the domain in which the IAS server computer is a member. Next, configure the IAS server computer to read the properties of user accounts in other domains by using the **netsh ras add registeredserver** command or the Active Directory Users And Computers snap-in.

Copying the Configuration of the Primary IAS Server to the Secondary IAS Server

To copy the configuration of the primary IAS server to the secondary IAS server, do the following:

1. On the primary IAS server computer, type **netsh aaaa show config > *path\file*.txt** at a command prompt, which stores the configuration settings, including registry settings, in a text file. The path can be a relative, an absolute, or a network path.

2. Copy the file created in step 1 to the secondary IAS server.

3. On the secondary IAS server computer, type **netsh exec *path\file*.txt** at a command prompt, which imports all the settings configured on the primary IAS server into the secondary IAS server.

You cannot copy the IAS settings from an IAS server running Windows Server 2003 to an IAS server running Windows 2000 Server.

Best Practices If you change the IAS server configuration in any way, use the Internet Authentication Service snap-in to change the configuration of the IAS server that is designated as the primary configuration server and then use the previous procedure to synchronize those changes on the secondary IAS server.

Configuring Wireless Network (IEEE 802.11) Policies Group Policy Settings

With the Wireless Network (IEEE 802.11) Policies Group Policy extension provided in Windows Server 2003, you can specify a list of preferred networks and their settings to automatically configure wireless LAN settings for wireless clients running Windows XP (SP1 or later) or Windows Server 2003. For each preferred network, you can specify association settings (such as the Service Set Identifier [SSID] and WEP usage) and authentication settings (such as the use of 802.1X authentication and the authentication protocol).

▶ **To configure Wireless Network (IEEE 802.11) Policies Group Policy settings for EAP-TLS authentication**

1. Open the Active Directory Users And Computers snap-in.

2. In the console tree, double-click Active Directory Users And Computers, right-click the domain or domain system container that contains your wireless computer accounts, and then click Properties.

3. On the Group Policy tab, click the appropriate Group Policy object (the default object is Default Domain Policy) and then click Edit.

4. In the console tree, open Computer Configuration; then Windows Settings; then Security Settings; then Wireless Network (IEEE 802.11) Policies.

5. On the Action menu, click Create Wireless Network Policy. The Wireless Network Policy Wizard will guide you through the creation of a wireless network policy. After it is created, double click the wireless network policy in the details pane.

6. Change settings on the General tab as needed.

7. On the Preferred Networks tab, click Add to add a preferred network.

8. On the Network Properties tab of the New Preferred Settings Properties dialog box, type the wireless network name (the SSID) and change the WEP settings as needed.

9. On the IEEE 802.1X tab, change 802.1X settings as needed.

10. In EAP Type, click Smart Card Or Other Certificate.

11. Click Settings.

12. On the Smart Card Or Other Certificate dialog box, configure server validation settings as needed.

13. Click OK to save changes to EAP properties.

14. Click OK to save changes to the new preferred network.

15. Click OK to save changes to the Wireless Network (802.11) policy.

The next time your Windows XP (SP1 and later) and Windows Server 2003 wireless clients update computer configuration Group Policy, their wireless network configuration is automatically configured.

Configuring Wireless Access Points

Before you configure the wireless APs in your network, you must first make sure they are deployed in a way that provides full coverage of your wireless network. For more information on deploying APs, see Chapter 7, "Wireless AP Placement."

Configure your wireless APs to support WEP encryption and 802.1X authentication. Additionally, configure the RADIUS client on your wireless APs with the following settings:

- The IP address or name of a primary RADIUS server, the shared secret, UDP ports for authentication and accounting, and failure detection settings.

- The IP address or name of a secondary RADIUS server, the shared secret, UDP ports for authentication and accounting, and failure detection settings.

To balance the load of RADIUS traffic between the primary and secondary IAS servers, configure half of the wireless APs with the primary IAS server as their primary RADIUS server and the secondary IAS server as their secondary RADIUS server;

configure the other half with the secondary IAS server as their primary RADIUS server and the primary IAS server as their secondary RADIUS server.

Configuring Wireless Client Computers

To configure wireless client computers, complete the tasks described in the following sections:

- Install the computer certificate.

- Install the user certificate.

- Configure 802.1X authentication for EAP-TLS.

Installing the Computer Certificate

For computer authentication with EAP-TLS, you must install a computer certificate on the wireless client computer. For installation on a wireless client computer running Windows Server 2003, Windows XP, or Windows 2000, connect to the organization's intranet by using an Ethernet port, and do the following:

- If the domain is configured for autoenrollment of computer certificates, each computer that is a member of the domain requests a computer certificate when computer Group Policy is refreshed. To force a refresh of computer Group Policy for a computer running Windows Server 2003 or Windows XP, restart the computer or type **gpupdate /target:computer** at a command prompt. To force a refresh of computer Group Policy for a computer running Windows 2000, restart the computer or type **secedit /refreshpolicy machine_policy** at a command prompt.

- If the domain is not configured for autoenrollment, you can request a computer certificate using the Certificates snap-in (this procedure is described in the "Obtaining and Installing a Computer Certificate" section of this chapter), or you can execute a CAPICOM script to install a computer certificate. For information about CAPICOM, see *http://msdn.microsoft.com/*.

Note An enterprise organization's information technology (IT) group can install a computer certificate before the computer, typically a laptop, is delivered to its user.

Installing the User Certificate

For user authentication with EAP-TLS, you must use a locally installed user certificate or a smart card. The locally installed user certificate can be obtained by autoenrollment, Web enrollment, requesting the certificate using the Certificates snap-in, importing a certificate file, or running a CAPICOM program or script. An organization's IT group or security group is usually responsible for issuing smart cards to users.

The easiest ways to install user certificates assume that network connectivity already exists, such as using an Ethernet port. When users connect to the intranet, they can obtain a user certificate through autoenrollment or by submitting a user certificate request using Web enrollment or the Certificates MMC snap-in. Alternately, they can run a CAPICOM program or script provided by the network administrator. The user logon script can be used to automate the execution of the CAPICOM program or script.

If you have configured autoenrollment of user certificates, the wireless user must update User Configuration Group Policy to obtain a user certificate. If you do not use autoenrollment for user certificates, you can obtain a user certificate by doing one of the following procedures (described in the following sections):

- Install via Web enrollment.

- Request a certificate.

- Install from a certificate file on a floppy disk.

Installing User Certificates via Web Enrollment

To submit a user certificate request via the Web, do the following:

1. Open Internet Explorer.

2. Connect to *http://servername/certsrv*, where *servername* is the name of the CA computer. The CA must also be running Internet Information Services (IIS).

3. Click Request A Certificate and then click Next.

4. On the Choose Request Type Web page, select the type of certificate you want to request under User Certificate Request and click Next.

5. On the Identifying Information Web page, do one of the following:

   - If you see the message "All The Necessary Identifying Information Has Already Been Collected. You May Now Submit Your Request," click Submit.

   Or

   - Enter your identifying information for the certificate request and click Submit.

6. If you see the Certificate Issued Web page, click Install This Certificate.

7. Close Internet Explorer.

Requesting a Certificate

To request a certificate using the Certificates snap-in, do the following:

1. Open a Microsoft Management Console (MMC) that contains Certificates – Current User.

2. In the console tree, right-click Personal, point to All Tasks, and then click Request New Certificate to start the Certificate Request Wizard.

3. In the Certificate Request Wizard, select the type of certificate you want to request. If you selected the Advanced check box:

   * Choose the cryptographic service provider (CSP) you will use.

   * Choose the key length (measured in bits) of the public key associated with the certificate.

   * Do not enable strong private key protection. Enabling strong private key protection requires user intervention (such as typing in a password) when the private key is used, which interferes with automatic access to wireless networks.

   * If you have more than one CA available, select the name of the CA that will issue the certificate.

4. Type a friendly name for your new certificate.

5. After the Certificate Request Wizard successfully finishes, click OK.

Installing from a Certificate File on a Floppy Disk

Another method of installing a user certificate is to export the user certificate onto a floppy disk and then import it onto the wireless client computer. For a floppy disk-based enrollment, perform the following:

1. Obtain a user certificate for the wireless client's user account from the CA through Web-based enrollment.

2. Open an MMC console containing Certificates – Current User.

3. Open Personal and then open Certificates.

4. In the details pane, right-click the certificate you want to export, point to All Tasks, and then click Export.

5. On the Welcome To The Certificate Export Wizard page, click Next.

6. On the Export Private Key page, click Export The Private Key. (This option appears only if the private key is marked as exportable and you have access to the private key.) Click Next.

7. On the Export File Format page, select Personal Information Exchange – PKCS (.PFX) as the export file format. Select other options as needed and then click Next.

8. On the Password page, type a password in Password and Confirm Password to protect the private key in the certificate and then click Next.

9. On the File To Export page, type the certificate filename or click Browse to specify the name and location of the certificate file. Click Next.

10. On the Completing The Certificate Export Wizard page, click Finish.

11. On the wireless client computer, open an MMC console containing Certificates – Current User.

12. Open the Personal folder.

13. On the Action menu, point to All Tasks and then click Import.

14. On the Welcome To The Certificate Export Wizard page, click Next.

15. For File Name on the File To Import page, either type the name of the certificate file stored in step 9 or click Browse to locate it.

16. On the Password page, type the password used to protect the private key in Password. Do not select Enable Strong Private Key Protection. If you intend to move this certificate in the future, click Mark This Key as Exportable.

17. On the Certificate Store page, click Next.

18. On the Completing The Certificate Import Wizard page, click Finish.

Configuring 802.1X Authentication for EAP-TLS

If you have configured Wireless Network (IEEE 802.11) Policies Group Policy settings and specified the use of EAP-TLS authentication for your wireless network— the Smart Card Or Other Certificate authentication method—no other configuration for wireless clients running Windows XP (SP1 or later) or Windows Server 2003 is needed.

▶ **To manually configure EAP-TLS authentication on a wireless client running Windows XP (SP1 or later) or Windows Server 2003**

1. Obtain the properties of the wireless connection in the Network Connections folder. Click the Wireless Networks tab, click the name of the wireless network in the list of preferred networks, and then click Properties.

2. Click the Authentication tab and select Enable IEEE 802.1X Authentication For This Network and the Smart Card Or Other Certificate EAP type.

3. Click Properties.

4. In the Smart Card Or Other Certificate dialog box, click Use a Certificate On This Computer to use a locally installed user certificate or Use My Smart Card for a smart card-based user certificate.

5. Select Validate Server Certificate to validate the computer certificate of the IAS server. If you want to specify the names of the authentication servers that must perform validation, select Connect To These Servers and type the server names.

6. Click OK to save changes to the Smart Card Or Other Certificate EAP type.

▶ **To manually configure EAP-TLS authentication on a wireless client running Windows XP (prior to SP1)**

1. Obtain properties of the wireless connection in the Network Connections folder.

2. On the Authentication tab, select Enable Network Access Control Using IEEE 802.1X and the Smart Card Or Other Certificate EAP type. Both of these configuration settings are enabled by default.

3. Click Properties. The Smart Card Or Other Certificate dialog box displays.

4. In the Smart Card Or Other Certificate dialog box, click Use A Certificate On This Computer to use a locally installed user certificate.

5. Select Validate Server Certificate to validate the computer certificate of the IAS server (enabled by default). If you want to specify how the names of the authentication servers end, select Connect Only If Server Name Ends With and type the string.

6. Click OK to save changes to the Smart Card Or Other Certificate EAP type.

▶ **To configure EAP-TLS authentication on a wireless client running Windows 2000 and Microsoft 802.1X Authentication Client**

1. Obtain properties of the wireless connection in the Dial-up And Network Connections folder.

2. On the Authentication tab, select Enable Network Access Control Using IEEE 802.1X (enabled by default) and the Smart Card Or Other Certificate EAP type.

3. Click Properties. The Smart Card Or Other Certificate dialog box displays.

4. In the Smart Card Or Other Certificate dialog box, click Use A Certificate On This Computer to use a locally installed user certificate or Use My Smart Card for a smart card–based user certificate.

5. Select Validate Server Certificate to validate the computer certificate of the IAS server (enabled by default). If you want to specify the names of the authentication servers that must perform validation, select Connect To These Servers and type the server names.

6. Click OK to save changes to the Smart Card Or Other Certificate EAP type.

Summary

This chapter described the detailed steps for configuring secure wireless access by using the EAP-TLS authentication protocol. Computers running Windows 2000 or Windows Server 2003 are used in the authentication infrastructure for domain controllers, CAs, and RADIUS servers (running IAS). A computer certificate is installed on each IAS server, and both a computer and user certificate is installed on Windows wireless clients. Windows wireless clients are then configured to use EAP-TLS authentication by using the Wireless Network (IEEE 802.11) Policies Group Policy setting or through manual configuration.

Chapter 9
Case Study: The Microsoft Wireless Network

This chapter describes how Microsoft implemented its secure wireless network using 802.11b and Extensible Authentication Protocol-Transport Layer Security (EAP-TLS) authentication. As an early adopter of wireless technology, Microsoft faced several challenges in deploying a secure and reliable global wireless infrastructure. Microsoft now has more than 30,000 wireless clients, and the wireless network is a key piece of its corporate-connected infrastructure.

History of the Microsoft Wireless LAN

Demand for wireless access to enterprise LANs is fueled by the growth of mobile computing devices such as laptops and personal digital assistants (PDAs) and by a desire by users for continual connections to the network without being restricted to "plug-in areas" that do not move with their work. Microsoft's dedication to providing end user connectivity anytime and anywhere drives its wireless product enhancements (as well as its commitment to providing a secure and reliable enterprise wireless networking infrastructure).

Microsoft was the first large enterprise to embrace wireless LAN (WLAN) technology as an alternative to wire-attached laptop units. With the IEEE 802.11 WLAN standard newly ratified as an international standard, Microsoft readily endorsed the IEEE 802.11b extension to the newly published standard (ratified September 16, 1999) and began deploying IEEE 802.11b in December of 1999 throughout its Redmond corporate campus. Since then, Microsoft has actively worked to improve and to lead efforts with the IEEE 802.11 standards body to enhance and refine areas of data privacy, authentication, and network reliability.

Shortly after the IEEE 802.11b ratification, the IEEE 802.1 MAC Bridging group began working on the IEEE 802.1X extension to the 802.1 bridging standard in support of authenticated port access to LAN-based networks such as IEEE 802.3 (Ethernet), IEEE 802.5 (token ring), Fiber Distributed Data Interface (FDDI), and IEEE 802.11.

Microsoft initially offered wireless connectivity as a supplement to the ubiquitous wired connectivity. Although it was not designed to be an end user's primary network connectivity device, the WLAN service soon became a highly desired connectivity choice that enabled impromptu discussions, software demonstrations, and ability to take work to meetings—all of which had a positive impact on worker productivity.

After the initial Redmond campus rollout finished, Microsoft had the largest enterprise WLAN network in the world, but it also immediately had to solve the deployment, integration, and maintenance issues of a large WLAN network. From the initial deployment of 2,800 wireless access points (APs) and 19,000 wireless network adapters, Microsoft had to deal with issues of security and scalability from the start. For example, Microsoft realized that Media Access Control (MAC) address filtering and early virtual private network (VPN) solutions would not be a scalable final solution to support a global WLAN.

The initial rollout of 802.11b on the Redmond campus used static Wired Equivalent Privacy (WEP) 128-bit encryption keys for data confidentiality and IEEE 802.11 shared key authentication. News of ongoing security compromises of WEP and shared key authentication prompted Microsoft to take an aggressive stance toward the security of its WLAN infrastructure. The result of this stance is the current WLAN deployment that uses 802.1X, certificate-based EAP-TLS authentication, and per-session WEP keys.

Microsoft continues to lead the security efforts in both authentication and data confidentiality in the IEEE 802.11i security task group. Microsoft also realizes the benefits to other areas of functionality and provides contributions to support end user requirements for *world mode* operation of wireless network adapters and an inter-wireless AP protocol that uses connect blocks of session association information.

Note World mode operation enables a wireless network adapter to operate in different countries, each of which can define the use of the S-Band Industrial, Scientific, and Medical (ISM) frequency band for 802.11b wireless networking. Different countries divide the S-Band ISM into different channels and define different transmission power requirements. Wireless APs and wireless network adapters support world mode operation.

Microsoft WLAN Technologies

The Microsoft WLAN utilizes the following technologies:

- IEEE 802.11b

- IEEE 802.1X

- EAP-TLS authentication

- RADIUS

- Active Directory directory service

- X.509 Certificates

Design and Deployment Considerations

Microsoft's deployment of wireless connectivity is for production access into the enterprise corporate intranet (hereafter known as *Corpnet*). Once on the Microsoft Corpnet, no firewalls restrict employees or other authorized users from accessing all network and corporate resources.

Performance

Because the WLAN was designed to supplement—not replace—Microsoft's wired Ethernet LAN infrastructure, two to four users on average share 11 Mbps of bandwidth per wireless AP. Real throughput fluctuates between 4–6.5 Mbps. The result of this design rule is that for a fully loaded AP (25 users), the user experience is similar to using a home DSL or cable modem connection.

An additional technique was used to ensure high performance in dense areas, such as executive briefing conference rooms and training areas, in which large numbers of users are located in a very densely populated area. By reducing transmit power of the wireless APs from 30 milliwatts (mW) to 15 or 5 mW (or even as low as 1 mW), smaller coverage areas were created. The reduction in transmission power allows a greater number of wireless APs to be placed in the same area. For example, in a room for 200 people, in which only three wireless APs can normally be placed with full power without coverage area overlap issues, additional lower-power wireless APs are used, resulting in a smaller number of wireless clients per wireless AP and better average bandwidth available per wireless client.

Scalability

Microsoft's WLAN design is based on a 20-meter diameter coverage area, which ensures redundant coverage against the potential failure of a single wireless AP and provides seamless roaming within a building. Microsoft's Operations and Technology Group (OTG) verified wireless AP installation for conformance with an internally developed commissioning checklist. It also checked the coverage and network connectivity of each wireless AP. On the engineering side, Microsoft was concerned about decreased coverage area size, overlapping coverage areas via channel configuration, and mitigating Bluetooth (BT) interference.

Roaming and Mobility

In Microsoft's WLAN deployment, all the wireless APs within each building are on the same IP subnet, so intra-building wireless roaming is seamless. When wireless clients associate with different wireless APs, the DHCP renewal process renews the lease on the existing TCP/IP configuration. Inter-building roaming and the DHCP renewal process cause a change in the IP address configuration, which can cause problems for applications that cannot gracefully handle a change in the IP address or other configuration. In either case, because EAP-TLS and certificates are used for authentication, the user is never prompted to authenticate to the WLAN.

Security

Elements of the security design include the following, which are discussed in the following sections:

- Authentication

- Eavesdropping

- Rogue wireless APs

Authentication

Microsoft chose EAP-TLS using user and computer certificates that are stored on the computer as the authentication method for wireless connectivity for the following reasons:

- EAP-TLS does not require any dependencies on the user account's password.

- EAP-TLS authentication occurs automatically, usually with no intervention by the user.

- EAP-TLS uses certificates, which provide a relatively strong authentication mechanism.

- The EAP-TLS exchange is protected with public key cryptography and is not susceptible to offline dictionary attacks.

- The EAP-TLS authentication process results in mutually determined keying material for data encryption (the WEP unicast session encryption key) and signing.

Eavesdropping

Wireless traffic on the Microsoft WLAN is protected from eavesdropping in the following ways:

- EAP messages for IEEE 802.1X negotiation are sent as clear text. However, the use of EAP-TLS and public key encryption prevents the eavesdropper from obtaining the information needed to masquerade as either the wireless client or the authenticating server.

- After EAP-TLS negotiation is complete, all traffic sent between an authenticated wireless client and its associated wireless AP is encrypted with either the WEP multicast/global or unicast session key.

By monitoring the 802.1X exchange and 802.11 control and data traffic, an eavesdropper listening to wireless traffic could obtain the following types of information:

- Names of the computer or user accounts involved in each EAP-TLS negotiation

- Wireless client and wireless AP MAC addresses

- MAC addresses of nodes on the wireless AP subnets

- Times of association and disassociation

An eavesdropper could use such information to do long-term traffic profiling and analysis that might provide user or device details.

For an eavesdropper listening on the wired network, sensitive attributes of RADIUS messages sent between the wireless APs and the RADIUS servers and proxies are protected with the RADIUS shared secret.

Rogue Wireless APs

The Microsoft WLAN is protected from rogue wireless APs by the use of EAP-TLS, which provides mutual authentication of the wireless client and the authenticating RADIUS server. To masquerade as a Microsoft corporate wireless AP, a rogue AP would require a security relationship with a Microsoft OTG RADIUS server, which is defined and controlled by the configuration of the wireless AP as a RADIUS client on the RADIUS server or proxy and a RADIUS shared secret. If a wireless AP does not have this security relationship and configuration, it cannot exchange RADIUS messages with the RADIUS server, and thus cannot authenticate 802.1X wireless clients. It is possible for the rogue wireless AP to be configured as the RADIUS client of a rogue RADIUS server. However, Microsoft wireless clients validate the certificate of the RADIUS server by default. Therefore, if the RADIUS server of the wireless AP cannot provide a valid certificate and proof of knowledge of its corresponding private key, the wireless client terminates the connection.

Deploying the Wireless Network

Microsoft's deployment of wireless access occurred in four phases, as discussed in the following sections.

- Phase 1: Pre-installation

- Phase 2: Installation

- Phase 3: Delivery

- Phase 4: Rollout to Microsoft users

Phase 1: Pre-Installation

Pre-installation involved the following steps:

1. Developing a wireless AP location plan based on design guidelines in which 95 percent of the installations require no specialized antennas.

2. Performing field-verification of proposed wireless AP locations to check for physical interference.

3. Presenting the final locations to a Microsoft OTG designer for approval prior to starting installation.

Phase 2: Installation

Physical installation of the wireless APs involved the following steps:

1. Enclosing wireless APs and antennas within plenum-rated enclosures to meet fire safety code requirements.

2. Configuring central, low-voltage power supply on backup power using uninterruptible power supplies.

3. Building out RADIUS infrastructure.

Phase 3: Delivery

Delivery involved the following steps:

1. Spot-checking wireless AP installation for conformance with commissioning checklist.

2. Verifying radio frequency (RF) coverage and network connectivity of each wireless AP.

3. Delivering "as-built" documents, reflecting the final placement of each wireless AP.

Phase 4: Rollout to Microsoft Users

The rollout to Microsoft users involved the following steps:

1. Creating a Cryptographic API Component Object Model (CAPICOM) script to install certificates.

2. Creating a Web site to host information about instructions, updated drivers, and the CAPICOM script.

3. Telling users of the Web site how to obtain wireless access.

To obtain the computer and user certificates required for wireless connectivity to the Microsoft corporate wireless network, the computer, typically a wireless laptop computer, must first connect to the Microsoft Corpnet using an Ethernet connection.

More Info   For more information about CAPICOM, see the topic titled "Cryptography, CryptoAPI, and CAPICOM" at *http://msdn.microsoft.com*.

Current Deployment and Infrastructure

There are currently more than 3,200 wireless APs of the Microsoft WLAN installed worldwide, and the magnitude of this deployment created unique challenges for Microsoft in the areas of security and authentication. Microsoft OTG enlisted several departments to create and deploy its 802.11 WLAN solution: End User Services (EUS), Corporate Security, Enterprise Network Engineering, and Corporate Server support groups provided integration testing and deployment of the secure Microsoft WLAN.

The current WLAN deployment consists of the following:

- Active Directory domain controllers
- Windows Server 2003 certification authorities (CAs)
- Wireless clients running Windows XP
- Cisco Aironet 340 and 350 Series Access Points
- RADIUS servers and proxies running Windows Server 2003

Active Directory Domain Controllers

The Microsoft Corpnet uses native mode domains with domain controllers running a member of the Windows Server 2003 family. During the transition to Windows Server 2003, there were domain controllers running Windows 2000 Server with Service Pack 2 (SP2) and the required patches for Active Directory to allow computer accounts to have dial-in properties and the SChannel certificate mapper installed (these patches are now part of Windows 2000 SP3). Within the Microsoft Corpnet, there are the following Active Directory forests:

- Corpnet.ms.com
- NT.Dev
- Win.SE
- Win.Deploy

The corpnet.ms.com forest contains the corpnet.ms.com domain and a series of child domains that represent the major geographical regions of the Microsoft Corporation. This forest structure is shown in Figure 9-1.

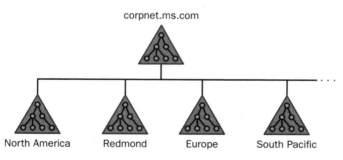

Figure 9-1. *The structure of the corpnet.ms.com forest.*

As defined by the forest structure for Active Directory, a member server of any domain within the forest can validate the credentials of any account in any domain in the forest. For example, a member server in the Redmond domain can validate the user or computer credentials for accounts in the North America, Europe, South Pacific, and other child domains.

> **More Info** For more information about the Microsoft Corpnet Active Directory infrastructure, search for the white paper titled "Windows 2000: Designing and Deploying Active Directory Service for the MS Internal Corpnet" at *http://www.microsoft.com/technet.*

The remote access permission on the Dial-In tab of user and computer accounts is set to Control Access Through Remote Access Policy. Because it was a Microsoft corporate decision that all valid domain machine and user accounts are allowed wireless access, the dial-in properties of the account are ignored for the evaluation of authorization and the determination of connection constraints. There is no global or universal group for all the accounts that have wireless access. (For more information, see "RADIUS Servers and Proxies Running Windows Server 2003," later in this chapter.)

Windows Server 2003 CAs

To issue user and computer certificates for wireless access and provide certificate revocation list (CRL) publication, the existing Microsoft PKI was used. To conform to Microsoft-recommended PKI best practices, the Microsoft PKI consists of the following:

- An offline root CA

- A level of offline intermediate CAs

- A level of online issuing CAs

This PKI hierarchy is shown in Figure 9-2.

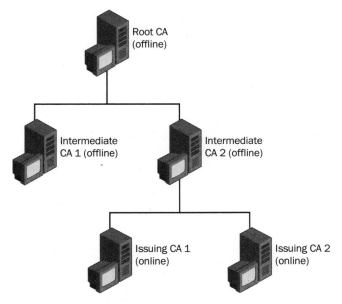

Figure 9-2. *Hierarchy for the Microsoft PKI.*

This PKI provides flexibility and insulates the root CA from attempts to compromise its private key by malicious users. All CAs in the Microsoft PKI are running on a Windows Server 2003 member server.

> **More Info**   For more information about PKI, see the Windows 2000 Security Services Web site at *http://www.microsoft.com/windows2000/technologies /security/default.asp* and the Windows Server 2003 Security Services Web site at *http://www.microsoft.com/windowsserver2003/technologies/security/ default.mspx.*

To issue computer certificates, autoenrollment—using the Automatic Certificate Request Settings in the Computer Configuration Group Policy—was configured on the appropriate domain system containers for all of the forests. All member computers requested and obtained a computer certificate from the appropriate issuing CA after automatically updating Computer Configuration Group Policy settings.

To issue user certificates, Microsoft OTG staff created a CAPICOM script. Because autoenrollment of user certificates was not possible with Windows 2000 enterprise CAs that were originally in place, the other alternatives were Web enrollment using the Certificates snap-in to request or import a user certificate or the use of a CAPICOM script. The use of CAPICOM scripts was chosen because it required no user intervention for selecting certificate settings.

To educate Microsoft users and provide a location from which the CAPICOM script could be launched, Microsoft OTG staff created an internal Web site. The CAPICOM script verifies whether a user or computer certificate is already installed. If not, the script causes the computer to request a user or computer certificate from an appropriate issuing CA.

The computer certificate (installed through autoenrollment) and the user certificate (installed through the CAPICOM script) are obtained while the computer is connected to the Microsoft Corpnet using an Ethernet connection.

Wireless Clients Running Windows XP

At Microsoft, the operating system platform for wireless clients is Microsoft Windows XP, which includes built-in support for 802.11 and 802.1X. A wireless client user uses the Windows XP Wireless Zero Configuration (WZC) service to connect to the Microsoft corporate wireless network. Default settings enable WEP encryption, the use of 802.1X authentication, and the EAP-TLS authentication method using user and computer certificates. All wireless network adapters used at Microsoft support the WZC service.

If Microsoft users have a wireless network at home, the WZC service enables them to have both wireless networks in their list of preferred wireless networks: the Microsoft corporate wireless network and their home wireless network. While at work, their wireless laptop connects to the Microsoft corporate network; while at home, their wireless laptop connects to their home wireless network. Each wireless network can have its own configuration, including wireless network type (infrastructure vs. ad hoc) and authentication and encryption settings.

Cisco Aironet 340 and 350 Series Access Points

The Microsoft WLAN uses Cisco Aironet 340 and 350 Series Access Points that are running Wireless IOS release 11.21 or later. The wireless APs are initially installed with a minimal configuration designed to provide TCP/IP and Simple Network Management Protocol (SNMP) access. A Microsoft-designed, PERL-based SNMP script is launched and configures standard settings for the wireless AP and individual settings such as channel number and signal power, which are extracted from a relational database. Access point firmware and radio firmware software are deployed by upgrading a single wireless AP in each building and then use the "distribute image" capability of the wireless APs to transfer that image to all wireless APs within the building.

All wireless APs are configured as RADIUS clients to two RADIUS servers, each of which is a member server in a child domain of the corpnet.ms.com forest. There are no wireless APs that use the RADIUS servers in the NT.Dev, Win.SE, or Win.Deploy forests. This configuration is shown in Figure 9-3.

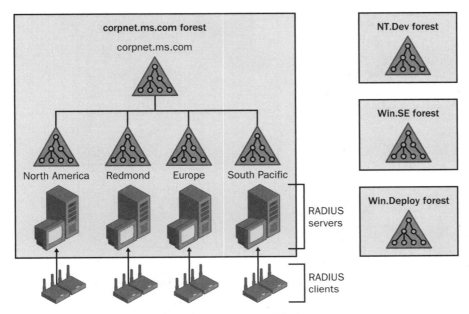

Figure 9-3. *Configuration of wireless APs as RADIUS clients.*

Although the wireless APs are configured with a primary and secondary RADIUS server, the behavior of the wireless APs is to use the primary RADIUS server exclusively unless it becomes unavailable, at which time they switch to the secondary RADIUS server and use it exclusively. If the secondary RADIUS server becomes unavailable, the wireless APs switch back to the primary RADIUS server and use it exclusively. To balance the load of all authentications for all wireless APs in a domain, approximately half of the wireless APs are configured with specific primary and secondary RADIUS servers (for example, primary is RAD1 and secondary is RAD2). The other half of the wireless APs are configured with the opposite primary and secondary RADIUS servers (for example, primary is RAD2 and secondary is RAD1). This manual configuration of the wireless APs assures that the RADIUS authentication load is approximately split in half between the two RADIUS servers in the domain (assuming that both RADIUS servers are available).

RADIUS Servers and Proxies Running Windows Server 2003

The RADIUS infrastructure for the Microsoft WLAN consists of pairs of domain member servers, each running Windows Server 2003 and Internet Authentication Service (IAS). The IAS servers act as RADIUS servers, RADIUS proxies, or both. Pairs are used to provide failover support in case one of the members of the pair becomes unavailable.

The RADIUS infrastructure is shown in Figure 9-4.

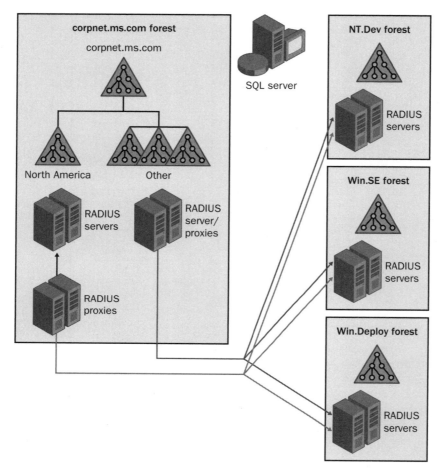

Figure 9-4. *RADIUS infrastructure for the Microsoft WLAN.*

North America Child Domain

North America contains most of the wireless APs and accounts being authenticated. To accommodate this heavy load, IAS servers are deployed as RADIUS proxies to handle all the RADIUS traffic. The RADIUS proxies provide load balancing of RADIUS traffic to the RADIUS servers and allow for the scaling out of the authentication infrastructure without having to reconfigure each wireless AP.

A pair of IAS servers acting as RADIUS proxies route messages in the following way:

- For accounts in the corpnet.ms.com forest, the IAS servers route messages from the wireless APs in North America to the North America RADIUS servers.

- For accounts in the NT.Dev, Win.SE, or Win.Deploy forests, the IAS servers route messages from wireless APs in North America to the RADIUS servers in the appropriate forest.

This routing is accomplished by the configuration of the following connection request policies in the following order:

1. For authentication requests for which the User-Name attribute ends with corp-net.ms.com, forward traffic to the NorthAmerica remote RADIUS server group (consisting of the two RADIUS servers in the North America domain).

2. For authentication requests for which the User-Name attribute ends with NT.Dev.ms.com, forward traffic to the NT.Dev remote RADIUS server group (consisting of the two RADIUS servers in the NT.Dev.ms.com forest).

3. For authentication requests for which the User-Name attribute ends with Win.SE.ms.com, forward traffic to the Win.SE remote RADIUS server group (consisting of the two RADIUS servers in the Win.SE.ms.com forest).

4. For authentication requests for which the User-Name attribute ends with Win.Deploy.ms.com, forward traffic to the Win.Deploy remote RADIUS server group (consisting of the two RADIUS servers in the Win.Deploy.ms.com forest).

5. For Windows XP (prior to SP1), the format for computer account names sent during computer authentication is Domain/ComputerAccount. In contrast, the format for user accounts names sent during user authentication is User-Account@Domain.Forest.

   To accommodate the different format for computer account names, additional connection request policies were created for each domain that matched the computer account name and forwarded the RADIUS traffic to the appropriate remote RADIUS server group. For example, a connection request policy for the computer accounts in the North America domain was configured as follows: For authentication requests for which the User-Name attribute begins with NorthAmerica/, forward traffic to the NorthAmerica remote RADIUS server group. For another example, a connection request policy for the computer accounts in the NT.Dev domain was configured as follows: For authentication request for which the User-Name attribute begins with NT.Dev/, forward traffic to the NT.Dev remote RADIUS server group.

   With Windows XP (SP1 and later), Windows Server 2003, and Windows 2000, the format for computer account names sent during computer authentication is ComputerAccount@Domain.Forest, and additional connection request policies for computer accounts are not needed.

A layer of RADIUS proxies is used in the North America domain to provide load balancing of authentication requests to the IAS servers in the NorthAmerica remote RADIUS server group for wireless APs in the entire North America region (not including the Redmond corporate campus). For the IAS servers acting as RADIUS servers in the North America domain, a single connection request policy is used to perform authentication at the IAS server for all authentication requests for which the User-Name attribute ends with corpnet.ms.com.

> **More Info** For more information about using Windows Server 2003 IAS as a RADIUS proxy and the configuration of connection request policies, see Chapter 4, "RADIUS, IAS, and Active Directory."

Other Child Domains

A pair of IAS servers acting as RADIUS server/proxies in the other child domains of the corpnet.ms.com forest perform the following:

- For accounts in the corpnet.ms.com forest, the IAS server performs authentication.

- For accounts in the NT.Dev, Win.SE, or Win.Deploy forests, messages are forwarded to the RADIUS servers in the appropriate forest.

Forwarding of authentication requests to RADIUS servers in other forests is accomplished by the configuration of the following connection request policies in the following order:

1. For authentication requests for which the User-Name attribute ends with corpnet.ms.com, perform authentication on this server.

2. For authentication requests for which the User-Name attribute ends with NT.Dev.ms.com, forward traffic to the NT.Dev remote RADIUS server group.

3. For authentication requests for which the User-Name attribute ends with Win.SE.ms.com, forward traffic to the Win.SE remote RADIUS server group.

4. For authentication requests for which the User-Name attribute ends with Win.Deploy.ms.com, forward traffic to the Win.Deploy remote RADIUS server group.

To accommodate the different format for computer account names, additional connection request policies were created for each domain that matched the computer account name and forwarded the RADIUS traffic to the appropriate remote RADIUS server group.

NT.Dev, Win.SE, and Win.Deploy Forests

In the NT.Dev, Win.SE, and Win.Deploy forests, a pair of IAS servers acting as RADIUS servers performs the following:

- For accounts in the forest, the IAS server performs authentication.

This authentication is accomplished by the configuration of the following connection request policy:

- For authentication requests for which the User-Name attribute ends with the forest name, perform authentication on this server.

Wireless Remote Access Policy Settings

For each IAS server that performs authentication and authorization as a RADIUS server, a wireless remote access policy is configured with the following settings:

- Conditions: NAS-Port-Type=Wireless-IEEE 802.11.

- Permissions: Grant Remote Access Permission.

- Profile, Dial-In Constraints tab: Minutes Server Can Remain Idle Before It Is Disconnected (Idle-Timeout) is set to 120. This setting forces a reauthentication for a wireless connection that has no activity for two hours.

- Profile, Authentication tab: Extensible Authentication Protocol and the Smart Card Or Other Certificate EAP type selected. Clear all other check boxes.

- Profile, Encryption tab: Clear all other check boxes except the Strongest check box. This setting forces all wireless connections to use 128-bit encryption.

- Profile, Advanced tab: Ignore-User-Dialin-Properties attribute is set to True.

  To simplify the evaluation of authorization and the evaluation of connection constraints for wireless and to ensure that wireless connections can be made, the wireless remote access policies for all the IAS servers acting as RADIUS servers are configured to ignore the settings on the Dial-In tab of computer and user accounts.

Centralized Logging to a SQL Server

Using the new SQL logging feature of Windows Server 2003 IAS, all connection information is logged to a central SQL server for analysis (refer to Figure 9-4).

Summary

The Microsoft WLAN is a secure wireless network that uses a combination of IEEE 802.11b, IEEE 802.1X, EAP-TLS certificate-based authentication, RADIUS, certificates, and Active Directory. The wireless clients run Windows XP, and the servers for the certificate and authentication infrastructure run Windows Server 2003. Computer certificates are deployed to wireless computers using autoenrollment. User certificates and Windows XP wireless configuration information is deployed to wireless computers through an internal Web site and a CAPICOM script. The RADIUS infrastructure uses a combination of RADIUS servers and proxies to load balance and route RADIUS traffic for different Active Directory forests.

Chapter 10
Intranet Wireless Deployment Using PEAP-MS-CHAP v2

PEAP-Microsoft Challenge Authentication Protocol version 2 (PEAP-MS-CHAP v2) is used for password-based wireless authentication when a Public Key Infrastructure (PKI) is not practical or available to issue computer and user certificates to all the wireless clients. This chapter describes the steps needed to deploy secure wireless using PEAP-MS-CHAP v2 authentication.

Required Components

The following components are required for an intranet wireless deployment using PEAP-MS-CHAP v2:

- **Wireless client computers running Windows.** Wireless client computers must be running Microsoft Windows XP Service Pack 1 (SP1) and later, Windows Server 2003, or Windows 2000 with Microsoft 802.1X Authentication Client.

- **At least two Internet Authentication Service servers.** At least two Internet Authentication Service (IAS) servers (one primary and one secondary) are recommended to provide fault tolerance for Remote Authentication Dial-In User Service (RADIUS)–based authentication. If only one IAS server is configured and it becomes unavailable, wireless access clients cannot connect. By using two IAS servers and configuring all wireless access points (APs)—acting as the RADIUS clients—for both the primary and secondary IAS servers, the wireless APs can detect when the primary RADIUS server is unavailable and then automatically fail over to the secondary IAS server. You can use either Windows Server 2003 or Windows 2000 Server IAS. IAS servers running Windows 2000 must have SP3 or later and Microsoft 802.1X Authentication Client installed. IAS is not included with Windows Server 2003, Web Edition.

- **Active Directory directory service domains.** Active Directory domains contain the user accounts, computer accounts, and dial-in properties that each IAS server requires to authenticate credentials and evaluate authorization. Although not a requirement, IAS should be installed on Active Directory domain controllers to optimize IAS authentication and authorization response times and minimize network traffic.

    You can use either Windows Server 2003 or Windows 2000 Server domain controllers. Windows 2000 domain controllers must have SP3 or later installed.

- **Computer certificates installed on the IAS servers.** To authenticate the IAS server to the wireless client during phase 1 of PEAP-based authentication, a computer certificate must be installed on the IAS server computers. The phases of PEAP authentication are described in Chapter 2, "Wireless Security."

- **Root certification authority certificates on each wireless client.** If not already installed, you must install root certification authority (CA) certificates for the issuing CA of the computer certificates being used by the IAS servers on the wireless client computers so that the computer certificates of the IAS servers are trusted for authentication.

- **Wireless remote access policy.** A remote access policy is configured for wireless connections so that wireless users and their computers can access the organization's intranet.

- **Multiple wireless APs.** Multiple wireless APs provide wireless access in different coverage areas of an organization. The wireless APs must support IEEE 802.1X, Wired Equivalent Privacy (WEP), RADIUS, and, optionally, Wi-Fi Protected Access (WPA).

Figure 10-1 shows the components of PEAP-MS-CHAP v2 authentication.

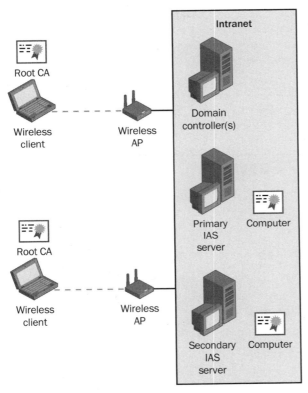

Figure 10-1. *The components of PEAP-MS-CHAP v2 authentication.*

Configuring Active Directory for Accounts and Groups for Wireless Access

To configure Active Directory user and computer accounts and groups for wireless access, do the following:

1. If you are using Windows 2000 domain controllers, install Windows 2000 SP3 or later on all domain controllers.

2. Ensure that all users that are making wireless connections have a corresponding user account.

3. Ensure that all computers that are making wireless connections have a corresponding computer account.

4. Set the remote access permission on user and computer accounts to the appropriate setting: either Allow Access or Control Access Through Remote Access Policy. The remote access permission setting is on the Dial-In tab on the properties of a user or computer account in the Active Directory Users And Computers snap-in.

5. Organize your wireless access user and computer accounts into the appropriate groups. For a native-mode domain, you can use universal and nested global groups. For example, create a universal group named WirelessUsers that contains global groups of wireless user and computer accounts for intranet access.

Best Practices Use a native-mode domain and universal and global groups to organize your wireless accounts into a single nested group.

Configuring the IAS Servers

To configure the IAS servers for PEAP-MS-CHAP v2 authentication, you must do the following, as described in the following sections:

- Configure the primary IAS server.
- Configure a remote access policy for wireless access.
- Configure the secondary IAS server.

Configuring the Primary IAS Server

To configure the primary IAS server on a computer, do the following tasks:

1. Obtain and install a computer certificate.
2. Install IAS and configure IAS server properties.
3. Configure IAS with RADIUS clients.

These tasks are described in the following sections.

Obtaining and Installing a Computer Certificate

If you are using computer certificate autoenrollment and Windows 2000 IAS, you can force a refresh of computer configuration Group Policy by typing **secedit /refreshpolicy machine_policy** from a command prompt on the primary IAS computer. If you are using computer certificate autoenrollment and Windows Server 2003 IAS, force a refresh of computer configuration Group Policy by typing **gpupdate /target:computer** from a command prompt.

If you are using a commercial CA or your PKI does not support autoenrollment of computer certificates, obtain the computer certificate and then follow the procedure described below.

▶ **To install a computer certificate on the primary IAS server**

1. Click Start, click Run, type **mmc**, and then click OK.
2. On the File menu, click Add/Remove Snap-In and then click Add.

3. Under Snap-In, double-click Certificates, click Computer Account, and then click Next.

4. Do one of the following:

   • If you logged on to the IAS server, click Local Computer and then click Finish.

   • If you are configuring the IAS server from a remote computer, click Another Computer and type the name of the computer, or click Browse to select the computer name and then click Finish.

5. Click Close.

   Certificates (Local Computer or *Computer Name*) appears on the list of selected snap-ins for the new console.

6. In the console tree, double-click Certificates (Local Computer or *Computer Name*) and then double-click Personal.

7. Point to All Tasks, and then click Import.

8. The Welcome To The Certificate Import Wizard page of the Certificate Import Wizard displays. Click Next.

9. On the File To Import page, type the filename of the certificate file provided by the commercial CA in File Name, or click Browse and use the Browse dialog box to locate it.

10. Click Next. On the Certificate Store page, click Place All Certificates in the Following Store. By default the Personal folder should be displayed as the import location.

11. Click Next. On the Completing the Certificate Import Wizard page, click Finish.

Best Practices   It is also possible to import a certificate by double-clicking a certificate file that is stored in a folder or sent in an email message. Although this works for certificates created with Windows CAs, this method might not work for third-party CAs. The recommended method of importing certificates is to use the Certificates snap-in.

Installing IAS and Configuring IAS Server Properties

To install IAS, do the following:

1. Open Add Or Remove Programs in Control Panel.

2. Click Add/Remove Windows Components.

3. In the Windows Components Wizard dialog box, double-click Networking Services under Components.

4. In the Networking Services dialog box, select Internet Authentication Service, shown in the following figure.

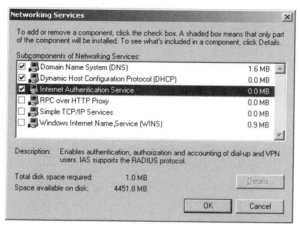

5. Click OK and then click Next.

6. If prompted, insert your Windows product compact disc.

7. After IAS is installed, click Finish and then click Close.

This procedure is the same for Windows 2000 Server IAS and Windows Server 2003 IAS. If you are using Windows 2000 IAS, you must also do the following:

1. Install Windows 2000 SP3 or later.

2. Install Microsoft 802.1X Authentication Client.

More Info You can obtain Windows 2000 SP3 or later from *http: //www.microsoft.com/windows2000/downloads/servicepacks/*.

You can obtain Microsoft 802.1X Authentication Client from *http: //support.microsoft.com/default.aspx?scid=kb;en-us;313664*.

The primary IAS server computer must be able to access account properties in the appropriate domains. If IAS is being installed on a domain controller, no additional configuration is required in order for IAS to access account properties in the domain to which it belongs. If IAS is not installed on a domain controller, you must configure the primary IAS server computer to read the properties of user accounts in the domain. You can do this by following the procedure described below.

▶ **To configure the primary IAS server computer to read the properties of user accounts in the domain**

1. Click Start, point to Programs, point to Administrative Tools, and then click Internet Authentication Service.

2. In the console tree, right-click Internet Authentication Service (Local), and then click Register Server in Active Directory.

   A Register Internet Authentication Server In Active Directory dialog box appears.

3. Click OK.

Alternately, you can do either of the following:

- Use the **netsh ras add registeredserver** command.

Or

- Add the computer account of the IAS server to the RAS and IAS servers security group with the Active Directory Users And Computers snap-in.

If the IAS server authenticates and authorizes wireless connection attempts for user accounts in other domains, verify that the other domains have a two-way trust with the domain in which the IAS server computer is a member. Next, configure the IAS server computer to read the properties of user accounts in other domains by using the **netsh ras add registeredserver** command or the Active Directory Users And Computers snap-in.

If there are accounts in other domains and those domains do not have a two-way trust with the domain in which the IAS server computer is a member, you must configure a RADIUS proxy between the two untrusted domains. If there are accounts in other Active Directory forests, you must configure a RADIUS proxy between the forests. For more information, see Chapter 11, "Additional Intranet Wireless Deployment Configurations."

Tip   You do not need to use a RADIUS proxy if you are using PEAP-MS-CHAP v2 and Windows NT 4.0-style user names (for example, microsoft\user1).

If you want to store authentication and accounting information for connection analysis and security investigation purposes, enable logging for accounting and authentication events. Windows 2000 IAS can log information to a local file. Windows Server 2003 IAS can log information to a local file and to a Structured Query Language (SQL) Server database.

▶ **To enable and configure logging for Windows 2000 IAS**

1. In the console tree of the Internet Authentication snap-in, click Remote Access Logging.

2. In the details pane, double-click Local File.

3. On the Settings tab, select one or more check boxes for recording authentication and accounting requests in the IAS log files:

   - To capture accounting requests and responses, select the Log Accounting Requests check box.

- To capture authentication requests, access-accept packets, and access-reject packets, select the Log Authentication Requests check box.

- To capture periodic status updates, such as interim accounting packets, select the Log Periodic Status check box.

4. On the Local File tab, select the log file format and new log time period and then type the log file directory as needed.

▶ **To enable and configure local file logging for Windows Server 2003 IAS**

1. In the console tree of the Internet Authentication snap-in, click Remote Access Logging.

2. In the details pane, double-click Local File.

3. On the Settings tab, select one or more check boxes for recording authentication and accounting requests in the IAS log files:

- To capture accounting requests and responses, select the Accounting Requests check box.

- To capture authentication requests, access-accept packets, and access-reject packets, select the Authentication Requests check box.

- To capture periodic status updates, such as interim accounting packets, select the Periodic Status check box.

4. On the Log File tab, type the log file directory as needed and select the log file format and new log time period.

▶ **To enable and configure SQL Server database logging for Windows Server 2003 IAS**

1. In the console tree of the Internet Authentication snap-in, click Remote Access Logging.

2. In the details pane, double-click SQL Server.

3. On the Settings tab, select one or more check boxes for recording authentication and accounting requests in the IAS log files:

- To capture accounting requests and responses, select the Accounting Requests check box.

- To capture authentication requests, access-accept packets, and access-reject packets, select the Authentication Requests check box.

- To capture periodic status updates, such as interim accounting packets, select the Periodic Status check box.

4. In Maximum Number Of Connections, type the maximum number of simultaneous sessions that IAS can create with the SQL Server.

5. To configure a SQL data source, click Configure.

6. On the Data Link Properties dialog box, configure the appropriate settings for the SQL Server database.

If needed, configure additional UDP ports for authentication and accounting messages that are sent by RADIUS clients (the wireless APs). By default, IAS uses UDP ports 1812 and 1645 for authentication messages and UDP ports 1813 and 1646 for accounting messages.

▶ To configure Windows 2000 IAS for different UDP ports

1. In the console tree of the Internet Authentication snap-in, right-click Internet Authentication Service and then click Properties.

2. Click the RADIUS tab, configure the UDP port numbers for your RADIUS authentication traffic in Authentication and the UDP port numbers for your RADIUS accounting traffic in Accounting.

▶ To configure Windows Server 2003 IAS for different UDP ports

1. In the console tree of the Internet Authentication snap-in, right-click Internet Authentication Service and then click Properties.

2. Click the Ports tab and then configure the UDP port numbers for your RADIUS authentication traffic in Authentication and the UDP port numbers for your RADIUS accounting traffic in Accounting.

   To use multiple port settings for authentication or accounting traffic, separate the port numbers with commas. You can also specify an IP address to which the RADIUS messages must be sent with the following syntax: IPAddress:UDPPort. For example, if you have multiple network adapters and you want to receive only RADIUS authentication messages sent to the IP address of 10.0.0.99 and UDP port 1812, you type **10.0.0.99:1812** in Authentication. However, if you specify IP addresses and copy the configuration of the primary IAS server to the secondary IAS server, you must modify the ports on the secondary IAS server to either remove the IP address of the primary IAS server or change the IP address to that of the secondary IAS server.

Configuring IAS with RADIUS Clients

You must configure the primary IAS server with the wireless APs as RADIUS clients.

▶ To add a RADIUS client corresponding to a wireless AP for Windows 2000 IAS

1. In the console tree of the Internet Authentication snap-in, right-click Clients, and then click New Client.

2. On the Add Client dialog box, type a name for the wireless AP in Friendly Name.

3. Click Next. On the Add RADIUS Client dialog box, type the IP address or DNS name of the wireless AP in Client Address (IP or DNS). If you type a DNS domain name, click Verify to resolve the name to the correct IP address for the wireless AP. Type the RADIUS shared secret for this combination of IAS server and wireless AP in Shared Secret, and then type it again in Confirm Shared Secret.

4. Click Finish.

▶ **To add a RADIUS client for Windows Server 2003 IAS**

1. Right-click RADIUS Clients and then click New RADIUS Client.

2. On the Name And Address page, type a name for the wireless AP in Friendly Name.

3. In Client Address (IP Or DNS), type the IP address or DNS host name. If you type a DNS host name, click Verify to resolve the name to the correct IP address for the wireless AP.

4. Click Next. On the Additional Information page, type the shared secret for this combination of IAS server and wireless AP in Shared Secret and then type it again in Confirm Shared Secret.

5. Click Finish.

If you are using IAS on a computer running Windows Server 2003, Enterprise Edition, and Windows Server 2003, Datacenter Edition, and you have multiple wireless APs on a single subnet (for example, in an Extended Service Set [ESS] configuration), you can simplify RADIUS client administration by specifying an address range instead of specifying the IP address or DNS name of a single RADIUS client. All the RADIUS clients in the range must be configured to use the same RADIUS server and shared secret.

The address range for RADIUS clients is expressed in the network prefix length notation $w.x.y.z/p$, in which $w.x.y.z$ is the dotted decimal notation of the address prefix and p is the prefix length (the number of high-order bits that define the network prefix). This notation is also known as Classless Inter-Domain Routing (CIDR) notation. An example is 192.168.21.0/24, which indicates all addresses from 192.168.21.1 to 192.168.21.255. To convert from subnet mask notation to network prefix length notation, p is the number of high-order bits set to one in the subnet mask. If you do not use this feature, it is a good security practice to use a different shared secret for each wireless AP.

Best Practices   Use as many RADIUS shared secrets as you can. Each shared secret should be a random sequence of upper- and lowercase letters, numbers, and punctuation that is at least 22 characters long. To ensure randomness, use a random character-generation program to determine shared secrets.

Using IPSec to Secure RADIUS Traffic

To ensure the maximum security for RADIUS messages, it is recommended that you use Internet Protocol security (IPSec) with certificate authentication; and Encapsulating Security Payload (ESP) to provide data confidentiality, data integrity, and data origin authentication for RADIUS traffic sent between the IAS servers and the wireless APs. Windows 2000 and Windows Server 2003 support IPSec. To secure RADIUS traffic sent from wireless APs, the wireless APs must also support IPSec.

Configuring a Wireless Remote Access Policy

The procedure for configuring a wireless remote access policy is different for Windows 2000 IAS and Windows Server 2003 IAS.

Configuring Windows 2000 IAS

To create a new remote access policy for wireless intranet access for Windows 2000 IAS, do the following:

1. In the console tree of the Internet Authentication snap-in, right-click Remote Access Policies and then click New Remote Access Policy.

2. On the Policy Name page, type the name of the policy in Policy Friendly Name.

3. On the Conditions page, click Add.

4. On the Select Attribute dialog box, double-click NAS-Port-Type.

5. In the Available Types list, add Wireless-IEEE 802.11 and Wireless-Other to the list of Selected Types, and then click OK.

   If SP3 or later is not installed on the IAS server, you do not see the Wireless-IEEE 802.11 and Wireless-Other NAS port types.

6. On the Select Attribute dialog box, double-click Windows-Groups.

7. On the Groups dialog box, click Add.

8. On the Select Groups dialog box, click the names of your wireless groups and click Add.

9. Click OK to close the Select Groups dialog box.

10. Click OK to close the Groups dialog box. An example of the resulting Conditions page is shown in the following figure.

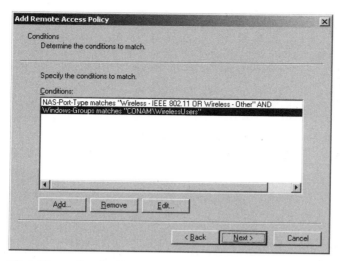

11. Click Next. On the Permissions page, click Grant Remote Access Permission.

12. Click Next. On the User Profile page, click Edit Profile.

13. On the Authentication tab, select the Extensible Authentication Protocol check box and click the Protected EAP (PEAP) EAP type.

   If Microsoft 802.1X Authentication Client is not installed on the IAS server, Protected EAP (PEAP) does not appear in the list of EAP types.

14. Click Configure. In the Protected EAP Properties dialog box, ensure that the name of the computer certificate installed on the IAS server is visible in Certificate Issued.

Note If you cannot select the certificate, the cryptographic service provider for the certificate does not support SChannel. SChannel support is required for IAS to use the certificate for EAP-TLS authentication.

   If there are multiple computer certificates installed on the IAS server, select the correct one in Certificate Issued. The Secured Password (EAP-MSCHAPv2) PEAP type is selected by default.

15. Click OK.

16. Clear the Microsoft Encrypted Authentication Version 2 (MS-CHAP v2) and Microsoft Encrypted Authentication (MS-CHAP) check boxes. The resulting configuration is shown in the following figure.

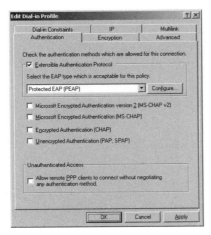

17. On the Encryption tab, clear the No Encryption check box.

18. Click OK.

19. When prompted with a Dial-In Settings message box, click No.

20. On the User Profile page, click Finish.

By default, adding a new remote access policy for Windows 2000 IAS places the new remote access policy at the bottom of the list of existing remote access policies. Therefore, to ensure that the new wireless remote access policy is used, move the new wireless remote access policy so that it is the first in the list (using the up arrow in the toolbar).

Configuring Windows Server 2003 IAS

To create a remote access policy for wireless access for Windows Server 2003 IAS, do the following:

1. From the console tree of the Internet Authentication Service snap-in, right-click Remote Access Policies and then click New Remote Access Policy.

2. On the Welcome To The New Remote Access Policy Wizard page, click Next.

3. On the Policy Configuration Method page, type the name of the policy in Policy Name.

4. Click Next. On the Access Method page, select Wireless.

5. Click Next. On the User Or Group Access page, select Group.

6. Click Add. In the Select Groups dialog box, type the names of your wireless groups in Enter The Object Names to Select.

7. Click OK. Your wireless groups are added to the list of groups on the Users Or Groups page.

8. Click Next. On the Authentication Methods page, the Protected EAP (PEAP) authentication is selected by default and configured to use PEAP-MS-CHAP v2.

9. Click Next. On the Completing The New Remote Access Policy page, click Finish.

If the wireless APs require vendor-specific attributes (VSAs), you must add the VSAs to the remote access policy.

▶ **To add a VSA to the wireless remote access policy**

1. In the console tree of the Internet Authentication Service snap-in, click Remote Access Policies.

2. Double-click the wireless remote access policy.

3. Click Edit Profile, click the Advanced tab, and then click Add. A list of pre-defined attributes displays in the Add Attribute dialog box.

4. Look at the list of available RADIUS attributes to determine whether your vendor-specific attribute is already in it. If it is, double-click it and then configure it as specified in your wireless AP documentation.

5. If the vendor-specific attribute is not in the list of available RADIUS attributes, double-click Vendor-Specific. The Multivalued Attribute Information dialog box displays.

6. Click Add. The Vendor-Specific Attribute Information dialog box displays.

7. To specify the network access server vendor for your wireless AP from the list, click Select From List and then select the wireless AP vendor for which you are configuring the VSA.

8. If the vendor is not listed, click Enter Vendor Code and then type the vendor code in the space provided.

More Info If you do not know the vendor code for your wireless AP, see RFC 1007 for a list of SMI Network Management Private Enterprise Codes.

9. Specify whether the attribute conforms to the RFC 2865 VSA specification. If you are not sure, see your wireless AP documentation. If your attribute conforms, click Yes. It Conforms and then click Configure Attribute. The Configure VSA (RFC Compliant) dialog box displays.

10. In Vendor-Assigned Attribute Number, type the number that is assigned to the attribute (the numbers available are 0 through 255). In Attribute Format, specify the format for the attribute; in Attribute Value, type the value that you assign to the attribute.

11. If the attribute does not conform, click No. It Does Not Conform and then click Configure Attribute. The Configure VSA (Non-RFC-Compliant) dialog box displays.

12. In Hexadecimal Attribute Value, type the value for the attribute.

This procedure is the same for Windows 2000 IAS and Windows Server 2003 IAS.

Best Practices   If you manage the remote access permission of user and computer accounts on a per-account basis, use remote access policies that specify a connection type. If you manage the remote access permission through the remote access policy, use remote access policies that specify a connection type and group. The recommended method is to manage remote access permission through the remote access policy.

Configuring the Secondary IAS Server

To configure the secondary IAS server on a computer, do the following, as described in the following sections:

1. Obtain and install a computer certificate.

2. Install IAS and configure the secondary IAS server computer to read the properties of user accounts.

3. Copy the configuration of the primary IAS server to the secondary IAS server.

Obtaining and Installing a Computer Certificate

If you use computer certificate autoenrollment and Windows 2000 IAS, force a refresh of computer Group Policy by typing **secedit /refreshpolicy machine_policy** from a command prompt. If you use computer certificate autoenrollment and Windows Server 2003 IAS, force a refresh of computer Group Policy by typing **gpupdate /target:computer** from a command prompt.

If you use a commercial CA or if your PKI does not support autoenrollment of computer certificates, obtain the computer certificate and use the certificate import procedure in the "Configuring the Primary IAS Server" section of this chapter to install the computer certificate on the secondary IAS server.

Installing IAS and Configuring the Secondary IAS Server Computer to Read the Properties of User Accounts

For a description of how to install IAS on the secondary IAS server computer and to configure it to read the properties of user accounts in the appropriate domains, see the "Configuring the Primary IAS Server" section of this chapter.

Copying the Configuration of the Primary IAS Server to the Secondary IAS Server

To copy the configuration of the primary IAS server to the secondary IAS server, do the following:

1. On the primary IAS server computer, type **netsh aaaa show config > *path\file*.txt** at a command prompt. This command stores the configuration settings, including registry settings, in a text file. The path can be relative, absolute, or a network path.

2. Copy the file created in step 1 to the secondary IAS server.

3. On the secondary IAS server computer, type **netsh exec *path\file*.txt** at a command prompt. This command imports all the settings configured on the primary IAS server into the secondary IAS server.

You cannot copy the IAS settings from an IAS server running Windows Server 2003 to an IAS server running Windows 2000 Server.

Best Practices If you change the IAS server configuration in any way, use the Internet Authentication Service snap-in to change the configuration of the IAS server that is designated as the primary configuration server and then use the previous procedure to synchronize those changes on the secondary IAS server.

Configuring Wireless Network (IEEE 802.11) Policies Group Policy Settings

By using the Wireless Network (IEEE 802.11) Policies Group Policy extension provided in Windows Server 2003, you can specify a list of preferred networks and their settings to automatically configure wireless LAN settings for wireless clients running Windows XP (SP1 or later) or Windows Server 2003. For each preferred network, you can specify association settings (such as the Service Set Identifier [SSID] and WEP usage) and authentication settings (such as the use of 802.1X authentication and the authentication protocol).

▶ **To configure Wireless Network (IEEE 802.11) Policies Group Policy settings for PEAP-MS-CHAP v2 authentication**

1. Open the Active Directory Users And Computers snap-in.

2. In the console tree, double-click Active Directory Users And Computers, right-click the domain or domain system container that contains your wireless computer accounts, and then click Properties.

3. On the Group Policy tab, click the appropriate Group Policy object (the default object is Default Domain Policy) and then click Edit.

4. In the console tree, open Computer Configuration; then Windows Settings, then Security Settings; then Wireless Network (IEEE 802.11) Policies.

5. On the Action menu, click Create Wireless Network Policy. The Wireless Network Policy Wizard will guide you through the creation of a wireless network policy. After it is created, double click the wireless network policy in the details pane.

6. Change settings on the General tab as needed.

7. On the Preferred Networks tab, click Add to add a preferred network.

8. On the Network Properties tab of the New Preferred Settings Properties dialog box, type the wireless network name (the SSID) and change WEP settings as needed.

9. On the IEEE 802.1X tab, change 802.1X settings as needed. In EAP Type, click Protected EAP (PEAP).

10. Click Settings. On the Protected EAP Properties dialog box, configure server validation settings as needed. For Select Authentication Method, the Secured Password (EAP-MSCHAP v2) PEAP type is selected by default.

11. If you are using PEAP fast reconnect, select the Enable Fast Reconnect check box.

12. Click OK to save changes to the PEAP properties.

13. Click OK to save changes to the new preferred network. Click OK to save changes to the Wireless Network (802.11) policy.

The next time your Windows XP (SP1 and later) and Windows Server 2003 wireless clients update computer configuration Group Policy, their wireless network configuration is automatically configured.

Configuring Wireless Access Points

Before you can configure the wireless APs in your network, you must first make sure they are deployed in a way that provides full coverage of your wireless network. For more information on deploying APs, see Chapter 7, "Wireless AP Placement."

Configure your wireless APs to support WEP encryption, WPA encryption (optionally), and 802.1X authentication. Additionally, configure the RADIUS client on your wireless APs with the following settings:

- The IP address or name of a primary RADIUS server, the shared secret, UDP ports for authentication and accounting, and failure detection settings.

- The IP address or name of a secondary RADIUS server, the shared secret, UDP ports for authentication and accounting, and failure detection settings.

To balance the load of RADIUS traffic between the primary and secondary IAS servers, configure half of the wireless APs with the primary IAS server as their primary RADIUS server and the secondary IAS server as their secondary RADIUS server. Configure the other half of the wireless APs with the secondary IAS server as their primary RADIUS server and the primary IAS server as their secondary RADIUS server.

Configuring Wireless Client Computers

To configure wireless client computers, complete the tasks described in the following sections:

- Install the root CA certificate (if needed).
- Configure 802.1X authentication for PEAP-MS-CHAP v2.

Installing the Root CA Certificate

If the root CA certificate of the issuer of the computer certificates installed on the IAS servers is already installed as a root CA certificate on your wireless clients, no other configuration is necessary. If your issuing CA is a Windows 2000 Server or Windows Server 2003 online root enterprise CA, the root CA certificate is automatically installed on each domain member computer through Group Policy.

▶ **To verify whether the correct root CA certificate is installed on your wireless clients**

1. Determine the root CA from the computer certificates installed on the IAS servers.

2. Check to see whether a certificate for the root CA is installed on your wireless clients.

▶ **To determine the root CA from the computer certificates installed on the IAS servers**

1. Click Start, click Run, type **mmc**, and then click OK.

2. On the File menu, click Add/Remove Snap-In and then click Add.

3. Under Snap-In, double-click Certificates, click Computer Account, and then click Next.

4. Do one of the following:

   - If you logged on to the IAS server, click Local Computer and then click Finish.

   - If you are configuring the IAS server from a remote computer, click Another Computer and type the name of the computer, or click Browse to select the computer name and then click Finish.

5. Click Close.

Certificates (Local Computer or *Computer Name*) appears on the list of selected snap-ins for the new console.

6. In the console tree, double-click Certificates (Local Computer or *Computer Name*), double-click Personal, and then click Certificates.

7. In the details pane, double-click the computer certificate used for wireless authentication.

8. On the Certification Path tab, note the name at the top of the certification path. This is the name of the root CA.

▶ **To see whether a certificate for the root CA is installed on your wireless client**

1. Click Start, click Run, type **mmc**, and then click OK.

2. On the File menu, click Add/Remove Snap-In, and then click Add.

3. Under Snap-In, double-click Certificates, click Computer Account, and then click Next.

4. Do one of the following:

   ● If you logged on to the wireless client computer, click Local Computer and then click Finish.

   ● If you are configuring the wireless client computer from a remote computer, click Another Computer and type the name of the computer, or click Browse to select the computer name, and then click Finish.

5. Click Close.

   Certificates (Local Computer or *Computer Name*) appears on the list of selected snap-ins for the new console.

6. In the console tree, double-click Certificates (Local Computer or *Computer Name*), double-click Trusted Root Certification Authorities, and then click Certificates. Examine the list of certificates in the details pane for a name(s) matching the root CA for the computer certificate issued to the IAS server(s).

If a certificate for the root CA is not installed, you must install the root CA certificate(s) of the issuer(s) of the computer certificate of the authenticating servers on each wireless client for the Windows operating systems that do not contain them. The easiest way to install a root CA certificate on all your wireless clients is through Group Policy, as described below.

▶ **To install a root CA certificate on a wireless client using Group Policy**

1. In the console tree of the Certificates snap-in on an IAS server, double-click Certificates (Local Computer), double-click Trusted Root Certification Authorities, and then click Certificates.

2. In the details pane, right-click the root CA certificate of the issuing CA of computer certificates on the IAS server, point to All Tasks, and then click Export.

3. On the Welcome to the Certificate Export Wizard page of the Certificate Export Wizard, click Next.

4. On the Export File Format page, click Cryptographic Message Syntax Standard–PKCS #7 Certificates (.PB7).

5. Click Next. On the File To Export page, type the filename for the exported certificate or click Browse to specify a location and filename.

6. Click Next. On the Completing The Certificate Export Wizard page, click Next and click OK.

7. Open the Active Directory Users And Computers snap-in.

8. In the console tree, double-click Active Directory Users And Computers, right-click the appropriate domain system container, and then click Properties.

9. On the Group Policy tab, click the appropriate Group Policy object (the default object is Default Domain Policy) and then click Edit.

10. In the console tree, open Computer Configuration; then Windows Settings; then Security Settings; then Public Key Policies. The Public Key Policies node is shown in the following figure.

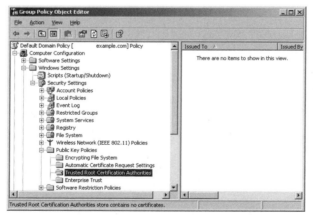

11. Right-click Trusted Root Certification Authorities and then click Import.

12. In the Certificate Import Wizard, specify the file that was saved in step 5.

13. Repeat steps 8–12 for all appropriate domain system containers.

The next time the wireless client computers update their computer configuration Group Policy, the root CA certificate of the issuing CA of computer certificates on the IAS servers is installed in their local computer certificate store.

▶ **To manually install a root CA certificate on a wireless client**

1. Export the root CA certificate to .PB7 file by following steps 1–6 of the previous procedure.

2. In the console tree of the Certificates (Local Computer) snap-in on the wireless client computer, double-click Certificates (Local Computer), double-click Trusted Root Certification Authorities, and then click Certificates.

3. Right-click Certificates, point to All Tasks, and then click Import.

4. The Welcome to the Certificate Import Wizard page of the Certificate Import Wizard displays. Click Next.

5. On the File To Import page, type the filename of the certificate file saved in step 1 in File Name, or click Browse and use the Browse dialog box to locate it.

6. Click Next. On the Certificate Store page, click Place All Certificates In The Following Store. By default, the Trusted Root Certification Authorities folder should display as the import location.

7. Click Next. On the Completing The Certificate Import Wizard page, click Finish.

Configuring 802.1X Authentication for PEAP-MS-CHAP v2

If you configured Wireless Network (IEEE 802.11) Policies Group Policy settings and specified the use of PEAP-MS-CHAP v2 authentication for your wireless network—the Protected EAP (PEAP) type with the Secured Password (EAP-MSCHAP v2) authentication method—no other configuration for wireless clients running Windows XP (SP1 or later) or Windows Server 2003 is needed.

▶ **To manually configure PEAP-MS-CHAP v2 authentication on a wireless client running Windows XP (SP1 or later) or Windows Server 2003**

1. Obtain properties of the wireless connection in the Network Connections folder. Click the Wireless Networks tab; then click the name of the wireless network in the list of preferred networks and click Properties.

2. Click the Authentication tab and then select Enable Network Access Control Using IEEE 802.1X (enabled by default) and the Protected EAP (PEAP) EAP type.

3. Click Properties. The Protected EAP Properties dialog box displays.

4. In the Protected EAP Properties dialog box, the Validate Server Certificate check box is selected by default. If you want to specify the names of the

authentication servers that must perform validation, select Connect To These Servers and type the names. The Secured Password (EAP-MSCHAP v2) PEAP authentication method is selected by default.

5. To enable PEAP fast reconnect, select the Enable Fast Reconnect check box.

▶ **To configure PEAP-MS-CHAP v2 authentication on a wireless client running Windows 2000 and Microsoft 802.1X Authentication Client**

1. Obtain properties of the wireless connection in the Dial-Up and Network Connections folder.

2. Click the Authentication tab and then select Enable Network Access Control Using IEEE 802.1X (enabled by default) and the Protected EAP (PEAP) EAP type.

3. Click Properties. The Protected EAP Properties dialog box displays.

4. In the Protected EAP Properties dialog box, the Validate Server Certificate check box is selected by default. If you want to specify the names of the authentication servers that must perform validation, select Connect To These Servers and type the names. The Secured Password (EAP-MSCHAP v2) PEAP authentication method is selected by default.

5. To enable PEAP fast reconnect, select the Enable Fast Reconnect check box.

Note By default, the PEAP-MS-CHAP v2 authentication uses your Windows logon credentials for wireless authentication. If you are connecting to a wireless network that uses PEAP-MS-CHAP v2 and you want to specify different credentials, click Configure and clear the Automatically Use My Windows Logon Name And Password check box. Windows 2000 IAS does not support fast reconnect.

Summary

This chapter described the detailed steps for configuring secure wireless access using the PEAP-MS-CHAP v2 authentication protocol. Computers running Windows 2000 or Windows Server 2003 are used in the authentication infrastructure for domain controllers and RADIUS servers (running IAS). A computer certificate is installed on each IAS server. Windows wireless clients are configured to use PEAP-MS-CHAP v2 authentication and the root CA certificate for the computer certificates that are installed on the IAS servers.

Chapter 11
Additional Intranet Wireless Deployment Configurations

Chapter 8, "Intranet Wireless Deployment Using EAP-TLS," and Chapter 10, "Intranet Wireless Deployment Using PEAP-MS-CHAP v2," describe the typical secure intranet wireless deployments using either Extensible Authentication Protocol-Transport Layer Security (EAP-TLS) or Protected EAP-Microsoft Challenge Handshake Authentication Protocol version 2 (PEAP-MS-CHAP v2) and a set of two Internet Authentication Service (IAS) servers. This chapter describes the following additional intranet wireless deployment configurations:

- Internet access for business partners

- Cross-forest authentication

- Using RADIUS proxies to scale authentications

- Using both EAP-TLS and PEAP-MS-CHAP v2 authentication

Internet Access for Business Partners

Most wireless access points (APs) in use today exhibit the following behaviors:

- When the wireless AP receives an Access-Accept message, the connection is allowed.

- When the wireless AP receives an Access-Reject message, the connection is denied.

To allow a business partner, vendor, or other non-employee (we will use the term *business partner* throughout this chapter to include all three types of users) to gain access to a separate network (such as the Internet) by using the same wireless infrastructure that allows employees access to the organization's intranet, the connection request must result in an Access-Accept message from the RADIUS server. It must also contain information that informs the wireless AP that traffic for this wireless connection must be handled differently. Typically, this information is in the form of RADIUS attributes that specify IP packet filtering or a virtual LAN (VLAN) ID.

Note A *VLAN* is the grouping of traffic by a Layer 2 or Layer 3 network device to form a logical link or subnet, regardless of the physical configuration of the nodes attached to the device. Wireless APs use VLANs to group the traffic of wireless clients for specific physical or logical links attached to the wireless AP. Each grouping of traffic is assigned a VLAN ID. For example, VLAN ID 0 is assigned to all authenticated user connections and the organization intranet; VLAN ID 1 is assigned to business partner connections and the Internet.

Because IP packet filtering is specific to the wireless AP and requires the configuration of RADIUS vendor-specific attributes (VSAs), we describe only VLAN IDs as the mechanism by which the wireless AP separates intranet traffic from Internet traffic.

To get an Access-Accept message from the RADIUS server, you must use guest access, or the business partner must have a valid account and use valid credentials, as discussed in the following sections.

Using Guest Access

Guest access occurs when wireless clients are connected without sending a user identity. The wireless client does not provide a username or credentials to the wireless AP, so the wireless AP does not include user identity (the User-Name attribute) or credential attributes in the Access-Request message. When the IAS server receives an Access-Request message that contains no user identity attributes, it verifies whether unauthenticated access is enabled for the remote access policy that matches the connection attempt. If a user identity attribute is not included, the IAS server uses the Guest account to obtain user account dial-in properties and group membership to evaluate authorization.

As previously mentioned, restricted or alternate network access for guest access clients is typically supported by wireless APs through the use of VLANs. For example, to the wireless AP, VLAN 0 is for the organization intranet and VLAN 1 is for the Internet. To specify a VLAN identifier for unauthenticated access, you must configure the Tunnel-Type and Tunnel-Pvt-Group-ID attributes on the advanced properties of the appropriate remote access policy.

Guest access for wireless connections uses EAP-TLS to perform a one-way authentication of the IAS server certificate. The IAS server sends its computer certificate for validation by the wireless client. The wireless client does not send a username or a certificate.

Note PEAP-MS-CHAP v2 does not allow one-way authentication or guest access.

The following processes enable guest access for wireless clients, as described in the next sections:

- Configuring a wireless guests group that contains the guest account.
- Configuring your wireless APs for the VLAN attached to the Internet.
- Configuring a wireless remote access policy for guest access.
- Configuring Windows wireless clients for unauthenticated access.

Configuring a Wireless Guests Group that Contains the Guest Account

To configure a wireless guests group, do the following:

1. From the console tree of the Active Directory Users And Computers snap-in, open the domain container and then open the Users folder.

2. In the details pane, double-click the Guest account.

3. On the Account tab, clear the Account Is Disabled check box in Account Options.

4. On the Dial-In tab, click either Allow Access or Control Access Through Remote Access Policy for the remote access permission. Click OK.

5. In the console tree, right-click Users, point to New, and then click Group.

6. In the New Object – Group dialog box, type the name of the wireless guests group in Group name (for example: **WirelessGuests**), and then click OK.

7. In the details pane, double-click the newly created group.

8. Click the Members tab and then click Add.

9. In the Select Users, Contacts, Users, Or Groups dialog box, type **guest** in Enter The Object Names To Select.

10. Click OK. The Guest user account is added to the wireless guests group.

11. Click OK to save changes to the wireless guests group.

Tip   If you want to enable guest access and use another account that serves the same purpose for guest access, create a user account and set the remote access permission to either Allow Access or Control Access Through Remote Access Policy and then set the registry value HKEY_LOCAL_MACHINE\System\CurrentControlSet\Services\RemoteAccess\Policy\Default User Identity on each IAS server to the name of the account. Changes to this registry setting do not take effect until the Internet Authentication Service restarts. Add this account to the wireless guests group.

Configuring Wireless APs for the VLAN Attached to the Internet

Configure your switching infrastructure to create a VLAN that is attached to the Internet. On the wireless AP, configure the VLAN ID of the VLAN that is attached to the Internet. For more information, see your switch and wireless AP documentation. VLANs are not supported by all wireless APs.

Configuring a Wireless Remote Access Policy for Guest Access

To configure a wireless remote access policy for unauthenticated Internet access for business partners, create a new custom remote access policy with the following settings:

- **Policy name.**   Unauthenticated wireless access to Internet (example).

- **Conditions.**   NAS-Port-Type=Wireless-Other or Wireless-IEEE 802.11, Windows-Groups=WirelessGuests (example).

- **Permissions.**   Select Grant Remote Access Permission.

- **Profile, Authentication tab.**   For Windows 2000 IAS, select Extensible Authentication Protocol and the Smart Card Or Other Certificate EAP Type. If you have multiple computer certificates installed on the IAS server, click Configure and then select the appropriate computer certificate. Select the Allow Remote PPP Clients To Connect Without Negotiating Any Authentication Method check box. Clear all other check boxes.

  For Windows Server 2003 IAS, click EAP Methods and add the Smart Card Or Other Certificate EAP Type. If you have multiple computer certificates installed on the IAS server, click Edit and then select the correct computer certificate. Select the Allow Clients to Connect Without Negotiating An Authentication Method check box. Clear all other check boxes.

- **Profile, Encryption tab.**   Clear the No Encryption check box. Select all other check boxes.

- **Profile, Advanced tab (if the wireless AP supports VLANs).**   Add the Tunnel-Type attribute with the value of "Virtual LANs (VLAN)".

  Add the Tunnel-Pvt-Group-ID attribute with the value of the VLAN ID of the VLAN that is connected to the Internet.

If the wireless APs require additional VSAs, you must add them to the remote access policy. For more information, see the "Configuring a Wireless Remote Access Policy" section of Chapter 8 or Chapter 10.

Configuring Windows Wireless Clients for Unauthenticated Access

The procedure for configuring a Windows wireless client depends on whether the Windows wireless client supports the Wireless Zero Configuration (WZC) service (Windows XP, Windows Server 2003) or not (Windows 2000).

Note   The Wireless Zero Configuration service is known as the Wireless Configuration service in Windows Server 2003.

For Windows wireless clients that support the WZC service, unauthenticated access is configured as follows:

1. When the business partner starts the computer, the WZC service scans for preferred networks. Assuming that the user does not already have your wireless network in the list of preferred networks, a prompt displays to select a wireless network from the notification area of the desktop.

2. When the business partner selects your wireless network, the initial authentication fails because the user does not have a valid set of certificates to perform EAP-TLS two-way authentication.

3. When the business partner clicks the notification of authentication failure, the settings of your wireless network display. The user must now configure the 802.1X settings to allow for unauthenticated access:

   - For computers running Windows XP, the business partner must select the Authenticate As Guest When User Or Computer Information Is Unavailable check box on the Authentication tab of the properties of the wireless network adapter in Network Connections.

   - For computers running Windows XP (SP1 and later) and Windows Server 2003, the business partner user must select the Authenticate As Guest When User Or Computer Information Is Unavailable check box on the Authentication tab of the properties of your wireless network.

For Windows wireless clients running Windows 2000, use the following steps to configure unauthenticated access:

1. When the computer starts, the business partner must use the wireless configuration software supplied with the wireless adapter to configure an association to your wireless network. Because the default EAP type for 802.1X authentication is EAP-TLS, authentication fails because no valid certificate is installed.

2. The business partner user must obtain the properties of the wireless network adapter in Network And Dial-Up Connections.

3. From the Authentication tab, the business partner user must select the Authenticate As Guest When User Or Computer Information Is Unavailable check box.

When the changes to the wireless network adapter or wireless network are saved, Windows attempts a new authentication using unauthenticated access and can access the Internet.

Note The preceding procedure assumes that the business partner computer has a root certification authority (CA) certificate installed that can validate the certificate of the authenticating IAS server. If not, you must provide a copy of the root CA certificate to the business partner to be installed in the Trusted Root Certification Authorities Local Computer store. Otherwise, unauthenticated access does not work.

The advantage of guest access is that there is no administrative overhead for managing user and computer accounts. The disadvantage is that anyone within range of your wireless network can use your wireless network to access the Internet, unless they are required to install a root CA certificate.

Using Validated Access

For validated access for business partners, you must create computer and user accounts and issue certificates—user and computer certificates for EAP-TLS authentication and root CA certificates for PEAP-MS-CHAP v2 authentication (if needed)—to each business partner. Next, create a global group with these accounts as members so that you can manage wireless access using a group-based remote access policy. For example, create a WirelessInternetUsers universal group that contains global groups of business partner user and computer accounts.

To configure a wireless remote access policy for validated Internet access for business partners, create a new custom remote access policy for wireless Internet access with the following settings:

- **Policy name.** Wireless access to Internet (example).

- **Conditions.** NAS-Port-Type=Wireless-Other or Wireless-IEEE 802.11, Windows-Groups=WirelessInternetUsers (example).

- **Permissions.** Select Grant Remote Access Permission.

- **Profile, Authentication tab.** Configure the EAP type for EAP-TLS (as described in Chapter 8) or PEAP-MS-CHAP v2 (as described in Chapter 10), as needed. Clear all other check boxes.

- **Profile, Encryption tab.** Clear the No Encryption check box. Select all other check boxes.

- **Profile, Advanced tab (if the wireless AP supports VLANs).** Add the Tunnel-Type attribute with the value of "Virtual LANs (VLAN)".

  Add the Tunnel-Pvt-Group-ID attribute with the value of the VLAN ID of the VLAN that is connected to the Internet.

If the wireless APs require additional VSAs, you must add them to the appropriate remote access policies. For more information, see the "Configuring a Wireless Remote Access Policy" section of Chapter 8 or Chapter 10.

The advantage of using validated access is that only specific business partners can access the Internet using your wireless network. The disadvantage is that there is more administrative overhead in managing user and computer accounts and issuing certificates.

Cross-Forest Authentication

Because IAS uses Active Directory to validate credentials and obtain user and computer account properties, a RADIUS proxy must be placed between the wireless APs and the IAS server computers when the user and computer accounts for wireless client computers and users exist in the following authentication databases:

- Two different Active Directory forests that do not trust each other.

- Two different domains that do not trust each other.

- Two different domains that have a one-way trust.

If you are using EAP-TLS authentication, you must use a RADIUS proxy, even if the forests have a two-way, transitive trust relationship.

Note   You do not need to use a RADIUS proxy if you use PEAP-MS-CHAP v2 and Windows NT 4.0-style usernames (for example: microsoft\user1).

When an access client sends user credentials, a *username* is often included, which includes two elements:

- Identification of the user account name

- Identification of the user account location

For example, for the username user1@example.com, user1 is the user account name, and example.com is the location of the user account. The identification of the location of the user account is known as a *realm*, which has different forms:

- **The realm name can be a prefix.**   For example\user1, example is the name of a Windows NT 4.0 domain.

- **The realm name can be a suffix.**   For user1@example.com, example.com is either a DNS domain name or the name of an Active Directory-based domain.

The username is passed from the wireless client to the wireless AP during the authentication phase of the connection attempt. This username becomes the User-Name RADIUS attribute in the Access-Request message sent by the wireless AP to its configured RADIUS server, which is a RADIUS proxy in this configuration. When the RADIUS proxy receives the Access-Request message, configured policies on the RADIUS proxy determine the RADIUS server to which the Access-Request message is forwarded based on the realm name.

Figure 11-1 shows IAS RADIUS proxies forwarding RADIUS messages between wireless APs and multiple IAS servers in two different Active Directory forests.

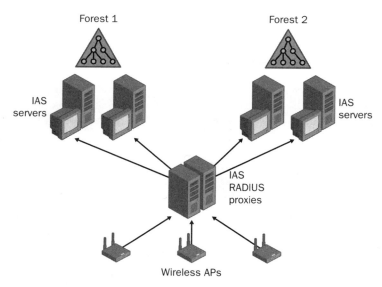

Figure 11-1. *Using IAS RADIUS proxies for cross-forest authentication.*

The following configuration is for an organization that uses the following:

- **Active Directory domains.** Active Directory domains contain the user accounts, passwords, and dial-in properties that each IAS server requires to authenticate user credentials and evaluate authorization.

- **At least two IAS servers in each forest.** At least two IAS servers (one primary and one secondary) can provide fault tolerance for RADIUS-based authentication, authorization, and accounting in each forest. If only one RADIUS server is configured and it becomes unavailable, wireless clients for that forest cannot be authenticated. By using at least two IAS servers and configuring the IAS RADIUS proxies for both the primary and secondary IAS servers, the IAS RADIUS proxies can detect when the primary IAS server is unavailable and then automatically fail over to the secondary IAS server.

- **A wireless remote access policy.** A wireless remote access policy is configured to authorize wireless connections based on group membership.

- **At least two IAS RADIUS proxies.** At least two IAS RADIUS proxies can provide fault tolerance for RADIUS requests that are sent from the wireless APs.

▶ To deploy the configuration just described

1. Configure the certificate infrastructure.

2. Configure the Active Directory forests for accounts and groups.

3. Configure the primary IAS server on a computer in the first forest.

4. Configure the secondary IAS server on another computer in the first forest.

5. Configure the primary IAS server on a computer in the second forest.

6. Configure the secondary IAS server on another computer in the second forest.

7. Configure the primary IAS RADIUS proxy.

8. Configure the secondary IAS RADIUS proxy.

9. Configure RADIUS authentication and accounting on wireless APs.

10. Configure wireless client computers.

Windows 2000 IAS does not support RADIUS proxy functionality. You must use Windows Server 2003 IAS for the RADIUS proxies needed for cross-forest authentication.

This configuration requires creating at least five RADIUS shared secrets:

- Because typical wireless APs allow the configuration of only a single RADIUS shared secret for both their primary and secondary RADIUS servers, one shared secret is needed for each wireless AP and the primary and secondary IAS RADIUS proxies.

- Because we copy the configuration of the primary IAS proxy to the secondary IAS RADIUS proxy, the following additional RADIUS shared secrets are needed:

    - Between the primary and secondary IAS RADIUS proxies and the primary IAS server in the first forest.

    - Between the primary and secondary IAS RADIUS proxies and the secondary IAS server in the first forest.

    - Between the primary and secondary IAS RADIUS proxies and the primary IAS server in the second forest.

    - Between the primary and secondary IAS RADIUS proxies and the secondary IAS server in the second forest.

Configuring the Certificate Infrastructure

For EAP-TLS authentication, follow the instructions in the "Configuring the Certificate Infrastructure" section of Chapter 8.

Configuring the Active Directory Forests for Accounts and Groups

Follow the instructions in the "Configuring Active Directory for Accounts and Groups" section of either Chapter 8 or Chapter 10 for each forest. Configuring the accounts and groups is the same when using either EAP-TLS or PEAP-MS-CHAP v2.

Configuring the Primary IAS Server on a Computer in the First Forest

To configure the primary IAS server on a computer in the first forest for EAP-TLS authentication, perform the steps described in the following sections of Chapter 8 on a computer in the first forest:

- "Obtaining and Installing a Computer Certificate"

- "Installing IAS and Configuring IAS Server Properties"

- "Configuring Windows 2000 IAS" or "Configuring Windows Server 2003 IAS" sections of "Configuring a Wireless Remote Access Policy"

To configure the primary IAS server on a computer in the first forest for PEAP-MS-CHAP v2 authentication, perform the steps described in the following sections of Chapter 10 on a computer in the first forest:

- "Obtaining and Installing a Computer Certificate"

- "Installing IAS and Configuring IAS Server Properties"

- "Configuring Windows 2000 IAS" or "Configuring Windows Server 2003 IAS" sections of "Configuring a Wireless Remote Access Policy"

Next, configure the primary IAS server in the first forest with the primary and secondary IAS RADIUS proxies as RADIUS clients. To do this, perform the steps in the "Configuring IAS with RADIUS Clients" section of Chapter 8 or Chapter 10 (instead of the wireless APs, add the primary and secondary IAS RADIUS proxies as RADIUS clients).

Configuring the Secondary IAS Server on Another Computer in the First Forest

To configure the secondary IAS server on another computer in the first forest, follow the instructions in the "Configuring the Secondary IAS Server" section of Chapter 8 (for EAP-TLS authentication) or Chapter 10 (for PEAP-MS-CHAP v2 authentication).

Configuring the Primary IAS Server on a Computer in the Second Forest

To configure the primary IAS server on a computer in the second forest for EAP-TLS authentication, perform the steps in the following sections of Chapter 8 on a computer in the second forest:

- "Obtaining and Installing a Computer Certificate"

- "Installing IAS and Configuring IAS Server Properties"

- "Configuring Windows 2000 IAS" or "Configuring Windows Server 2003 IAS" sections of "Configuring a Wireless Remote Access Policy"

To configure the primary IAS server on a computer in the second forest for PEAP-MS-CHAP v2 authentication, perform the steps in the following sections of Chapter 10 on a computer in the second forest:

- "Obtaining and Installing a Computer Certificate"

- "Installing IAS and Configuring IAS Server Properties"

- "Configuring Windows 2000 IAS" or "Configuring Windows Server 2003 IAS" sections of "Configuring a Wireless Remote Access Policy"

Next, configure the primary IAS server in the second forest with the primary and secondary IAS RADIUS proxies as RADIUS clients. To do this, follow the instructions in the "Configuring IAS with RADIUS Clients" section of Chapter 8 or Chapter 10 (instead of the wireless APs, add the primary and secondary IAS RADIUS proxies as RADIUS clients).

Configuring the Secondary IAS Server on Another Computer in the Second Forest

To configure the secondary IAS server on another computer in the second forest, perform the steps in the "Configuring the Secondary IAS Server" section of Chapter 8 (for EAP-TLS authentication) or Chapter 10 (for PEAP-MS-CHAP v2 authentication).

Configuring the Primary IAS RADIUS Proxy

To configure the primary IAS RADIUS proxy, do the following:

1. On a computer running Windows Server 2003, install IAS as an optional networking component. The computer on which IAS is installed is not required to be dedicated to forwarding RADIUS messages. For example, you can install IAS on a file server. Because the primary IAS RADIUS proxy computer is not performing authentication or authorization of wireless connections, it can be a member of a domain of either forest.

2. If needed, configure additional UDP ports for RADIUS messages that are sent by the wireless APs. By default, IAS uses UDP ports 1812 and 1645 for authentication and UDP ports 1813 and 1646 for accounting.

3. Add the wireless APs as RADIUS clients of the IAS RADIUS proxy using the instructions described in the "Configuring IAS with RADIUS Clients" section of Chapter 8 or Chapter 10.

4. In the console tree of the Internet Authentication Service snap-in, open Connection Request Processing.

5. Right-click Remote RADIUS Server Groups and then click New Remote RADIUS Server Group.

6. On the Welcome To The New Remote RADIUS Server Group Wizard page, click Next.

7. On the Group Configuration page, click Custom and type the group name for the IAS servers in the first forest in Group Name (for example: **RADIUS Servers in Forest1**). Click Next.

8. On the Add Servers page, click Add.

9. On the Address tab, type the IP address or name of the primary IAS server in the first forest. If you specify a name, click Verify to resolve the name to an IP address.

10. On the Authentication/Accounting tab, type the shared secret between the primary and secondary IAS RADIUS proxies and the primary IAS server in the first forest.

11. Click OK to add the server to the list of servers in the group.

12. On the Add Servers page, click Add.

13. On the Address tab, type the IP address or name of the secondary IAS server in the first forest.

14. On the Authentication/Accounting tab, type the shared secret between the primary and secondary IAS RADIUS proxies and the secondary IAS server in the first forest.

15. Click OK to add the server to the list of servers in the group.

16. Click Next.

17. On the Completing The New Remote RADIUS Server Group page, click Finish. The New Connection Request Policy Wizard automatically runs.

18. On the Welcome To The New Connection Request Policy Wizard page, click Next.

19. On the Policy Configuration Method page, click A Typical Policy For A Common Scenario and then type the name for the connection request policy in Policy Name (for example: **Forward Requests to RADIUS Servers in Forest1**). Click Next.

20. On the Request Authentication Page, click Forward Connection Requests To A Remote RADIUS Server For Authentication. Click Next.

21. On the Realm Name page, type the realm name for all names in the first forest (for example: **forest1.example.com**). Select the newly created remote RADIUS server group for the IAS servers in the first forest in Server Group. Click Next.

22. On the Completing The New Connection Request Policy Wizard page, click Finish.

23. Right-click Remote RADIUS Server Groups and then click New Remote RADIUS Server Group.

24. On the Welcome To The New Remote RADIUS Server Group Wizard page, click Next.

25. On the Group Configuration page, click Custom and type the group name for the IAS servers in the second forest in Group Name (for example: **RADIUS Servers in Forest2**). Click Next.

26. On the Add Servers page, click Add.

27. On the Address tab, type the IP address or name of the primary IAS server in the second forest. If you specify a name, click Verify to resolve the name to an IP address.

28. On the Authentication/Accounting tab, type the shared secret between the primary and secondary IAS RADIUS proxies and the primary IAS server in the second forest.

29. Click OK to add the server to the list of servers in the group.

30. On the Add Servers page, click Add.

31. On the Address tab, type the IP address or name of the secondary IAS server in the second forest.

32. On the Authentication/Accounting tab, type the shared secret between the primary and secondary IAS RADIUS proxies and the secondary IAS server in the second forest.

33. Click OK to add the server to the list of servers in the group.

34. Click Next.

35. On the Completing The New Remote RADIUS Server Group page, click Finish.

36. On the Welcome To The New Connection Request Policy Wizard page, click Next.

37. On the Policy Configuration Method page, click A Typical Policy For A Common Scenario and then type the name for the Connection Request Policy in Policy Name (for example: **Forward Requests to RADIUS Servers in Forest2**). Click Next.

38. On the Request Authentication Page, click Forward Connection Requests To A Remote RADIUS Server For Authentication. Click Next.

39. On the Realm Name page, type the realm name for all names in the second forest (for example: **forest2.example.com**). Select the newly created remote RADIUS server group for the IAS servers in the second forest in Server Group. Click Next.

40. On the Completing The New Connection Request Policy Wizard page, click Finish.

Configuring the Secondary IAS RADIUS Proxy

To configure the secondary IAS RADIUS proxy on another computer, do the following:

1. On a computer running Windows Server 2003, install IAS as an optional networking component.

   The computer on which IAS is installed is not required to be dedicated to forwarding RADIUS messages. For example, you can install IAS on a file server. Like the primary IAS RADIUS proxy, the secondary IAS RADIUS proxy computer can be a member of a domain of either forest because it is not performing authentication or authorization of wireless connections.

2. On the primary IAS RADIUS proxy computer, type **netsh aaaa show config > *path\file*.txt** at the command prompt.

   This command stores the configuration settings, including registry settings, in a text file. The path can be relative, absolute, or a network path.

3. Copy the file created in step 2 to the secondary IAS RADIUS proxy.

4. On the secondary IAS RADIUS proxy computer, type **netsh exec *path\file*.txt** at a command prompt.

   This command imports all the settings configured on the primary IAS RADIUS proxy into the secondary IAS RADIUS proxy.

The default load-balancing settings of the RADIUS servers in the two remote RADIUS server groups allow each IAS RADIUS proxy to distribute the authentication request load equally to the two IAS servers in each forest.

Configuring RADIUS Authentication on the Wireless APs

Deploy your wireless APs to provide coverage for all the areas that require access to your wireless network. For more information, see Chapter 7, "Wireless AP Placement."

Configure your wireless APs to support Wired Equivalent Policy (WEP) or Wi-Fi Protected Access (WPA) encryption and 802.1X authentication. Additionally, configure the RADIUS client on your wireless APs with the following settings:

- The IP address or name of a primary RADIUS server, the shared secret, UDP ports for authentication and accounting, and failure-detection settings.

- The IP address or name of a secondary RADIUS server, the shared secret, UDP ports for authentication and accounting, and failure-detection settings.

To balance the load of RADIUS traffic between the primary and secondary IAS RADIUS proxies, configure half of the wireless APs with the primary IAS RADIUS proxy as their primary RADIUS server and the secondary IAS RADIUS proxy as their secondary RADIUS server. Configure the other half of the wireless APs with the secondary IAS RADIUS proxy as their primary RADIUS server and the primary IAS RADIUS proxy as their secondary RADIUS server.

Configuring Wireless Client Computers

To configure the wireless client computer, follow the instructions in the "Configuring Wireless Client Computers" section of Chapter 8 (for EAP-TLS) or Chapter 10 (for PEAP-MS-CHAP v2).

Using RADIUS Proxies to Scale Authentications

When performing authentication for a large number of wireless clients using EAP-TLS and certificates, the volume of authentication traffic needed to keep wireless clients connected can be substantial. In a large deployment, it is best to attempt to spread the load of authentication traffic among multiple IAS server computers. Because you cannot rely on the wireless APs to consistently or adequately spread their authentication traffic among multiple RADIUS servers, intermediate IAS RADIUS proxies can provide this function.

Without RADIUS proxies, each wireless AP sends its RADIUS requests to one or multiple RADIUS servers and detects unavailable RADIUS servers. The wireless AP might or might not be balancing the load of RADIUS traffic across multiple RADIUS servers. By using IAS RADIUS proxies, consistent load balancing is used to spread the load of authentication, authorization, and accounting traffic across all the IAS servers in the organization. Additionally, there is a consistent scheme for failure detection and RADIUS server *failover* (the detection of an unavailable RADIUS server and avoidance of its use for future authentication requests) and *failback* (the detection that a previously unavailable RADIUS server is available).

The following configuration is for an organization that uses the following:

- **Active Directory domains.** Active Directory domains contain the user accounts, passwords, and dial-in properties that each IAS server requires to authenticate user credentials and evaluate authorization.

- **Multiple IAS servers.** To balance the load of RADIUS authentication, authorization, and accounting traffic, there are multiple IAS servers.

- **A wireless remote access policy.** A wireless remote access policy is configured to authorize wireless connections based on group membership.

- **Two IAS RADIUS proxies.** Two IAS RADIUS proxies provide fault tolerance for RADIUS requests that are sent from the wireless APs.

Figure 11-2 shows the use of IAS RADIUS proxies to balance the load of RADIUS traffic from wireless APs across multiple IAS servers.

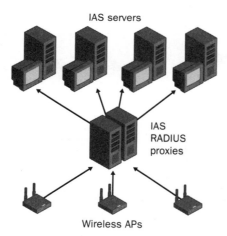

IAS servers

IAS RADIUS proxies

Wireless APs

Figure 11-2. *Using IAS RADIUS proxies to load balance RADIUS traffic.*

▶ **To deploy the configuration just described**

1. Configure the certificate infrastructure.

2. Configure the Active Directory for accounts and groups.

3. Configure IAS as a RADIUS server on multiple computers.

4. Configure the primary IAS RADIUS proxy.

5. Configure the secondary IAS RADIUS proxy.

6. Configure RADIUS authentication and accounting on wireless APs.

7. Configure wireless client computers.

This configuration requires the creation of the following RADIUS shared secrets:

- A different shared secret is needed between each wireless AP and the set of primary and secondary IAS RADIUS proxies. Because typical wireless APs allow the configuration of only a single RADIUS shared secret for both their primary and secondary RADIUS servers, and because we copy the configuration of the primary IAS proxy to the secondary IAS RADIUS proxy, we cannot use different shared secrets between a wireless AP and the primary and secondary IAS RADIUS proxies.

- A different shared secret is needed between each IAS server and the set of primary and secondary IAS RADIUS proxies. Because we copy the configuration of the primary IAS proxy to the secondary IAS RADIUS proxy, we cannot use different shared secrets between the primary and secondary IAS RADIUS proxies and each IAS RADIUS server.

Configuring the Certificate Infrastructure

For EAP-TLS authentication, follow the instructions in the "Configuring the Certificate Infrastructure" section of Chapter 8.

Configuring Active Directory for Accounts and Groups

Follow the steps in the "Configuring Active Directory for Accounts and Groups" section of Chapter 8 or Chapter 10.

Configuring IAS as a RADIUS Server on Multiple Computers

To configure IAS on each IAS server computer for EAP-TLS authentication, perform the steps in the following sections of Chapter 8 on each IAS server computer:

- "Obtaining and Installing a Computer Certificate"

- "Installing IAS and Configuring IAS Server Properties"

- "Configuring Windows 2000 IAS" or "Configuring Windows Server 2003 IAS" sections of "Configuring a Wireless Remote Access Policy"

To configure IAS on each IAS server computer for PEAP-MS-CHAP v2 authentication, perform the steps in the following sections of Chapter 10 on each IAS server computer:

- "Obtaining and Installing a Computer Certificate"

- "Installing IAS and Configuring IAS Server Properties"

- "Configuring Windows 2000 IAS" or "Configuring Windows Server 2003 IAS" sections of "Configuring a Wireless Remote Access Policy"

Next, configure each IAS server computer with the primary and secondary IAS RADIUS proxies as RADIUS clients. To do this, perform the steps in the "Configuring IAS with RADIUS Clients" section of Chapter 8 or Chapter 10 (instead of the wireless APs, add the primary and secondary IAS RADIUS proxies as RADIUS clients).

Note Each IAS server is configured separately rather than configuring an initial IAS server and copying its configuration to other IAS server computers. This process is done so that different RADIUS shared secrets can be used between the IAS RADIUS proxies and the IAS server computers.

Configuring the Primary IAS RADIUS Proxy

To configure the primary IAS RADIUS proxy, do the following:

1. On a computer running Windows Server 2003, install IAS as an optional networking component.

   The computer on which IAS is installed is not required to be dedicated to forwarding RADIUS messages. For example, you can install IAS on a file server.

2. If needed, configure additional UDP ports for RADIUS messages that are sent by the wireless APs.

   By default, IAS uses UDP ports 1812 and 1645 for authentication and UDP ports 1813 and 1646 for accounting.

3. Add the wireless APs as RADIUS clients of the IAS RADIUS proxy using the steps described in the "Configuring IAS with RADIUS Clients" section of Chapter 8 or Chapter 10.

4. In the console tree of the Internet Authentication Service snap-in, open Connection Request Processing.

5. Right-click Remote RADIUS Server Groups, and then click New Remote RADIUS Server Group.

6. On the Welcome To The New Remote RADIUS Server Group Wizard page, click Next.

7. On the Group Configuration page, click Custom and type the group name for the RADIUS servers in Group Name (for example: **RADIUS Servers in example.com Domain**). Click Next.

8. On the Add Servers page, click Add.

9. On the Address tab, type the IP address or name of an IAS server. If you specify a name, click Verify to resolve the name to an IP address.

10. On the Authentication/Accounting tab, type the shared secret between the primary and secondary IAS RADIUS proxies and the IAS server.

11. Click OK to add the server to the list of servers in the group.

12. Repeat steps 8 through 11 for each IAS server in the domain.

13. Click Next.

14. On the Completing The New Remote RADIUS Server Group page, click Finish.

15. On the Welcome To The New Connection Request Policy Wizard page, click Next.

16. On the Policy Configuration Method page, click A Typical Policy For A Common Scenario and then type the name for the Connection Request Policy in Policy Name (for example: **Forward Requests to RADIUS Servers in the example.com Domain**). Click Next.

17. On the Request Authentication Page, click Forward Connection Requests To A Remote RADIUS Server For Authentication. Click Next.

18. On the Realm Name page, type the realm name for all names in the domain or forest (for example: **example.com**) and clear the Before Authentication, Remove Realm Name From The User Name check box. Select the newly created remote RADIUS server group for all IAS servers in the domain in Server Group. Click Next.

19. On the Completing The New Connection Request Policy Wizard page, click Finish.

Configuring the Secondary IAS RADIUS Proxy

To configure the secondary IAS RADIUS proxy on another computer, do the following:

1. On a computer running Windows Server 2003, install IAS as an optional networking component. The computer on which IAS is installed is not required to be dedicated to forwarding RADIUS messages. For example, you can install IAS on a file server.

2. On the primary IAS RADIUS proxy computer, type **netsh aaaa show config > *path\file*.txt** at a command prompt.

   This command stores the configuration settings, including registry settings, in a text file. The path can be relative, absolute, or a network path.

3. Copy the file created in step 2 to the secondary IAS RADIUS proxy computer.

4. On the secondary IAS RADIUS proxy computer, type **netsh exec *path\file*.txt** at a command prompt. This command imports all the settings configured on the primary IAS RADIUS proxy into the secondary IAS RADIUS proxy.

The default load-balancing settings of the RADIUS servers in the remote RADIUS server group cause each IAS RADIUS proxy to distribute the authentication request load equally to all the IAS servers in the domain.

Configuring RADIUS Authentication on the Wireless APs

Deploy your wireless APs to provide coverage for all the areas that require access to your wireless network. (For more information, see Chapter 7.)

Configure your wireless APs to support WEP or WPA encryption and 802.1X authentication. Additionally, configure the RADIUS client on your wireless APs with the following settings:

- The IP address or name of a primary RADIUS server, the shared secret, UDP ports for authentication and accounting, and failure-detection settings.

- The IP address or name of a secondary RADIUS server, the shared secret, UDP ports for authentication and accounting, and failure-detection settings.

To balance the load of RADIUS traffic between the primary and secondary IAS RADIUS proxies, configure half of the wireless APs with the primary IAS RADIUS proxy as their primary RADIUS server and the secondary IAS RADIUS proxy as their secondary RADIUS server. Configure the other half of the wireless APs with the secondary IAS RADIUS proxy as their primary RADIUS server and the primary IAS RADIUS proxy as their secondary RADIUS server.

Configuring Wireless Client Computers

To configure the wireless client computer, follow the instructions in the "Configuring Wireless Client Computers" section of Chapter 8 (for EAP-TLS) or Chapter 10 (for PEAP-MS-CHAP v2).

Using EAP-TLS and PEAP-MS-CHAP v2

Although a typical secure wireless configuration uses either EAP-TLS or PEAP-MS-CHAP v2, there are situations that require the simultaneous use of both authentication methods. For example, if you use PEAP-MS-CHAP v2 exclusively and then deploy a certificate infrastructure for EAP-TLS authentication, you need to support both types as you transition from the password-based PEAP-MS-CHAP v2 authentication method to the certificate-based EAP-TLS authentication method.

The way in which you configure the IAS servers to simultaneously support both EAP-TLS and PEAP-MS-CHAP v2 authentication for wireless connections depends on whether you are using Windows 2000 IAS or Windows Server 2003 IAS.

Configuring Windows 2000 IAS for Both EAP-TLS and PEAP-MS-CHAP v2 Authentication

Because Windows 2000 IAS remote access policies do not allow for the configuration of multiple EAP types, it is necessary to create two different remote access policies: one that requires EAP-TLS authentication and one that requires PEAP-MS-CHAP v2 authentication. To differentiate the two types of wireless access, you must create two different groups: one for the user and computer accounts that are using EAP-TLS authentication and one for the user and computer accounts that are using PEAP-MS-CHAP v2 authentication.

To configure a wireless remote access policy for users using EAP-TLS authentication, create a remote access policy with the following settings:

- **Policy name.** EAP-TLS authenticated wireless access (example).
- **Conditions.** NAS-Port-Type=Wireless-Other or Wireless-IEEE 802.11, Windows-Groups=WirelessEAP-TLS (example).
- **Permissions.** Select Grant Remote Access Permission.
- **Profile, Authentication tab.** Select the Extensible Authentication Protocol check box and the Smart Card Or Other Certificate EAP Type. Clear all other check boxes.
- **Profile, Encryption tab.** Clear the No Encryption check box. Select all other check boxes.

To configure a wireless remote access policy for users using PEAP-MS-CHAP v2 authentication, create a remote access policy with the following settings:

- **Policy name.** PEAP-MS-CHAP v2 authenticated wireless access (example).
- **Conditions.** NAS-Port-Type=Wireless-Other or Wireless-IEEE 802.11, Windows-Groups=WirelessPEAP-MS-CHAPv2 (example).
- **Permissions.** Select Grant Remote Access Permission.
- **Profile, Authentication tab.** Select the Extensible Authentication Protocol check box and the Protected EAP (PEAP) EAP Type. Clear all other check boxes.
- **Profile, Encryption tab.** Clear the No Encryption check box. Select all other check boxes.

Windows 2000 and Per-Policy EAP Types

Windows 2000 IAS does not allow for per-policy configuration of a specific EAP type. For example, if you use EAP-TLS for both virtual private network (VPN) and wireless authentication, you must configure the properties of the EAP-TLS type so that authentication will work for both VPN and wireless connections. The computer certificate selected for EAP-TLS authentication must be usable for both types of connections. For example, if EAP-TLS authentication for VPN connections must use one computer certificate and EAP-TLS authentication for wireless connections must use a different computer certificate, a single Windows 2000 IAS server cannot be used. You must use different sets of Windows 2000 IAS RADIUS servers for the different types of connection, or you must use Windows Server 2003 IAS, which allows per-policy configuration of EAP type properties.

Configuring Windows Server 2003 IAS for Both EAP-TLS and PEAP-MS-CHAP v2 Authentication

Windows Server 2003 IAS allows the configuration of multiple EAP types in a single remote access policy. Therefore, you configure the initial wireless remote access policy according to the instructions in Chapter 8 or Chapter 10. You can then configure the resulting remote access policy to support both EAP types—by using EAP-TLS first and then using PEAP-MS-CHAP v2.

For example, if you configure your IAS servers with the remote access policy described in Chapter 8, the remote access policy for EAP-TLS must be modified by using the following steps:

1. From the console tree of the Internet Authentication Service snap-in, open Remote Access Policies.

2. In the details pane, double-click the remote access policy for wireless connections.

3. Click Edit Profile.

4. From the Authentication tab, click EAP Methods.

5. In the Select EAP Providers dialog box, the EAP Types list should contain the Smart Card Or Other Certificate EAP Type.

6. Click Add, select Protected EAP (PEAP) in Authentication Methods and click OK. The Protected EAP (PEAP) EAP Type is added to the list of EAP Types after the Smart Card Or Other Certificate Type. The following figure shows the resulting configuration.

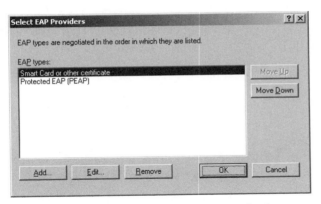

7. Click OK to save the changes to EAP methods.

8. Click OK to save the changes to the remote access policy profile.

9. Click OK to save changes to the remote access policy.

This is the correct order for the EAP types. You want IAS to attempt to negotiate EAP types from the most secure to the least secure. If you modify the remote access policy, as created in Chapter 10, use the preceding procedure to add the Smart Card or Other Certificate EAP Type to the list of EAP types. Then, in the Select EAP Providers dialog box, select the Smart Card Or Other Certificate EAP Type and click Move Up, so that it is first in the list of EAP types.

Summary

This chapter described the detailed steps for deploying secure wireless networks for configurations not described in Chapter 8 or Chapter 10. To deploy Internet access for business partners, you can configure either guest access or validated access. For guest access, the Guest account and a wireless guests group is used to specify Internet access. For validated access, business partners are given valid computer accounts, user accounts, and certificates to obtain a validated connection to the Internet.

To deploy secure wireless between forests, use a layer of IAS RADIUS proxies between the wireless APs and the IAS servers in each forest. To scale RADIUS traffic up, use a layer of IAS RADIUS proxies between the wireless APs and multiple IAS servers in the forest. To use both EAP-TLS and PEAP-MS-CHAP v2 authentication methods simultaneously, either create two groups and two remote access policies (for Windows 2000 IAS) or modify the existing remote access policy to allow both types of authentication (for Windows Server 2003 IAS).

Chapter 12
Secure Wireless Networks for the Home and Small Business

Using wireless networking in homes and small businesses has obvious benefits. With wireless networking, you do not have to install cabling to connect the separate computers together; and portable computers, such as laptops and notebook computers, can be moved around the house or small business office and maintain their connections to the network.

You can deploy IEEE 802.11 wireless LAN networks in your home or small business by using either infrastructure mode (a wireless access point [AP] is required) or ad hoc mode (a wireless AP is not required).

In infrastructure mode in a typical home or small business office, a single wireless AP is used to connect one or more computers that are either mobile (such as laptop or notebook computers) or stationary (such as a desktop computer in a room without network cabling) to each other, and to either an existing wired network (such as Ethernet) or the Internet.

Figure 12-1 shows an example of a single wireless AP wireless network in a home environment.

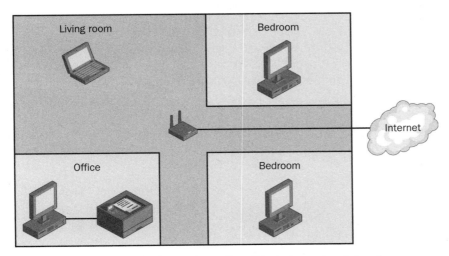

Figure 12-1. *An example of a single wireless AP wireless network in a home.*

In ad hoc mode, the wireless clients can connect directly together without needing a wireless AP or a connection to an existing wired network. Figure 12-2 shows an example of an ad hoc mode wireless network in a home environment.

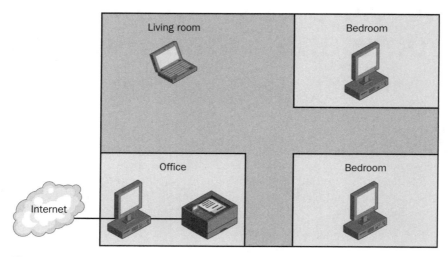

Figure 12-2. *An example of an ad hoc mode wireless network in a home.*

Enable and Configure Security on Your Wireless Network

One of the first steps of configuring a wireless network is to select a name for it. If you are creating a new wireless network, the name you choose should be different from the names of all other wireless networks within scanning range. For example, if you are creating a wireless network in your home, and your neighbor has already created a wireless network called HOME that is visible from the locations in your home, you must choose a name other than HOME. After you select a wireless network name and configure it for your wireless AP (infrastructure mode) or initial wireless client (ad hoc mode), that name is visible from any IEEE 802.11b wireless node within scanning range.

War driving is the practice of driving around business or residential neighborhoods to scan for wireless network names. People driving around the vicinity of your wireless network might be able to see your wireless network name, but whether they can do anything beyond viewing your wireless network name is determined by your use of wireless security.

If you have enabled and properly configured security on your wireless network, war drivers can see your network name and join your network; but they cannot send data, interpret the data sent on your wireless network, access the resources of your wireless or wired network (shared files, private Web sites), or use your Internet connection. Without wireless security enabled and properly configured, however, war drivers *can* do all of these things and more. For example, a malicious user might use your Internet connection to send e-mail or launch attacks against other computers. The malicious traffic can then be traced back to your home or small business.

It is for these reasons that Microsoft strongly urges you to enable and properly configure wireless security.

Wireless Security

Security for IEEE 802.11b consists of encryption and authentication, as described in the following sections.

Encryption

To encrypt wireless data, you can use Wired Equivalent Privacy (WEP); if your wireless networking components are Wi-Fi Protected Access (WPA)–enabled, you can use the Temporal Key Integrity Protocol (TKIP).

WEP Encryption

Securing physical access to the network is difficult because of the nature of wireless LAN networks. Unlike a wired network (in which a direct physical connection is required), anyone within range of a wireless AP or a wireless client can conceivably send and receive frames—as well as listen for other frames being sent—which makes eavesdropping on and remote sniffing of wireless network frames very easy.

WEP uses a shared secret key to encrypt the data of the sending node, and the receiving node uses the same WEP key to decrypt the data. For infrastructure mode, the WEP key must be configured on the wireless AP and all the wireless clients. For ad hoc mode, the WEP key must be configured on all the wireless clients.

As specified in the IEEE 802.11 standards, WEP uses a 40-bit secret key, and most wireless hardware for IEEE 802.11 supports the use of a 104-bit WEP key. If your hardware supports both, use a 104-bit key.

Strong Encryption with WEP

Some wireless vendors advertise a 128-bit wireless encryption key, which is the addition of a 104-bit WEP key with another number (a 24-bit number known as the *initialization vector*) used during the encryption process. Some wireless APs also support the use of a 152-bit wireless encryption key (a 128-bit WEP key added to the 24-bit initialization vector). Windows XP does not support the configuration of 128-bit WEP keys.

If you must use 152-bit wireless encryption keys, disable the Wireless Zero Configuration (WZC) service by clearing the Use Windows To Configure My Wireless Network Settings check box on the Wireless Networks tab of the properties of the wireless connection or wireless network adapter in Network Connections. Use the configuration tool provided with your wireless network adapter to configure the wireless network settings and the WEP key.

Choosing a WEP Key

The WEP key should be a random sequence of keyboard characters (upper- and lowercase letters, numbers, and punctuation) or hexadecimal digits (numbers 0–9 and letters A–F). The more random your WEP key, the safer it is to use for a longer period of time.

A WEP key based on a familiar word (such as your company name or your last name) or an easily remembered phrase is easy to guess. After malicious users discover your WEP key, they can decrypt received frames, send properly encrypted frames, and begin attacking your network.

Even if your WEP key is random, it is still subject to determination if a large amount of data encrypted with the same key is collected and analyzed. Therefore, it is recommended that you change your WEP key to a new random sequence periodically (for example, every three months).

WPA Encryption

TKIP in WPA dynamically determines a unique initial encryption key for each authenticated association, and changes the key for each wireless frame. TKIP does not require manual configuration of an encryption key.

Authentication

The following types of authentication are available for use with 802.11b networks, as described in the following sections:

- Open system
- Shared key
- IEEE 802.1X
- WPA with preshared key

Open System Authentication

Open system authentication is not really authentication because all it does is identify a wireless node using its wireless adapter hardware address. A *hardware address*, which is an address assigned to the network adapter during its manufacture, is used to address wireless frames.

In infrastructure mode, some wireless APs allow you to configure a list of allowed hardware addresses for open system authentication. However, it is a fairly simple matter for a malicious user to capture frames sent on your wireless network to determine the hardware address of allowed wireless nodes and then use that hardware address to perform open system authentication and join your wireless network.

In ad hoc mode, there is no equivalent of configuring the list of allowed hardware addresses in Windows XP or Windows Server 2003. Therefore, any hardware address can be used to perform open system authentication and join your ad hoc mode–based wireless network.

Shared Key Authentication

Shared key authentication verifies that the wireless client joining the wireless network has been configured with a secret key. During the authentication process, the wireless client proves that it has the secret key without actually sending the secret key. In infrastructure mode, all the wireless clients and the wireless AP use the same shared key; in ad hoc mode, all the wireless clients of the ad hoc wireless network use the same shared key.

IEEE 802.1X Authentication

The IEEE 802.1X standard enforces authentication of a network node before it can begin to exchange data with the network. Exchanging frames with the network is denied if the authentication process fails. IEEE 802.1X provides much stronger authentication than open system or shared key authentication.

The recommended solution for Windows wireless authentication is the use of EAP-Transport Layer Security (TLS) and certificates for authentication. To use EAP-TLS authentication for wireless connections, you must create an authentication infrastructure that consists of an Active Directory directory service domain, Remote Authentication Dial-In User Service (RADIUS) servers, and a certification authority (CA) to issue certificates to your RADIUS servers and wireless clients. This authentication infrastructure is appropriate for large businesses and enterprise organizations, but it is not practical for most homes or small business offices. If your home or small business office has an Active Directory domain controller, a RADIUS server, and a CA, and you want to deploy an EAP-TLS-authenticated wireless network, follow the instructions given in Chapter 8, "Intranet Wireless Deployment Using EAP-TLS."

If you have a domain controller and a RADIUS server, but no CA, you can purchase a computer certificate from a commercial CA, install it on your RADIUS server, and use Protected EAP (PEAP) and the Microsoft Challenge-Handshake Authentication Protocol, version 2 (MS-CHAP v2) EAP type. PEAP-MS-CHAP v2 uses passwords instead of certificates for credentials. The only certificate required when using PEAP-MS-CHAP v2 is the RADIUS server certificate, which is used to authenticate the RADIUS server and create a secure channel for communication between the wireless client and the RADIUS server.

More Info For more information about deploying secure wireless networks using PEAP-MS-CHAP v2 authentication, see Chapter 10, "Intranet Wireless Deployment Using PEAP-MS-CHAP v2."

WPA with Preshared Key Authentication

WPA supports two types of authentication:

- User-level 802.1X authentication using an EAP type

- Preshared key (PSK)

Preshared key authentication for WPA was designed specifically for the home and small office environment, in which an 802.1X authentication infrastructure is not present. With preshared key authentication, the wireless AP and the wireless clients are configured with the same key. When authenticating, the wireless clients provide proof that they have been configured with the correct preshared key.

Choosing a WPA Preshared Key

The WPA preshared key should be a random sequence of keyboard characters (upper- and lowercase letters, numbers, and punctuation) and can be up to 256 characters long. The longer and more random your preshared key, the safer it is to use for a longer period of time. A preshared key based on a familiar word (such as your company name, last name, or part of your home address) or an easily remembered phrase can be easily guessed. After malicious users have determined the WPA preshared key, they can begin attacking your network.

Because the initial TKIP encryption key is different for each association and changes with each wireless frame, you do not have to worry about malicious users accumulating a large amount of data and decrypting wireless frames. However, to prevent online dictionary attacks against your WPA preshared key, it is a good idea to change it periodically (for example, once every six months).

Recommended Authentication: WPA-PSK or Open System

For a secure wireless network that cannot use IEEE 802.1X authentication, the recommendation is to use one of the following:

- If your wireless network components are WPA-enabled, use WPA with pre-shared key authentication.

- If your wireless network components are not WPA-enabled, use open system authentication.

The use of open system authentication instead of shared key authentication in the absence of WPA might seem contradictory. Open system authentication is not really authentication, but identification; and shared key authentication requires knowledge of a shared secret key. Although shared key authentication might be a stronger authentication method than open system, using it actually makes your wireless communication less secure.

For most wireless implementations, including Windows XP, the shared key authentication secret key is the same as the WEP encryption key. The shared key authentication process consists of two messages: a challenge message sent by the authenticator and a challenge response message sent by the authenticating wireless client. A malicious user who captures both messages can use cryptanalysis methods to determine the shared key authentication secret key—and therefore the WEP encryption key. After the WEP encryption key is determined, the malicious user has full access to your network, as if WEP encryption were not enabled. Therefore, although shared key authentication is stronger than open system authentication, it weakens WEP encryption.

The tradeoff of using open system authentication is that anyone can easily join your network, unless your wireless AP has the capability to configure the list of allowed wireless clients by their hardware addresses. By joining the network, malicious users use up one of the available wireless connections, but they cannot send or decrypt received wireless frames without the WEP encryption key.

Wireless APs and Windows wireless clients support open system authentication. One advantage of using open system authentication is that it is always enabled for Windows XP wireless clients—no additional authentication configuration is needed.

For these reasons, open system authentication is recommended for the home or small office wireless network in the absence of WPA.

Using the Windows XP WZC Service

For home or small office wireless networks, you use the WZC service to discover your wireless network. However, because the default settings for a wireless network are either to automatically determine the WEP key (for a WEP-based network) or use WPA with 802.1X authentication, the initial authentication process fails. You must manually configure the settings for your wireless network after it is discovered with the WZC service.

Setting Up a Wireless Network with a Wireless Access Point

This section describes how to set up a wireless network for a home or small business when you use a wireless AP (infrastructure mode). To secure your infrastructure mode home or small business wireless network, you must use open system authentication with WEP encryption or WPA preshared key authentication with TKIP encryption.

Configuring the Wireless AP

If your wireless AP does not support WPA, you must do the following when configuring your wireless AP:

- Specify the wireless network name (SSID).

- Enable open system authentication.

- Enable WEP.

- Select a WEP key format.

  If you are typing the WEP key using keyboard characters, you must type five characters for a 40-bit WEP key and 13 characters for a 104-bit WEP key. If you are typing the WEP key using hexadecimal digits, you must type 10 hexadecimal digits for a 40-bit key and 26 hexadecimal digits for a 104-bit key. If you have the choice of the format of the WEP key, choose hexadecimal because hexadecimal digits allow more randomness for the WEP key. The more random your WEP key, the safer it is to use for a longer period of time.

- Select the WEP encryption key number.

  You must specify which key to use. IEEE 802.11b allows the use of up to four different WEP keys. A single WEP key is used when traffic is exchanged between the wireless AP and a wireless client. The key is stored in a specific memory position. In order for the receiver to correctly decrypt the incoming frame, both the sender and the receiver must use the same encryption key in the same memory position.

  Although it is possible to configure your wireless AP with all four keys and have different clients use different keys, this process can lead to configuration confusion. Instead, choose a specific key and a specific memory position to use for the wireless AP and all the wireless clients.

  The configuration of a specific encryption key is complicated by the fact that Windows XP (prior to Service Pack 1 [SP1]) refers to the encryption key memory positions using a *key index* and it numbers the key indexes starting at 0. Many wireless APs refer to the encryption key memory positions as *encryption keys* and number the keys starting at 1. In this case, you must make the Windows XP (prior to SP1) key index number indicate the same encryption key memory position as the encryption key number on the wireless AP; otherwise, the wireless AP and wireless clients cannot communicate. Table 12-1 shows this relationship.

The easiest configuration is to use the first encryption key memory position, which corresponds to Windows XP (prior to SP1) key index 0 (or Windows XP [SP1 and later] and Windows Server 2003 key index 1) and wireless AP encryption key 1.

- Specify the WEP key.

Note   Windows XP (SP1 and later) and Windows Server 2003 number the encryption key index starting at 1, which matches the encryption key numbers of many wireless APs.

Table 12-1.   Windows XP (Prior to SP1) Key Index and Wireless AP Encryption Key Numbers

Windows XP (Prior to SP1) Key Index Number	Wireless AP Encryption Key Number
0	1
1	2
2	3
3	4

If your wireless AP does support WPA, you must do the following when configuring your wireless AP:

- Specify the wireless network name (SSID).
- Enable WPA-PSK authentication.
- Enable TKIP.
- Specify the WPA preshared key.

Configuring the Windows Wireless Clients

Configuration of the Windows wireless clients depends on the following factors:

- Whether the wireless network adapter driver supports the WZC service.
- Whether the clients are running Windows XP (prior to SP1) or Windows XP (SP1 and later).
- Whether or not you use WPA.

Configuring Wireless Clients with WEP

If WPA is either not supported or not enabled for your wireless network components, there are several different types of configuration for Windows wireless clients, as follows:

- Your computer is running Windows XP (prior to SP1) and your wireless network adapter driver supports the WZC service.

- Your computer is running Windows XP (prior to SP1) or Windows Server 2003, and your wireless network adapter driver supports the WZC service.

- Your wireless network adapter driver does not support the WZC service.

Wireless Network Adapter Driver Supports the WZC Service with Windows XP (Prior to SP1)   Use the following procedure to configure Windows XP (prior to SP1) for your infrastructure mode wireless network when the wireless network adapter supports the WZC service:

1. Install your wireless network adapter in Windows XP, including installing the proper drivers for your wireless network adapter so it appears as a wireless connection in Network Connections.

2. When the computer is within range of the wireless AP operating in your home or small business, Windows XP should detect it and prompt you with a message in the notification area of your taskbar.

3. Click the notification message. If you are not notified, right-click the wireless network adapter in Network Connections and click View Available Wireless Networks.

   In either case, you should see a Connect To Wireless Network dialog box.

4. Click Advanced.

5. In the wireless network adapter properties dialog box, click your wireless network name and click Configure.

6. In the Wireless Network Properties dialog box, clear the The Key Is Provided For Me Automatically check box.

7. In Key Format, select the encryption key format as configured on wireless AP.

8. In Key Length, select the key size as configured on the wireless AP.

9. In Network Key, type the key as configured on the wireless AP.

10. In Key Index, select the key index corresponding to the encryption key memory position as configured on the wireless AP.

11. Click OK to save changes to the wireless network.

12. Click OK to save changes to the wireless network adapter.

Figure 12-3 shows an example of the Wireless Network Properties dialog box for a home wireless network with the following configuration:

- SSID is HOME-AP.

- WEP is enabled.

- Open system authentication is enabled.

- The WEP encryption key is 104 bits long, is in hexadecimal format, uses key index 0 (the first encryption key position), and consists of the sequence 8e7cd510fba7f71ef29abc63ce.

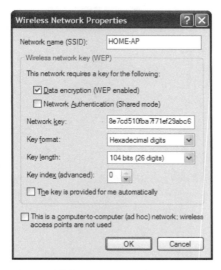

Figure 12-3. *Example of Windows XP (prior to SP1) configuration for an infrastructure mode wireless network.*

Wireless Network Adapter Driver Supports the WZC Service with Windows XP (SP1 and Later)

Use the following procedure to configure Windows XP (SP1 and later) or Windows Server 2003 for your infrastructure mode wireless network when the wireless network adapter supports the WZC service:

1. Install your wireless network adapter in Windows XP. This process includes installing the proper drivers for your wireless network adapter so it appears as a wireless connection in Network Connections.

2. When the computer is within range of the wireless AP operating in your home or small business, Windows XP should detect it and prompt you with a message in the notification area of your taskbar.

3. Click the notification message. If you are not notified, right-click the wireless network adapter in Network Connections and click View Available Wireless Networks.

   In either case, you should see a Wireless Network Connection dialog box.

4. Click Advanced.

5. In the wireless network adapter properties dialog box, click your wireless network name and click Configure.

6. On the Association tab of the Wireless Network Properties dialog box, clear the The Key Is Provided For Me Automatically check box.

7. In Network Key and Confirm Network Key, type the WEP encryption key as configured on the wireless AP.

8. In Key Index, select the key index corresponding to the encryption key memory position as configured on the wireless AP.

9. Click OK to save changes to the wireless network.

10. Click OK to save changes to the wireless network adapter.

Figure 12-4 shows an example of a Wireless Network Properties dialog box for a home wireless network with the following configuration:

- SSID is HOME-AP.

- Open system authentication is enabled.

- WEP is enabled.

- The WEP encryption key consists of the sequence 8e7cd510fba7f71ef29abc63ce and uses key index 0 (the first encryption key position).

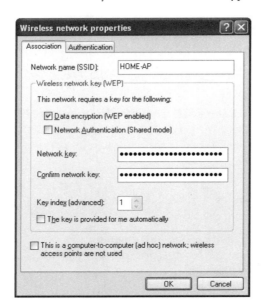

Figure 12-4. *Example of Windows XP (SP1 and later) properties of an infrastructure mode wireless network.*

Wireless Network Adapter Driver Does Not Support the WZC Service   If your wireless network adapter driver does not support the WZC service, you notice the following:

- The network adapter does not appear as a wireless connection in Network Connections; it appears as a LAN adapter, similar to an Ethernet connection.

- The properties of the wireless connection do not have a Wireless Networks tab.

- You do not receive a Windows XP notification area message indicating that wireless networks are available.

To get the most out of your Windows wireless experience, you should contact your wireless network adapter vendor to obtain the latest version of the drivers for Windows XP that support the WZC service. If new drivers are not available, or if you want to connect your computer to the wireless network while the drivers are being obtained, you must manually configure wireless network settings using the configuration software supplied with the wireless network adapter.

To configure your wireless network adapter, use the configuration software provided by the network adapter vendor to configure the following:

- SSID of your wireless network.

  The SSID must be the same as that configured on the wireless AP.

- Open system authentication (enabled).

- WEP encryption (enabled).

- WEP key size.

  Select the key size as configured on the wireless AP. If the wireless network adapter does not support the same encryption key length as the wireless AP, you must reconfigure the wireless AP. For example, if your wireless AP supports 40-bit and 104-bit WEP key sizes and your wireless network adapter supports only 40-bit keys, you must reconfigure the wireless AP to use a 40-bit WEP key.

- WEP key format.

  Select the same WEP key format as configured on the wireless AP. If the wireless network adapter does not support the same encryption key formats as the wireless AP, you must reconfigure the wireless AP. For example, if your wireless AP supports keyboard and hexadecimal WEP key formats, and your wireless network adapter supports only keyboard format, you must reconfigure the wireless AP to use keyboard format for the encryption keys.

- WEP key.

  Type the same encryption key as configured on the wireless AP.

- WEP key number.

  Specify the same encryption key number as configured on the wireless AP.

Configuring the Wireless Clients with WPA

This section describes how to configure your wireless client when WPA is supported and enabled on your wireless AP and your wireless clients.

> **Note** There is no procedure for configuring a computer running Windows XP (prior to SP1) for WPA. The Windows WPA Client can be installed only on computers running Windows XP (SP1 and later) and Windows Server 2003.

Wireless Network Adapter Driver Supports the WZC Service with Windows XP (SP1 and Later) Use the following procedure to configure Windows XP (SP1 and later) for your infrastructure mode wireless network when the wireless network adapter supports the WZC service:

1. Install your wireless network adapter in Windows XP. This process includes installing the proper drivers for your wireless network adapter so it appears as a wireless connection in Network Connections.

2. When the computer is within range of the wireless AP operating in your home or small business, Windows XP should detect it and prompt you with a message in the notification area of your taskbar.

3. Click the notification message. If you are not notified, right-click the wireless network adapter in Network Connections and click View Available Wireless Networks.

   In either case, you should see a Wireless Network Connection dialog box.

4. Click Advanced.

5. In the wireless network adapter properties dialog box, click your wireless network name and click Configure.

6. In Authentication in the Wireless Network Properties dialog box, select WPA-PSK. TKIP should already be selected in Data Encryption.

7. In Network Key and Confirm Network Key, type the WPA preshared key as configured on the wireless AP.

8. Click OK to save changes to the wireless network.

9. Click OK to save changes to the wireless network adapter.

Figure 12-5 shows an example of a Wireless Network Properties dialog box for a home wireless network with the following configuration:

- SSID is HOME-AP.

- WPA-PSK authentication is enabled.

- The WPA preshared key is 32 characters long and consists of the sequence 8d(Xo2$j%nfK039ksSs#06I[_C3!1~9z.

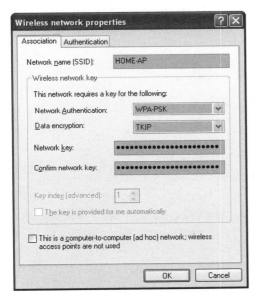

Figure 12-5. *Example of a WPA-enabled Windows XP (SP1 and later) configuration for an infrastructure mode wireless network.*

Wireless Network Adapter Driver Does Not Support the WZC Service   To configure your wireless network adapter, use the configuration software provided by the network adapter vendor to configure the following:

- SSID of your wireless network.

    The SSID must be the same as configured on the wireless AP.

- WPA preshared key authentication (enabled).

- TKIP encryption (enabled).

- WPA preshared key.

    Type the same WPA preshared key as configured on the wireless AP.

Setting Up a Wireless Network Without a Wireless Access Point

This section describes how to set up a wireless network for a home or small business when you are not using a wireless AP (ad hoc mode). For an ad hoc wireless network, you must set up an initial wireless client that assumes some of the responsibilities of a wireless AP with respect to beaconing the name of the ad hoc wireless network to other wireless network clients.

To secure your ad hoc mode home or small business wireless network, you must use open system authentication and WEP encryption.

Note WPA does not support ad hoc wireless networks.

Configuring the Initial Wireless Client

The configuration of the initial wireless client depends on the following factors:

- Whether the wireless network adapter driver supports the WZC service.

- Whether you are using Windows XP (prior to SP1) or Windows XP (SP1 and later).

Wireless Network Adapter Driver Supports the WZC Service with Windows XP (Prior to SP1)   Use the following procedure to configure the initial Windows XP (prior to SP1) wireless client for your ad hoc mode wireless network when the wireless network adapter supports the WZC service:

1. Install your wireless network adapter in Windows XP. This process includes installing the proper drivers for your wireless network adapter so it appears as a wireless connection in Network Connections.

2. Because there might not be any wireless networks in your home or small business location, you might not be prompted with a message in the notification area of your taskbar. If you are notified, click the notification. You should see a Connect To Wireless Network dialog box. Click Advanced.

3. If you are not notified, right-click the wireless network adapter in Network Connections and then click Properties.

4. On the Wireless Networks tab of the wireless network adapter properties dialog box, click Add under Preferred Networks.

5. In the Wireless Network Properties dialog box, type the name of your ad hoc wireless network in Network Name (SSID).

6. Select the Data Encryption (WEP Enabled) and This Is A Computer-To-Computer (Ad Hoc) Network check boxes. Clear the The Key Is Provided For Me Automatically check box.

7. In Key Format, select a key format.

8. In Key Length, select a key size.

9. In Network Key, type the WEP key.

10. In Key Index, select 0.

11. Click OK to save changes to the wireless network.

12. Click OK to save changes to the wireless network adapter.

Figure 12-6 shows an example of a Wireless Network Properties dialog box for a home ad hoc wireless network with the following configuration:

- SSID is HOME-AD HOC.

- WEP is enabled.

- Open system authentication is enabled.

- Ad hoc mode is enabled.

- The WEP encryption key is 104 bits long, is in hexadecimal format, uses key index 0 (the first encryption key position), and consists of the sequence 19a8bce753ed4e6a410b730fa4.

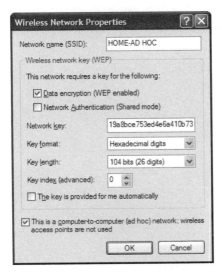

Figure 12-6. *Example of Windows XP (prior to SP1) configuration for an ad hoc mode wireless network.*

Wireless Network Adapter Driver Supports the WZC Service with Windows XP (SP1 and Later) Use the following procedure to configure the initial Windows XP (SP1 and later) or Windows Server 2003 wireless client for your ad hoc mode wireless network when the wireless network adapter supports the WZC service:

1. Install your wireless network adapter in Windows XP or Windows Server 2003. This process includes installing the proper drivers for your wireless network adapter so it appears as a wireless connection in Network Connections.

2. Because there might not be any wireless networks in your home or small business location, you might not be prompted with a message in the notification area of your taskbar. If you are notified, click the notification. You should see a Wireless Network Connection dialog box. Click Advanced.

3. If you are not notified, right-click the wireless network adapter in Network Connections and then click Properties.

4. On the Wireless Networks tab in the wireless network adapter properties dialog box, click Add under Preferred Networks.

5. On the Association tab in the Wireless Network Properties dialog box, type the name of your ad hoc wireless network in Network Name (SSID).

6. Select the Data Encryption (WEP Enabled) and This Is A Computer-To-Computer (Ad Hoc) Network check boxes. Clear the The Key Is Provided For Me Automatically check box.

7. In Network Key and Confirm Network Key, type the WEP key.

8. In Key Index, select 1.

9. Click OK to save changes to the wireless network.

10. Click OK to save changes to the wireless network adapter.

Figure 12-7 shows an example of a Wireless Network Properties dialog box for a home ad hoc wireless network with the following configuration:

- SSID is HOME-AD HOC.

- Open system authentication is enabled.

- WEP is enabled.

- Ad hoc mode is enabled.

- The WEP encryption key is 104 bits long, is in hexadecimal format, uses key index 1 (the first encryption key position), and consists of the sequence 19a8bce753ed4e6a410b730fa4.

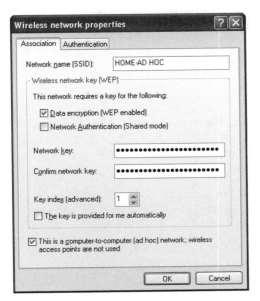

Figure 12-7. *Example of Windows XP (SP1 and later) configuration for an ad hoc mode wireless network.*

Wireless Network Adapter Driver Does Not Support the WZC Service   When the initial Windows wireless client does not support the WZC service, use the configuration software provided by the network adapter vendor to configure the following:

- SSID of your ad hoc wireless network.

- Ad hoc wireless network mode (enabled).

- Open system authentication (enabled).

- WEP encryption (enabled).

- WEP key size.

  For the best security, select 104-bit WEP keys.

- WEP key format.

  For the best security, select hexadecimal format.

- WEP encryption key memory position.

  For the easiest configuration, select the first encryption key memory position.

- WEP encryption key.

Configuring the Additional Windows XP Wireless Clients

The configuration of additional wireless clients depends on the following factors:

- Whether the wireless network adapter driver supports the WZC service.

- Whether you are using Windows XP (prior to SP1) or Windows XP (SP1 and later).

Wireless Network Adapter Driver Supports the WZC Service with Windows XP (Prior to SP1)   Use the following procedure to configure additional Windows XP (prior to SP1) wireless clients for your ad hoc mode wireless network when the wireless network adapter supports the WZC service:

1. Install your wireless network adapter in Windows XP. This process includes installing the proper drivers for your wireless network adapter so it appears as a wireless connection in Network Connections.

2. When the computer is within range of the initial wireless client in your home or small business, Windows XP should detect it and prompt you with a message in the notification area of your taskbar.

3. Click the notification message. If you are not notified, right-click the wireless network adapter in Network Connections and click View Available Wireless Networks.

   In either case, you should see a Connect To Wireless Network dialog box.

4. Click Advanced.

5. In the wireless network adapter properties dialog box, click your wireless network name and click Configure.

6. In the Wireless Network Properties dialog box, select the Data Encryption (WEP Enabled) check box and clear the The Key Is Provided For Me Automatically check box.

7. In Key Format, select the encryption key format as configured on the initial wireless client.

8. In Key Length, select the key size as configured on the initial wireless client.

9. In Network Key, type the key as configured on the initial wireless client.

10. In Key Index, select the index corresponding to the encryption key memory position on the initial wireless client.

11. Click OK to save changes to the wireless network.

12. Click OK to save changes to the wireless network adapter.

Wireless Network Adapter Driver Supports the WZC Service with Windows XP (SP1 and Later)   Use the following procedure to configure additional Windows XP (SP1 and later) wireless clients for your ad hoc mode wireless network when the wireless network adapter supports the WZC service:

1. Install your wireless network adapter in Windows XP. This process includes installing the proper drivers for your wireless network adapter so it appears as a wireless connection in Network Connections.

2. When the computer is within range of the initial wireless client in your home or small business, Windows XP should detect it and prompt you with a message in the notification area of your taskbar.

3. Click the notification message. If you are not notified, right-click the wireless network adapter in Network Connections and click View Available Wireless Networks.

   In either case, you should see a Wireless Network Connection dialog box.

4. Click Advanced.

5. In the wireless network adapter properties dialog box, click your wireless network name and click Configure.

6. On the Association tab, select the Data Encryption (WEP Enabled) check box and clear the The Key Is Provided For Me Automatically check box.

7. In Network Key and Confirm Network Key, type the WEP key as configured on the initial wireless client.

8. In Key Index, select the index corresponding to the encryption key memory position configured on the initial wireless client. For example, if the initial wireless client is running Windows XP (prior to SP1) and is using key index 0, set the key index to 1. If the initial wireless client is running Windows XP (SP1 and later) or Windows Server 2003 and is using key index 1, set the key index to 1.

9. Click OK to save changes to the wireless network.

10. Click OK to save changes to the wireless network adapter.

Wireless Network Adapter Driver Does Not Support the WZC Service   When additional Windows wireless clients do not support the WZC service, use the configuration software provided by the network adapter vendor to configure the following:

- SSID of your ad hoc wireless network.

  The SSID must be the same as configured on the initial wireless client.

- Ad hoc wireless network mode (enabled).

- Open system authentication (enabled).

- Enable WEP encryption (enabled).

- WEP key size.

Select the key size as configured on the initial wireless client. If the wireless network adapter does not support the same encryption key length as the initial wireless client, you must reconfigure the initial wireless client. For example, if the initial wireless client supports 40-bit and 104-bit WEP key sizes, and your wireless network adapter supports only 40-bit keys, you must reconfigure the initial wireless client to use a 40-bit WEP key.

- WEP key format.

Select the same WEP key format as configured on the initial wireless client. If the wireless network adapter does not support the same encryption key formats as the initial wireless client, you must reconfigure the initial wireless client. For example, if the initial wireless client supports keyboard and hexadecimal WEP key formats, and your wireless network adapter supports only keyboard format, you must reconfigure the initial wireless client to use keyboard format for the WEP encryption key.

- WEP key.

Type the same encryption key as configured on the initial wireless client.

- WEP encryption key memory position.

Select the same WEP encryption key memory position (or encryption key number) as configured on the initial wireless client.

Summary

Wireless networks enable location independence and roaming support for network connectivity in your home or small business. You can configure a wireless network by using a wireless AP (infrastructure mode) or using only wireless clients (ad hoc mode).

Wireless networks can also allow unintended access to your network. To provide security for your home or small office infrastructure mode wireless network in which 802.1X authentication is not practical, you must use either open system authentication with WEP encryption or WPA preshared key authentication with TKIP encryption. For the best security for your home or small office ad hoc mode wireless network, you must use open system authentication and WEP encryption. For the best security with WEP encryption, use a 104-bit WEP key that consists of a random sequence of 26 hexadecimal digits and change it periodically.

Chapter 13
RADIUS Infrastructure for Public Place Deployment

Wireless access to the Internet in public places—such as airports, coffee shops, and other locations—is another segment of wireless connectivity that is growing quickly. Laptop and notebook computer owners use a wireless Internet service provider (WISP) to connect to the Internet. Once on the Internet, wireless users can access public Web sites or use a virtual private network (VPN) technology to create a secure connection to their employer's network across the Internet.

The infrastructure required by the WISP to provide connectivity to the Internet spans a wide range of network services, including the following:

- **Dynamic Host Configuration Protocol (DHCP)** A DHCP infrastructure assigns unique Internet Protocol (IP) addresses and other configuration settings.

- **Domain Name System (DNS)** A DNS infrastructure provides name resolution services to allow wireless clients to use names (such as www.example.com) rather than IP addresses (such as 131.107.90.234), to connect to Internet resources.

- **World Wide Web** Web sites allow users to view information stored on a Web server and respond to information requested by the Web server. In many WISP deployments, a series of Web pages for user identification, enrollment, and billing is the mechanism by which a new customer obtains connectivity to the Internet.

- **Certification Authority (CA)** A CA is needed in the WISP's network infrastructure only if the customers of the WISP are required to use Extensible Authentication Protocol-Transport Layer Security (EAP-TLS) and certificates for authenticated connections. In most cases, WISPs will use Protected EAP-Microsoft Challenge Handshake Authentication Protocol version 2 (PEAP-MS-CHAP v2) and passwords for authenticated connections.

- **Remote Authentication Dial-In User Service (RADIUS)** RADIUS is used as the industry standard protocol to provide authentication, authorization, and accounting for wireless connections.

Figure 13-1 shows the set of components for a public place deployment.

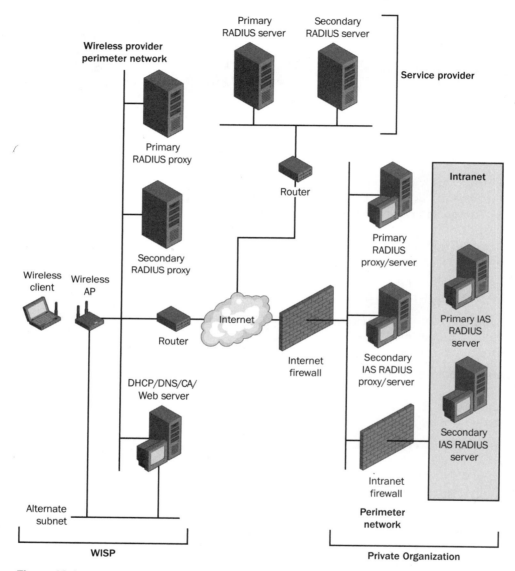

Figure 13-1. *Components of a public place deployment.*

At the time of the publication of this book, the configuration of DHCP, DNS, Web, and CA infrastructure for WISPs was not standardized. Because there are too many ways to configure these components to provide public wireless access to the Internet, and industry practices for their setup are evolving, they are not described in this chapter.

As an example, Figure 13-1 shows the use of a computer acting as a DHCP server, DNS server, and CA that is connected to an alternate subnet. Wireless clients that do not have valid credentials use this alternate subnet. Using unauthenticated access, the new wireless user is allowed access only to the alternate subnet—through which the wireless client can obtain an IP address, perform a signup process using Web pages, and even obtain a certificate. When the signup process is complete, the user is prompted to reauthenticate, at which time the wireless client uses the recently obtained credentials for an authenticated connection to gain access to the Internet.

Although the use of many network services on the WISP perimeter network is not standardized, the RADIUS infrastructure—consisting of RADIUS proxies and servers—works the same regardless of the other elements of the WISP's network service infrastructure. Therefore, this chapter describes only the RADIUS portion of a WISP's network and assumes the use of Internet Authentication Service (IAS).

Note   Microsoft is investigating the development of new wireless client components to better support the WISP scenario. For more information, see Appendix B, "Wireless ISPs and Windows Provisioning Services."

Components of a RADIUS Infrastructure for Public Place Wireless Access

Public place wireless access consists of the organizational entities listed below and shown in Figure 13-1.

- **WISP**   The WISP is the organization that provides the wireless connection to the Internet for WISP users. A WISP deploys wireless access points (APs) and a network infrastructure in a public place and generates revenue by either charging wireless users directly (as customers of the WISP) or charging a benefactor of the wireless user. The benefactor of a wireless user is typically either a communications service provider (such as a phone company) or a private organization (such as a corporation). The WISP has existing agreements with wireless user benefactors and relies on the benefactor to authenticate and authorize the wireless connection of the wireless user.

- **Service provider**   The service provider provides various telecommunications services (such as mobile phone access) for its customers. To provide seamless wireless access with WISPs, the service provider enters into agreements with WISPs to provide wireless access to its customers in exchange for a fee. The service provider then offers this additional service to its customers for an additional monthly fee. The service provider's customer signs up for the service and receives credentials to identify them (such as a certificate). After configuration of the credentials, the customer can connect to the wireless network of the WISP without being a customer of the WISP. During the authentication exchange, the WISP forwards the credentials of the wireless user to the service provider, who authenticates and authorizes the connection attempt. The wireless user does not have to sign up with the WISP and gets seamless wireless connectivity to the Internet. This type of public wireless access is useful for individuals who spend a lot of time in public places such as coffee shops and want to remain connected to the Internet.

- **Private organization**   In a manner similar to a service provider, the WISP enters into an agreement with a private organization to provide Internet access to the private organization's employees for a fee. When the employee attempts to connect to the WISP's network, the employee uses the private organization's credentials for authentication. During the authentication exchange, the WISP forwards the credentials of the wireless user to the private organization, who authenticates and authorizes the connection attempt. The wireless user does not have to sign up with the WISP and gets seamless wireless connectivity to the Internet. This type of public wireless access is useful for private organization employees who travel often and want to get wireless access to the Internet and the private organization from airports, conference centers, or hotels.

From a RADIUS perspective, the relevant portions of infrastructure are the following:

- A set of at least two RADIUS proxies that forwards RADIUS messages between the wireless APs of the WISP and the RADIUS servers of service providers or private organizations.

- A set of at least two RADIUS servers at each service provider that provides authentication, authorization, and accounting for wireless connections initiated by customers of the service provider.

- A set of at least two RADIUS servers or proxies in the perimeter network of each private organization that provides authentication, authorization, and accounting for wireless connections initiated by employees of the private organization.

- If RADIUS proxies are used in the perimeter network of the private organization, a set of at least two RADIUS servers is deployed within the private network's intranet.

To provide authentication, authorization, and accounting for its own customers, the WISP can configure its RADIUS proxy computers to act as both a RADIUS proxy (for wireless clients that have benefactors) and a RADIUS server (for wireless clients that either have an existing account with the WISP or enroll with the WISP upon their initial connection).

To ensure the maximum security for RADIUS messages, it is recommended that you use Internet Protocol security (IPSec) with certificate authentication and Encapsulating Security Payload (ESP) to provide data confidentiality, data integrity, and data origin authentication for RADIUS traffic sent between all the RADIUS components.

The most important RADIUS traffic to secure is that sent across the Internet. Windows 2000 and Windows Server 2003 support IPSec. To secure RADIUS traffic sent from wireless APs, the wireless APs must also support IPSec. If any of the RADIUS components are behind a Network Address Translator (NAT), you must use IPSec NAT traversal (NAT-T). Windows Server 2003 supports IPSec NAT-T.

Wireless ISP Configuration

The WISP must configure the following, as discussed in the next sections:

- Wireless APs

- Primary IAS RADIUS proxy

- Secondary IAS RADIUS proxy

Configuring the Wireless APs

Configure the RADIUS client on your wireless APs by using the following settings:

- The IP address or name of a primary RADIUS server, the shared secret, User Datagram Protocol (UDP) ports for authentication and accounting, and failure detection settings.

- The IP address or name of a secondary RADIUS server, the shared secret, UDP ports for authentication and accounting, and failure detection settings.

To balance the load of RADIUS traffic between the primary and secondary IAS RADIUS proxies, configure half the wireless APs with the primary IAS RADIUS proxy as their primary RADIUS server and the secondary IAS RADIUS proxy as their secondary RADIUS server. Configure the other half of the wireless APs with the secondary IAS RADIUS proxy as their primary RADIUS server and the primary IAS RADIUS proxy as their secondary RADIUS server.

Configuring the Primary IAS RADIUS Proxy

To configure the primary IAS RADIUS proxy on a computer, perform the following, as discussed in the next sections:

- Install IAS and configure IAS server properties

- Configure the primary IAS RADIUS proxy with RADIUS clients

- Configure connection request policies on the primary IAS RADIUS proxy

Installing IAS and Configuring IAS Server Properties

To install Windows Server 2003 IAS, do the following:

1. Open Add Or Remove Programs in Control Panel.

2. Click Add/Remove Windows Components.

3. In the Windows Components Wizard dialog box, double-click Networking Services under Components.

4. In the Networking Services dialog box, select Internet Authentication Service.

5. Click OK and then click Next.

6. If prompted, insert your Windows product compact disc.

7. After IAS is installed, click Finish and then click Close.

If the IAS RADIUS proxy computer is not acting as a RADIUS server performing authentication, authorization, and accounting for WISP customers, it does not have to belong to a domain or be registered in any domains—it can be a standalone server. If the IAS RADIUS proxy computer is acting as a RADIUS server, follow the instructions in Chapter 10, "Intranet Wireless Deployment Using PEAP-MS-CHAP v2" (for PEAP-MS-CHAP v2 authentication) or Chapter 8, "Intranet Wireless Deployment Using EAP-TLS" (for EAP-TLS authentication) to register it in the appropriate domains and configure an appropriate remote access policy.

If you want to store authentication and accounting information for connection analysis and security investigation purposes, enable logging for accounting and authentication events. Windows Server 2003 IAS can log information to a local file and to a Microsoft SQL (Structured Query Language) Server database.

▶ **To enable and configure local file logging for Windows Server 2003 IAS**

1. Click Start, point to Programs, point to Administrative Tools, and then click Internet Authentication Service.

2. In the console tree of the Internet Authentication snap-in, click Remote Access Logging.

3. In the details pane, double-click Local File.

4. On the Settings tab, select one or more check boxes for recording authentication and accounting requests in the IAS log files:

   • To capture accounting requests and responses, select the Accounting Requests check box.

   • To capture authentication requests, Access-Accept packets, and Access-Reject packets, select the Authentication Requests check box.

- To capture periodic status updates, such as interim accounting packets, select the Periodic Status check box.

5. Click Apply to save your changes to the Settings tab.

6. On the Log File tab, type the log file directory as needed and select the log file format and new log time period. Click OK.

▶ **To enable and configure SQL Server database logging for Windows Server 2003 IAS**

1. In the console tree of the Internet Authentication snap-in, click Remote Access Logging.

2. In the details pane, double-click SQL Server.

3. On the Settings tab, select one or more check boxes for recording authentication and accounting requests in the IAS log files:

- To capture accounting requests and responses, select the Accounting Requests check box.

- To capture authentication requests, Access-Accept packets, and Access-Reject packets, select the Authentication Requests check box.

- To capture periodic status updates, such as interim accounting packets, select the Periodic Status check box.

4. In Maximum Number Of Connections, type the maximum number of simultaneous sessions that IAS can create with the SQL Server.

5. To configure a SQL data source, click Configure.

6. In the Data Link Properties dialog box, configure the appropriate settings for the SQL Server database.

If needed, configure additional UDP ports for authentication and accounting messages that are sent by RADIUS clients (the wireless APs). By default, IAS uses UDP ports 1812 and 1645 for authentication messages and UDP ports 1813 and 1646 for accounting messages.

▶ **To configure Windows Server 2003 IAS for different UDP ports**

1. In the console tree of the Internet Authentication snap-in, right-click Internet Authentication Service and then click Properties.

2. Click the Ports tab; configure the UDP port numbers for your RADIUS authentication traffic in Authentication and the UDP port numbers for your RADIUS accounting traffic in Accounting.

To use multiple port settings for authentication or accounting traffic, separate the port numbers with commas. You can also specify an IP address to which the RADIUS messages must be sent with the following syntax: *IPAddress:UDPPort*. For example, if you have multiple network adapters and you want to receive only RADIUS authentication messages sent to the IP address of 10.0.0.99 and UDP port 1812, type **10.0.0.99:1812** in Authentication. However, if you specify IP addresses and copy the configuration of the primary IAS RADIUS proxy to the secondary IAS RADIUS proxy, you must modify the ports on the secondary IAS RADIUS proxy to either remove the IP address of the primary IAS RADIUS proxy or change the IP address to that of the secondary IAS RADIUS proxy. After configuring the port numbers, click OK.

Configuring the Primary IAS RADIUS Proxy with RADIUS Clients

You must configure the primary IAS RADIUS proxy with the wireless APs as RADIUS clients. To add a RADIUS client for Windows Server 2003 IAS, do the following:

1. In the console tree of the Internet Authentication snap-in, right-click RADIUS Clients and then click New RADIUS Client.

2. On the Name and Address page, type a name for the wireless AP for Friendly Name. In Client Address (IP Or DNS), type the IP address or DNS domain name. If you type a DNS domain name, click Verify to resolve the name to the correct IP address for the wireless AP.

3. Click Next. On the Additional Information page, type the shared secret for this combination of IAS RADIUS proxy and wireless AP in Shared Secret; then type it again in Confirm Shared Secret.

4. Click Finish.

If you are using IAS on a computer running either Windows Server 2003, Enterprise Edition, or Windows Server 2003, Datacenter Edition, and you have multiple wireless APs on a single subnet (for example, in an Extended Service Set [ESS] configuration), you can simplify RADIUS client administration by specifying an address range instead of specifying the IP address or DNS name of a single RADIUS client. All RADIUS clients in the range must be configured to use the same RADIUS server and shared secret.

The address range for RADIUS clients is expressed in the network prefix length notation $w.x.y.z/p$, where $w.x.y.z$ is the dotted decimal notation of the address prefix and p is the prefix length (the number of high-order bits that define the network prefix). This is also known as Classless Inter-Domain Routing (CIDR) notation. An example is 192.168.21.0/24, which indicates all addresses from 192.168.21.1 to 192.168.21.255. To convert from subnet mask notation to network prefix length notation, p is the number of high-order bits set to one in the subnet mask. If you are not using this feature, use a different shared secret for each wireless AP.

Best Practices Use as many RADIUS shared secrets as you can. Each shared secret should be a random sequence of upper- and lowercase letters, numbers, and punctuation that is at least 22 characters long. To ensure randomness, use a random character generation program to determine shared secrets.

Configuring Connection Request Policies on the Primary IAS RADIUS Proxy

To provide a temporary connection to the WISP's network for signup purposes or to forward RADIUS traffic to the RADIUS servers at a service provider or private organization, you must configure the following connection request policies:

- **A connection request policy that allows unauthenticated access.**   This connection request policy allows wireless users, who are not customers of the WISP and who do not have a known benefactor, to have access to a closed alternate subnet that contains the network services (such as DHCP, DNS, Web, CA) that allow the user to sign up with the WISP. When the sign-up process is complete, the user has credentials to obtain an authenticated connection and to access the Internet.

- **A connection request policy to forward RADIUS messages for each service provider.**   For each service provider with which the WISP has an agreement, a separate connection request policy must be created. The connection request policy is configured to forward requests to the RADIUS servers of the service provider based on the name of the service provider in the realm portion of the wireless client's account name. For information about realm names, see Chapter 4, "RADIUS, IAS, and Active Directory."

- **A connection request policy to forward RADIUS messages for each private organization.**   For each private organization with which the WISP has an agreement, a separate connection request policy must be created. The connection request policy is configured to forward requests to the RADIUS servers of the private organization based on the name of the private organization in the realm portion of the wireless client's account name.

Authenticated connections for wireless clients that are customers of the WISP will use the default connection request policy named Use Windows Authentication For All Users.

▶ **To configure a connection request policy for unauthenticated access**

1. From the console tree of the Internet Authentication Service snap-in, open Connection Request Processing, right-click Connection Request Policies, and then click New Connection Request Policy.

2. On the Welcome To The New Connection Request Policy Wizard page, click Next.

3. On the Policy Configuration Method page, select A Custom Policy and type the name of the policy in Policy Name.

4. Click Next. On the Policy Conditions page, click Add.

5. In Select Attribute, click Day And Time Restrictions and then click Add.

6. In Time of Day Constraints, click Permitted, and then click OK. Click Next.

7. On the Request Processing Method page, click Edit Profile.

8. On the Authentication tab, click Accept Users Without Validating Credentials.

9. On the Advanced tab, add the desired RADIUS attributes and configure their values for the method used to provide access to the alternate subnet. For example, WISPs commonly use either packet filtering or virtual LANs.

10. On the Edit Profile page, click OK.

11. On the Request Processing Method page, click Next.

12. On the Completing The New Connection Request Processing Policy Wizard page, click Finish.

13. If the WISP IAS RADIUS proxy computers are only acting as RADIUS proxies and not as RADIUS servers, right-click the connection request policy named Use Windows Authentication For All Users in the details pane and then click Delete. In Delete Connection Request Policy, click Yes.

▶ **To configure a connection request policy for a service provider**

1. From the console tree of the Internet Authentication Service snap-in, open Connection Request Processing, right-click Connection Request Policies, and then click New Connection Request Policy.

2. On the Welcome To The New Connection Request Policy Wizard page, click Next.

3. On the Policy Configuration Method page, select A Typical Policy For A Common Scenario and type the name of the policy in Policy Name.

4. Click Next. On the Request Authentication page, click Forward Connection Requests To A Remote RADIUS Server For Authentication.

5. Click Next. On the Realm Name page, type the realm name for the service provider in Realm Name and clear the Before Authentication, Remove Realm Name From The User Name check box.

6. Click New Group.

7. On the Welcome To The New Remote RADIUS Server Group Wizard page, click Next.

8. On the Group Configuration Method page, type the name of the remote RADIUS server group in Group Name.

9. Click Next. On the Add Servers page, type the IP address or DNS domain name of the service provider's primary RADIUS server in Primary Server, the IP address or DNS domain name of the service provider's secondary RADIUS server in Backup Server, and the RADIUS shared secret in both Shared Secret and Confirm Shared Secret.

10. Click Next. On the Completing The New Remote RADIUS Server Group Wizard page, click Finish.

11. On the Realm Name page, click Next.

12. On the Completing The New Connection Request Processing Policy Wizard, click Finish.

▶ **To configure a connection request policy for a private organization**

1. From the console tree of the Internet Authentication Service snap-in, open Connection Request Processing, right-click Connection Request Policies, and then click New Connection Request Policy.

2. On the Welcome To The New Connection Request Policy Wizard page, click Next.

3. On the Policy Configuration Method page, select A Typical Policy For A Common Scenario and type the name of the policy in Policy Name.

4. Click Next. On the Request Authentication page, click Forward Connection Requests To A Remote RADIUS Server For Authentication.

5. Click Next. On the Realm Name page, type the realm name for the private organization in Realm Name and clear the Before Authentication, Remove Realm Name From The User Name check box.

6. Click New Group.

7. On the Welcome to the New Remote RADIUS Server Group Wizard page, click Next.

8. On the Group Configuration Method Page, type the name of the remote RADIUS server group in Group Name.

9. Click Next. On the Add Servers page, type the IP address or DNS domain name of the private organization's primary RADIUS server or proxy in Primary Server, the IP address or DNS domain name of the private organization's secondary RADIUS server or proxy in Backup Server, and the RADIUS shared secret in both Shared Secret and Confirm Shared Secret.

10. Click Next. On the Completing The New Remote RADIUS Server Group Wizard page, click Finish.

11. On the Realm Name page, click Next.

12. On the Completing The New Connection Request Processing Policy Wizard, click Finish.

Configuring the Secondary IAS RADIUS Proxy

To install IAS, use the IAS installation procedure found in the "Configuring the Primary IAS RADIUS Proxy" section of this chapter. Like the primary IAS RADIUS proxy, the secondary IAS RADIUS proxy does not have to belong to a domain or be registered in any domains because it is not performing authentication and authorization. It can be a standalone server.

▶ **To copy the configuration of the primary IAS RADIUS proxy to the secondary IAS RADIUS proxy**

1. On the primary IAS RADIUS proxy computer, type **netsh aaaa show config > *path\file*.txt** at a command prompt. This command stores the configuration settings, including registry settings, in a text file. The path can be a relative, absolute, or network path.

2. Copy the file created in step 1 to the secondary IAS RADIUS proxy.

3. On the secondary IAS RADIUS proxy computer, type **netsh exec *path\file*.txt** at a command prompt. This command imports all the settings configured on the primary IAS RADIUS proxy into the secondary IAS RADIUS proxy.

Best Practices   If you change the IAS server configuration in any way, use the Internet Authentication Service snap-in to change the configuration of the IAS RADIUS proxy that is designated as the primary configuration server and then use this procedure to synchronize those changes on the secondary IAS RADIUS proxy.

Service Provider Configuration

The service provider can use IAS as a RADIUS server if the service provider is using a Windows NT Server 4.0 domain, an Active Directory directory service domain, or the local Security Accounts Manager (SAM) as the user account database for its customers.

Figure 13-2 shows the configuration of the service provider that is using IAS RADIUS servers.

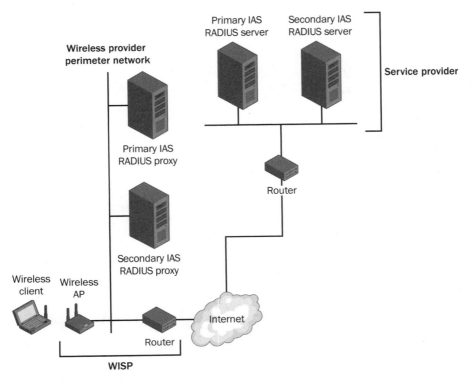

Figure 13-2. *Using IAS RADIUS servers at the service provider.*

To configure the primary and secondary IAS RADIUS server of the service provider to allow wireless access at the WISP for its customers, see Chapter 8 (for EAP-TLS authentication) or Chapter 10 (for PEAP-MS-CHAP v2 authentication).

Private Organization Configuration

The configuration of the RADIUS components in the private organization depends on whether RADIUS servers or RADIUS proxies are placed in the perimeter network.

Using IAS RADIUS Servers

The recommended configuration of IAS RADIUS servers in the perimeter network is that they have two network adapters—one attached to the Internet and one attached to the intranet. This configuration is recommended because it greatly simplifies packet filter configuration on the intranet firewall. Because the IAS RADIUS servers that are already attached to the intranet send their traffic directly to the intranet domain controllers, additional packet filters on the intranet firewall are not needed.

Figure 13-3 shows the configuration of the private organization when using IAS RADIUS servers on the perimeter network.

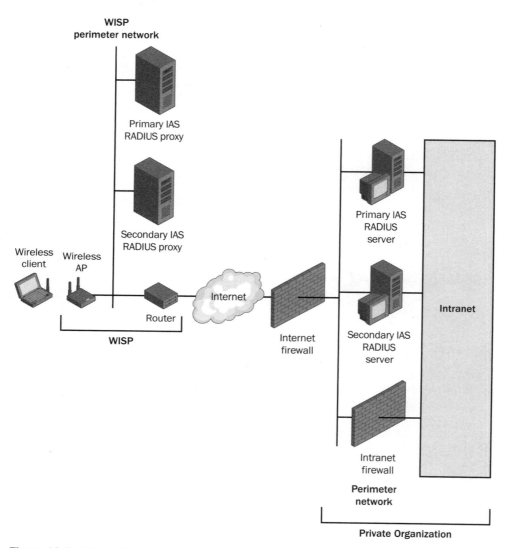

Figure 13-3. *Using IAS RADIUS servers on the perimeter network.*

The IAS RADIUS servers have two network adapters installed, but do not have routing enabled. It is not possible to use an IAS RADIUS server on the perimeter network as a router to reach the intranet. The RADIUS traffic that is received on the perimeter network interface of the IAS RADIUS server is sent to the destination address of the IAS RADIUS server. When it is received, the IAS RADIUS server contacts a domain controller on the intranet to verify credentials and obtain account properties.

Configuring Primary and Secondary IAS Servers on the Perimeter Network

To configure the primary and secondary IAS servers on the perimeter network to allow wireless access, see either Chapter 8 (for EAP-TLS authentication) or Chapter 10 (for PEAP-MS-CHAP v2 authentication). The RADIUS clients of the primary and secondary IAS RADIUS servers are the primary and secondary IAS RADIUS proxies of the WISP.

The primary and secondary IAS RADIUS servers on the perimeter network must be configured with additional routes to make the locations on the intranet reachable. Because the primary and secondary IAS RADIUS servers are connected to the Internet via the perimeter network interface, it must be configured with a default gateway; the IP address of the Internet firewall's perimeter network interface. The configuration of the default gateway creates a default route on the primary and secondary IAS RADIUS servers that effectively summarizes all the locations on the Internet. Because you cannot use multiple default gateways and you must be able to reach any Internet location, you cannot configure the intranet interface of the primary and secondary IAS RADIUS servers with a default gateway. Therefore, in order for the locations of the intranet to be reachable, you must configure the primary and secondary IAS RADIUS servers with a set of routes that summarizes all the locations of your intranet. For each route, use the **route add** *destination* **mask** *netmask gateway* **–p** command to add the route to the IP routing table of both the primary and secondary IAS RADIUS servers. For more information about the route command parameters, type **route add** at a command prompt.

Configuring Firewall Packet Filters

The Internet firewall must be configured with the appropriate packet filters to allow traffic to be exchanged between WISP RADIUS proxies and the IAS RADIUS servers. Because the IAS RADIUS servers are using their intranet interfaces to communicate with the domain controllers of the intranet, additional intranet firewall packet filters are not needed.

Internet Firewall Packet Filters   The following packet filters must be configured on the Internet firewall:

- For the input filters of the Internet interface and the output filters of the perimeter network interface, configure the following:

  - A packet filter that allows packets with the destination IP address set to the perimeter network IP address of the primary IAS RADIUS server and the destination UDP port set to 1812 (or an alternate UDP port used for RADIUS authentication traffic).

  - A packet filter that allows packets with the destination IP address set to the perimeter network IP address of the primary IAS RADIUS server and the destination UDP port set to 1813 (or an alternate UDP port used for RADIUS accounting traffic).

- A packet filter that allows packets with the destination IP address set to the perimeter network IP address of the secondary IAS RADIUS server and the destination UDP port set to 1812 (or an alternate UDP port used for RADIUS authentication traffic).

- A packet filter that allows packets with the destination IP address set to the perimeter network IP address of the secondary IAS RADIUS server and the destination UDP port set to 1813 (or an alternate UDP port used for RADIUS accounting traffic).

- For the output filters of the Internet interface and the input filters of the perimeter network interface, configure the following:

  - A packet filter that allows packets with the source IP address set to the perimeter network IP address of the primary IAS RADIUS server and the source UDP port set to 1812 (or an alternate UDP port used for RADIUS authentication traffic).

  - A packet filter that allows packets with the source IP address set to the perimeter network IP address of the primary IAS RADIUS server and the source UDP port set to 1813 (or an alternate UDP port used for RADIUS accounting traffic).

  - A packet filter that allows packets with the source IP address set to the perimeter network IP address of the secondary IAS RADIUS server and the source UDP port set to 1812 (or an alternate UDP port used for RADIUS authentication traffic).

  - A packet filter that allows packets with the source IP address set to the perimeter network IP address of the secondary IAS RADIUS server and the source UDP port set to 1813 (or an alternate UDP port used for RADIUS accounting traffic).

Using IAS RADIUS Proxies

The configuration of the RADIUS components and firewall packet filters when using IAS RADIUS proxies in the perimeter network depends on whether the IAS RADIUS proxies have a single network adapter attached to the perimeter network or two network adapters—one attached to the Internet and one attached to the intranet. Either configuration is possible because the traffic from the IAS RADIUS proxies to the IAS RADIUS servers on the intranet can be easily specified, unlike the configuration in which IAS RADIUS servers with a single network adapter are located in the perimeter network.

Figure 13-4 shows the configuration of the private organization when using IAS RADIUS proxies in the perimeter network.

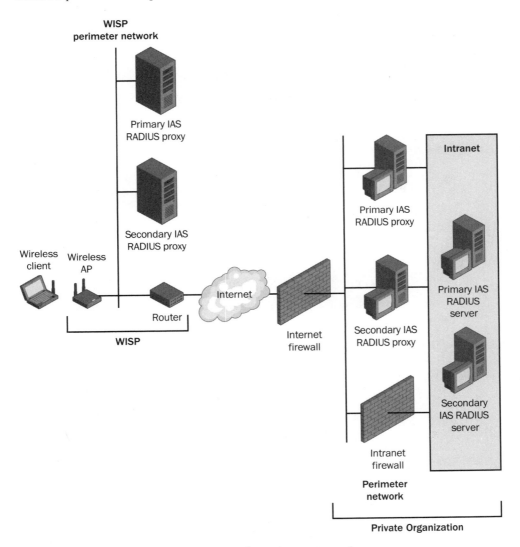

Figure 13-4. *Using IAS RADIUS proxies in the perimeter network.*

In the latter configuration, the IAS RADIUS proxies have two network adapters, but routing is not enabled. It is not possible to use an IAS RADIUS proxy on the perimeter network as a router to reach the intranet. The RADIUS traffic that is received on the perimeter network interface of the IAS RADIUS proxy is sent to the destination address of the IAS RADIUS proxy. When it is received, the IAS RADIUS proxy creates a new RADIUS message that is sent to an IAS RADIUS server on the intranet using the intranet interface.

Configuring the Primary IAS RADIUS Proxy on the Perimeter Network

To configure the primary IAS proxy on the perimeter network, follow the steps in the "Installing IAS and Configuring IAS Server Properties" section of this chapter. Next, you must configure the primary IAS proxy with RADIUS clients that correspond to the WISP primary and secondary IAS RADIUS proxies.

For the steps to configure RADIUS clients, see "Configuring the Primary IAS RADIUS Proxy with RADIUS Clients" in this chapter. Next, you must configure a connection request policy that forwards RADIUS messages to the IAS RADIUS servers on the intranet.

▶ **To configure a connection request policy to forward RADIUS messages to the IAS RADIUS servers on the intranet**

1. In the console tree of the Internet Authentication Service snap-in, double-click Connection Request Processing, right-click Connection Request Policies, and then click New Connection Request Policy.

2. On the Welcome To The New Connection Request Policy Wizard page, click Next.

3. On the Policy Configuration Method page, select A Typical Policy For A Common Scenario and type the name of the policy in Policy Name.

4. Click Next. On the Request Authentication page, click Forward Connection Requests to a Remote RADIUS Server for Authentication.

5. Click Next. On the Realm Name page, type the realm name for the private organization in Realm Name and clear the Before Authentication, Remove Realm Name From The User Name check box.

6. Click New Group.

7. On the Welcome To The New Remote RADIUS Server Group Wizard page, click Next.

8. On the Group Configuration Method Page, type the name of the remote RADIUS server group in Group Name.

9. Click Next. On the Add Servers page, type the IP address or DNS domain name of the primary IAS RADIUS server on the intranet in Primary Server, the IP address or DNS domain name of the secondary IAS RADIUS server on the intranet in Backup Server, and the RADIUS shared secret in both Shared Secret and Confirm Shared Secret. Click Next.

10. On the Completing The New Remote RADIUS Server Group Wizard page, click Finish.

11. On the Realm Name page, click Next.

12. On the Completing the New Connection Request Processing Policy Wizard, click Finish.

13. In the details pane, right-click the connection request policy named Use Windows Authentication For All Users and then click Delete. In Delete Connection Request Policy, click Yes.

The primary IAS RADIUS proxy on the perimeter network must be configured with additional routes to make the locations on the intranet reachable. For the set of routes that summarizes all of the locations of your intranet, use the **route add *destination* mask *netmask gateway* –p** command to add each route to the IP routing table of the primary IAS RADIUS proxy.

Configuring the Secondary IAS RADIUS Proxy on the Perimeter Network

After the primary IAS RADIUS server is configured, install IAS on the secondary IAS RADIUS proxy computer and copy the configuration of the primary IAS RADIUS proxy by using the steps described in the "Configuring the Secondary IAS RADIUS Proxy" section of this chapter.

For the set of routes that summarizes all the locations of your intranet, use the **route add *destination* mask *netmask gateway* –p** command to add each route to the IP routing table of the secondary IAS RADIUS proxy.

Configuring Primary and Secondary IAS Servers on the Intranet

To configure the primary and secondary IAS servers on the intranet to allow wireless access, see either Chapter 8 (for EAP-TLS authentication) or Chapter 10 (for PEAP-MS-CHAP v2 authentication). This configuration is the same regardless of whether the IAS RADIUS proxies on the perimeter network have one or two network adapters.

Configuring Firewall Packet Filters

The Internet and intranet firewalls must be configured with the correct packet filters that allow traffic to be exchanged between:

- The WISP IAS RADIUS proxies and the private organization's IAS RADIUS proxies (the Internet firewall) in the perimeter network.

- The private organization's IAS RADIUS proxies in the perimeter network and the IAS RADIUS servers located on the intranet (the intranet firewall).

Internet Firewall Packet Filters   Regardless of whether the IAS RADIUS proxies have one or two network adapters, the following packet filters must be configured on the Internet firewall:

- For the input filters of the Internet interface and the output filters of the perimeter network interface, configure the following:

  - A packet filter that allows packets with the destination IP address set to the perimeter network IP address of the primary IAS RADIUS proxy and the destination UDP port set to 1812 (or an alternate UDP port used for RADIUS authentication traffic).

- A packet filter that allows packets with the destination IP address set to the perimeter network IP address of the primary IAS RADIUS proxy and the destination UDP port set to 1813 (or an alternate UDP port used for RADIUS accounting traffic).

- A packet filter that allows packets with the destination IP address set to the perimeter network IP address of the secondary IAS RADIUS proxy and the destination UDP port set to 1812 (or an alternate UDP port used for RADIUS authentication traffic).

- A packet filter that allows packets with the destination IP address set to the perimeter network IP address of the secondary IAS RADIUS proxy and the destination UDP port set to 1813 (or an alternate UDP port used for RADIUS accounting traffic).

- For the output filters of the Internet interface and the input filters of the perimeter network interface, configure the following:

  - A packet filter that allows packets with the source IP address set to the perimeter network IP address of the primary IAS RADIUS proxy and the source UDP port set to 1812 (or an alternate UDP port used for RADIUS authentication traffic).

  - A packet filter that allows packets with the source IP address set to the perimeter network IP address of the primary IAS RADIUS proxy and the source UDP port set to 1813 (or an alternate UDP port used for RADIUS accounting traffic).

  - A packet filter that allows packets with the source IP address set to the perimeter network IP address of the secondary IAS RADIUS proxy and the source UDP port set to 1812 (or an alternate UDP port used for RADIUS authentication traffic).

  - A packet filter that allows packets with the source IP address set to the perimeter network IP address of the secondary IAS RADIUS proxy and the source UDP port set to 1813 (or an alternate UDP port used for RADIUS accounting traffic).

Intranet Firewall Packet Filters The configuration of packet filters on the intranet firewall depends on whether the IAS RADIUS proxies have one network adapter or two. If the IAS RADIUS proxies have two network adapters, the intranet firewall does not need to be configured with additional packet filters because the RADIUS traffic is sent directly to the intranet IAS RADIUS server by the IAS RADIUS proxies using their intranet interfaces.

If the IAS RADIUS proxies have only a single network adapter, the intranet firewall must be configured with the following packet filters:

- For the input filters of the perimeter network interface and the output filters of the intranet interface, configure the following:

  - A packet filter that allows packets with the source IP address set to the perimeter network IP address of the primary IAS RADIUS proxy, the destination IP address set to the primary IAS RADIUS server, and the destination UDP port set to 1812 (or an alternate UDP port used for RADIUS authentication traffic).

  - A packet filter that allows packets with the source IP address set to the perimeter network IP address of the primary IAS RADIUS proxy, the destination IP address set to the secondary IAS RADIUS server, and the destination UDP port set to 1812 (or an alternate UDP port used for RADIUS authentication traffic).

  - A packet filter that allows packets with the source IP address set to the perimeter network IP address of the primary IAS RADIUS proxy, the destination IP address set to the primary IAS RADIUS server, and the destination UDP port set to 1813 (or an alternate UDP port used for RADIUS accounting traffic).

  - A packet filter that allows packets with the source IP address set to the perimeter network IP address of the primary IAS RADIUS proxy, the destination IP address set to the secondary IAS RADIUS server, and the destination UDP port set to 1813 (or an alternate UDP port used for RADIUS accounting traffic).

  - A packet filter that allows packets with the source IP address set to the perimeter network IP address of the secondary IAS RADIUS proxy, the destination IP address set to the primary IAS RADIUS server, and the destination UDP port set to 1812 (or an alternate UDP port used for RADIUS authentication traffic).

  - A packet filter that allows packets with the source IP address set to the perimeter network IP address of the secondary IAS RADIUS proxy, the destination IP address set to the secondary IAS RADIUS server, and the destination UDP port set to 1812 (or an alternate UDP port used for RADIUS authentication traffic).

  - A packet filter that allows packets with the source IP address set to the perimeter network IP address of the secondary IAS RADIUS proxy, the destination IP address set to the primary IAS RADIUS server, and the destination UDP port set to 1813 (or an alternate UDP port used for RADIUS accounting traffic).

- A packet filter that allows packets with the source IP address set to the perimeter network IP address of the secondary IAS RADIUS proxy, the destination IP address set to the secondary IAS RADIUS server, and the destination UDP port set to 1813 (or an alternate UDP port used for RADIUS accounting traffic).

- For the output filters of the perimeter network interface and the input filters of the intranet interface, configure the following:

  - A packet filter that allows packets with the destination IP address set to the perimeter network IP address of the primary IAS RADIUS proxy, the source IP address set to the primary IAS RADIUS server, and the source UDP port set to 1812 (or an alternate UDP port used for RADIUS authentication traffic).

  - A packet filter that allows packets with the destination IP address set to the perimeter network IP address of the primary IAS RADIUS proxy, the source IP address set to the secondary IAS RADIUS server, and the source UDP port set to 1812 (or an alternate UDP port used for RADIUS authentication traffic).

  - A packet filter that allows packets with the destination IP address set to the perimeter network IP address of the primary IAS RADIUS proxy, the source IP address set to the primary IAS RADIUS server, and the source UDP port set to 1813 (or an alternate UDP port used for RADIUS accounting traffic).

  - A packet filter that allows packets with the destination IP address set to the perimeter network IP address of the primary IAS RADIUS proxy, the source IP address set to the secondary IAS RADIUS server, and the source UDP port set to 1813 (or an alternate UDP port used for RADIUS accounting traffic).

  - A packet filter that allows packets with the destination IP address set to the perimeter network IP address of the secondary IAS RADIUS proxy, the source IP address set to the primary IAS RADIUS server, and the source UDP port set to 1812 (or an alternate UDP port used for RADIUS authentication traffic).

  - A packet filter that allows packets with the destination IP address set to the perimeter network IP address of the secondary IAS RADIUS proxy, the source IP address set to the secondary IAS RADIUS server, and the source UDP port set to 1812 (or an alternate UDP port used for RADIUS authentication traffic).

  - A packet filter that allows packets with the destination IP address set to the perimeter network IP address of the secondary IAS RADIUS proxy, the source IP address set to the primary IAS RADIUS server, and the source UDP port set to 1813 (or an alternate UDP port used for RADIUS accounting traffic).

- A packet filter that allows packets with the destination IP address set to the perimeter network IP address of the secondary IAS RADIUS proxy, the source IP address set to the secondary IAS RADIUS server, and the source UDP port set to 1813 (or an alternate UDP port used for RADIUS accounting traffic).

Summary

Deploying an IAS-based RADIUS infrastructure for a wireless public place deployment consists of configuring RADIUS components at the WISP, the service provider, and the private organization. At the WISP, IAS RADIUS proxies are configured with RADIUS clients (the wireless APs) and with a set of connection request policies to provide unauthenticated access and to forward RADIUS traffic to RADIUS components at each service provider and private organization. At the service provider, IAS RADIUS servers provide authentication and authorization of wireless client access for the WISP. At the private organization, you can use either IAS RADIUS servers or IAS RADIUS proxies in your perimeter network. IAS RADIUS proxies in the perimeter network forward the RADIUS messages from the WISP to IAS RADIUS servers in the intranet.

Part III
Troubleshooting Wireless Networks

Chapter 14
Troubleshooting the Windows Wireless Client

When troubleshooting wireless connectivity, it is important to first determine whether some or all of your wireless clients are experiencing problems. If *all* of your wireless clients are experiencing problems, issues may exist in your authentication infrastructure. If *some* of your wireless clients are experiencing problems, issues may exist for your wireless access points (APs) or individual wireless clients.

In this chapter, we examine the troubleshooting tools of Microsoft Windows wireless clients to gather troubleshooting information and the common problems that can occur when obtaining authenticated wireless access for individual Windows wireless clients.

Troubleshooting Tools

The tools for troubleshooting wireless connections on Windows wireless clients are the following:

- **Network Connections folder**   The Network Connections folder is used to determine the status of the connection and its configuration.

- **Tracing**   Tracing is used to obtain detailed information of the behavior of internal components that perform Extensible Authentication Protocol (EAP) and 802.1X authentication.

- **Network Monitor**   Network Monitor is used to capture the network traffic sent between a wireless client and the wireless AP or another wireless client.

- **Wireless Monitor snap-in**   The Wireless Monitor snap-in, provided only with Windows Server 2003, is used to view available wireless APs and wireless client events.

Network Connections Folder

The Network Connections folder and the messages displayed in the notification area of the desktop provide information about the state of the authentication. If an authentication requires additional information from the user, such as selecting one of multiple user certificates, a text balloon appears that instructs the user. Within the Network Connections folder, the text under the name of the connection corresponding to the wireless network adapter describes the state of the authentication.

Figure 14-1 shows the information available for a successfully authenticated wireless connection in the Windows XP Network Connections folder.

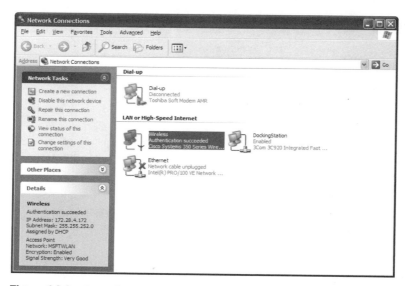

Figure 14-1. *A wireless network connection in the Network Connections folder.*

For Windows XP wireless clients, when you click the wireless connection, the Details area displays the authentication status, the Internet Protocol (IP) address configuration, and information about the connected wireless network and the current association.

When you obtain status on the connection, you can view information such as the signal speed on the General tab and the IP address configuration on the Support tab. If the wireless adapter is assigned an Automatic Private IP Addressing (APIPA) address in the range 169.254.0.0/16 or the configured alternate IP address, the wireless client is still associated with the wireless AP, but either authentication has failed or the Dynamic Host Configuration Protocol (DHCP) server is not available. If the authentication fails and the association is still in place, the wireless adapter is enabled and Transmission Control Protocol/Internet Protocol (TCP/IP) performs its normal configuration process. If a DHCP server is not found (either authenticated or not), Windows XP automatically configures an APIPA address or the alternate address.

For a Windows 2000 wireless client, you can use the Network And Dial-up Connections folder to view whether the connection corresponding to your wireless network adapter is authenticated. If authentication is successful, the connection icon appears normal. If authentication has failed, the connection icon has a red X through it. To view the IP address configuration of the connection corresponding to the wireless network adapter, type **ipconfig** at a command prompt.

Tracing

Windows XP, Windows Server 2003, and Windows 2000 have an extensive tracing capability that you can use to troubleshoot complex problems for specific components. The information in tracing files is typically useful only to Microsoft support engineers, who might request that you create trace files for a connection attempt during their investigation of a support issue. You can enable the components in Windows to log tracing information to files using the **netsh** command for specific components or for all components.

To enable and disable tracing for a specific component, the command is

netsh ras set tracing *component* **enabled | disabled**

in which *component* is a component in the list of components found in the registry under HKEY_LOCAL_MACHINE\SOFTWARE\Microsoft\Tracing. For example, to enable tracing for the IASRAD component, the command is

netsh ras set tracing iasrad enabled

To enable tracing for all components, the command is

netsh ras set tracing * enabled

Enabling tracing for all components produces a lot of log files for processes that are not related to wireless authentication, and can consume system resources. To obtain detailed information about the EAP authentication process for Windows XP or Windows Server 2003, enable tracing for just the EAP over LAN (EAPOL) and RASTLS components.

To enable tracing for EAPOL, the command is

netsh ras set tracing eapol enabled

To enable tracing for RASTLS, the command is

netsh ras set tracing rastls enabled

After these commands are issued, try the authentication process again and view the Eapol.log and Rastls.log files in the *SystemRoot*\Tracing folder.

To disable tracing for EAPOL and RASTLS, the respective commands are

netsh ras set tracing eapol disabled

netsh ras set tracing rastls disabled

To obtain detailed information about the EAP authentication process for Windows 2000, enable tracing for the RASTLS component.

Microsoft Network Monitor

You can use Microsoft Network Monitor, available in Microsoft Systems Management Server or the Windows 2000 Server and Windows Server 2003 families, or a commercial packet analyzer (also known as a network sniffer), to capture and view the authentication and data traffic sent and received by the wireless network adapter. Network Monitor includes 802.1X, EAPOL, and EAP parsers. A *parser* is a component included with Network Monitor that can separate the fields of a protocol header and display their structure and values. Without a parser, Network Monitor displays the hexadecimal bytes of a header, which you must parse manually.

For Windows wireless client authentications, you can use Network Monitor to capture the set of frames exchanged between the wireless client computer and the wireless AP during the wireless authentication process. You can then use Network Monitor to view the individual frames and determine why the authentication failed.

In the Windows 2000 Server and Windows Server 2003 families, Network Monitor is installed as an optional management and monitoring tool using Control Panel's Add/Remove Programs. Once installed, you can run Network Monitor from the Administrative Tools folder.

Figure 14-2 shows an example of the display of an EAP message in Network Monitor for an EAP-Transport Layer Security (EAP-TLS)-based wireless authentication.

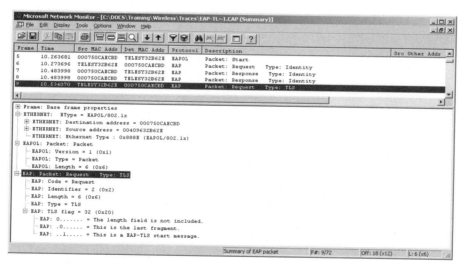

Figure 14-2. *Example of an EAP message in Network Monitor.*

Wireless Monitor Snap-in

For Windows Server 2003-based wireless clients, you can use the new Wireless Monitor snap-in to view wireless AP or wireless client information.

To add the Wireless Monitor snap-in to a console, do the following:

1. Click Start, click Run, type **mmc**, and then click OK.

2. Click File, click Add/Remove Snap-in, and then click Add.

3. In the Add Standalone Snap-In dialog box, click Wireless Monitor and then click Add.

4. Click Close and then click OK.

There are two main screens of information in the Wireless Monitor snap-in:

- Access Point Information

- Wireless Client Information

When you click Access Point Information in the console tree, the wireless network adapter scans for the available wireless APs within range and then displays them in the details pane, as shown in Figure 14-3.

Figure 14-3. *Wireless AP information in the Wireless Monitor snap-in.*

You can use the list of wireless APs to determine the visibility and parameters (such as signal strength, channel, and data rates) of specific wireless APs for a given location.

When you click Wireless Client Information in the console tree, the list of wireless events for the Wireless Zero Configuration (WZC) service and the EAPOL component displays in the details pane, as shown in Figure 14-4.

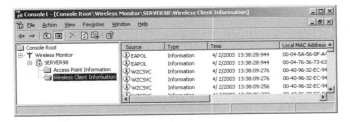

Figure 14-4. *Wireless client information in the Wireless Monitor snap-in.*

You can use these events to determine how the WZC service chooses to connect to a specific wireless AP and explore the details of the authentication process.

Common Connectivity and Authentication Problems

The following are some common problems with wireless connectivity and authentication that are encountered by a Windows wireless client:

- **Wireless network is not found.** If you have configured your wireless APs to suppress the beaconing of the Service Set Identifier (SSID), also known as the wireless network name, the WZC service cannot automatically connect to the wireless network. You must manually create a preferred wireless network with the correct SSID and associated settings. After the wireless network is created and added to your list of preferred networks, the wireless client should automatically connect.

  Verify that you are within range of the wireless AP for the wireless network by using tools provided by the wireless adapter vendor or (for Windows Server 2003) the Wireless Monitor snap-in. You can move the wireless AP or the wireless client, adjust the transmission power level on the wireless AP, or reposition or remove sources of radio frequency attenuation or interference.

- **The message "Windows Was Unable To Find A Certificate To Log You On To The Network" is displayed in the notification area.** The most typical cause for this message is that you do not have either a user or computer certificate installed. Depending on the registry value of HKEY_LOCAL_MACHINE\Software\Microsoft\EAPOL\Parameters\General \Global\AuthMode, you might need to have both installed. Verify that you have a computer certificate, a user certificate, or both installed using the Certificates snap-in.

  Another possible cause for this message is that you have certificates installed, but they either cannot be used for wireless authentication, or they cannot be validated by all of your Internet Authentication Service (IAS) Remote Authentication Dial-In User Service (RADIUS) servers. User and computer certificates must have a valid range of dates, must not be revoked, must have the Client Authentication purpose in the Enhanced Key Usage (EKU) field of the certificate, and must have the user principal name (UPN) of a valid user account or fully qualified domain name (FQDN) of valid computer account for the Subject Alternative Name field of the certificate. Additionally, verify that the root certification authority (CA) for the issuing CA of the user and computer certificates is installed in the Trusted Root Certification Authorities Local Computer store on each IAS RADIUS server.

- **Wireless network adapter seems stuck attempting to authenticate.** For EAP-TLS authentication with Windows XP (prior to SP1) wireless clients, if the wireless client is validating the server certificate (enabled by default) and the Connect If The Server Name Ends With string on the Smart Card And

Other Certificate Properties dialog box is incorrect, authentication will fail. To view the Smart Card And Other Certificate Properties dialog box, obtain properties of the network connection that corresponds to the wireless LAN network adapter, click the Authentication tab, and then click Properties.

For Windows XP (SP1 and later), Windows Server 2003, and Windows 2000 with the Microsoft 802.1X Authentication Client, you can specify the names of the servers that must authenticate the wireless client in Connect To These Servers, from the Smart Card Or Other Certificate EAP Properties dialog box. To view the Smart Card And Other Certificate Properties dialog box, obtain properties of the wireless network, click the Authentication tab, and then click Properties. The names of the servers must match the names of the authenticating servers, or authentication will fail.

Summary

The tools for troubleshooting wireless connection problems for an individual Windows wireless client consist of the Network Connections folder, tracing, Network Monitor, and the Wireless Monitor snap-in. Common problems for the Windows wireless client are the inability to find the correct wireless network, lack of a proper certificate, or misconfiguration of the server names from which the wireless client will accept certificates.

Chapter 15
Troubleshooting the Wireless AP

If you have multiple wireless access points (APs) and are unable to connect or authenticate with one of them, you might have a problem with that specific wireless AP. In this chapter, we examine the common troubleshooting tools of wireless APs and the common problems of connecting and authenticating with a wireless AP.

Wireless AP Troubleshooting Tools

Although the set of troubleshooting tools for wireless APs varies with each manufacturer and with each model, some of the more common troubleshooting tools are the following:

- Panel indicators

- Site survey software

- SNMP support

- Diagnostics

These tools are described in the following sections. Consult your wireless AP documentation for information about the set of troubleshooting tools provided with your wireless AP.

Panel Indicators

Most wireless APs have one or more indicators, status lights that are visible on the housing of the wireless AP, from which you can obtain a quick assessment of the wireless AP's hardware status. For example, you might see the following:

- An indicator to show that the wireless AP has electrical power.

- An indicator to show general operation status. For example, the indicator might show whether the wireless AP is associated with any wireless clients.

- An indicator to show wireless network traffic. This indicator might blink for each frame received on the wireless network.

- An indicator to show data collisions. If the blinking of this indicator seems excessive, evaluate the performance of the link using the methods suggested by the wireless AP vendor.

- An indicator to show wired network traffic. This indicator might blink for each frame received on the wired network.

Alternately, the wireless AP might have a liquid crystal display (LCD) panel that shows icons indicating its current status. Consult your wireless AP documentation for information about panel indicators and their interpretation.

Site Survey Software

Site survey software, which you use during the deployment of wireless APs to determine their optimal placement, is typically installed on a wireless-capable laptop computer from a CD-ROM provided by the wireless AP or wireless network adapter vendor.

As described in Chapter 7, "Wireless AP Placement," the site survey software is used to determine the coverage volume and where the data rate changes for each wireless AP. If wireless clients cannot connect to a specific wireless AP, use the site survey software to perform a site survey for that wireless AP. There might have been a change in the devices that create interference and objects that interfere with signal propagation since the original site survey and AP placement was done.

SNMP Support

Many wireless APs include a Simple Network Management Protocol (SNMP) agent with support for the following SNMP Management Information Bases (MIBs):

- IEEE 802.11 MIB

- IEEE 802.1 PAE (Port Access Entity) MIB

- SNMP Management MIB (described in RFC 1157)

- SNMP MIB II (described in RFC 1213)

- Bridge MIB (described in RFC 1286)

- Ethernet Interface MIB (described in RFC 1398)

- IETF Bridge MIB (described in RFC 1493)

- Remote Monitoring (RMON) MIB (described in RFC 1757)

- RADIUS Client Authentication MIB (described in RFC 2618)

The SNMP agent on the wireless AP can be used in conjunction with your existing SNMP-based network management infrastructure to configure your wireless APs, set trap conditions, and monitor loads on your wireless APs.

Diagnostics

Diagnostics for wireless APs can be of the following forms:

- Diagnostic facilities that are available through the main wireless AP configuration program, such as a Windows program provided on the wireless AP vendor product CD-ROM or a series of Web pages.

- Diagnostic facilities that are available through a command-line tool or facility, such as terminal access to the wireless AP.

The exact diagnostic facilities of a wireless AP vary from one wireless AP to another; however, the purpose of the diagnostics is to ensure that the wireless AP is operating properly (from a hardware standpoint) and to validate its current configuration.

Common Wireless AP Problems

The following are common problems with wireless APs:

- Unable to see the wireless AP.

- Unable to authenticate with the wireless AP.

- Unable to communicate beyond the wireless AP.

These common problems are discussed in detail in the following sections.

Unable to See the Wireless AP

If wireless clients are unable to see the wireless AP in a scan of wireless networks, one or more of the following may be happening.

- **The wireless AP is not beaconing.**   All wireless APs should be sending periodic beacon messages that contain the Service Set Identifier (SSID)—unless the wireless AP has been configured to suppress the SSID in the beacon message—and the wireless AP's capabilities (such as supported bit rates and security options). To verify that the wireless AP is beaconing, you can use the site survey software, the Wireless Monitor snap-in for Microsoft Windows Server 2003, or a packet sniffer that can capture wireless beacon frames. A simple packet sniffer that can capture beacon frames and other types of wireless management frames might be included on the CD-ROM provided by your wireless AP vendor.

Note   Microsoft Network Monitor cannot capture wireless beacon frames.

- **The wireless AP is not configured for the correct channel.**   If the wireless AP is using the same channel as an adjacent wireless AP, signal interference might be impairing the wireless clients' ability to connect. Change the wireless AP channel if needed.

- **The wireless AP is not advertising the correct set of capabilities.** Confirm that the wireless AP is configured to operate for the correct technology (802.11b, 802.11a, or 802.11g) and with the correct bit rates and authentication options, such as Wi-Fi Protected Access (WPA). By capturing the beacon frame with a network sniffer, you can compare the configured wireless options to those being advertised in the beacon frame.

- **The wireless AP has inadequate signal strength in the anticipated coverage volume.** Use your site survey software to confirm that the coverage volume of the wireless AP is that which is described in your plans after initially deploying the wireless APs (as described in Chapter 7). If there are new sources of signal attenuation, reflection, or interference, make the appropriate changes to the locations of either interfering equipment or the wireless AP.

Unable to Authenticate with the Wireless AP

If you have multiple wireless APs, and your wireless clients cannot authenticate with any of them, you might have a problem with your authentication infrastructure. See Chapter 16, "Troubleshooting the Authentication Infrastructure," for instructions on how to troubleshoot this situation. If you have multiple wireless APs, and the wireless clients cannot authenticate with an individual wireless AP, you need to troubleshoot the authentication-related configuration of the wireless AP. The three areas of authentication configuration you need to investigate are as follows:

- 802.1X configuration

- RADIUS configuration

- WPA configuration

802.1X Configuration

Ensure that the wireless AP has 802.1X authentication enabled. Some wireless APs might refer to 802.1X authentication as Extensible Authentication Protocol (EAP) authentication.

RADIUS Configuration

The Remote Authentication Dial-In User Service (RADIUS) configuration consists of the following elements:

- Wireless AP RADIUS configuration

- RADIUS server reachability

- RADIUS server configuration

- Internet Protocol Security (IPSec) for RADIUS traffic

These elements are described in the following sections.

Wireless AP RADIUS Configuration Ensure that the wireless AP has been properly configured for RADIUS. The wireless AP should contain the following configuration information:

- The IP address of a primary RADIUS server

- The destination User Datagram Protocol (UDP) ports for RADIUS traffic sent to the primary RADIUS server (UDP port 1812 for RADIUS authentication traffic and UDP port 1813 for RADIUS accounting traffic)

- The shared secret for the primary RADIUS server

- The IP address of a secondary RADIUS server

- The destination UDP ports for RADIUS traffic sent to the secondary RADIUS server

- The shared secret for the secondary RADIUS server

RADIUS Server Reachability Ensure that the primary and secondary RADIUS servers are reachable from the wireless AP by doing the following:

- If the wireless AP diagnostics has a ping facility—the capability to send an Internet Control Message Protocol (ICMP) Echo message to an arbitrary unicast IP destination—try pinging the IP address of the primary and secondary RADIUS servers.

- If the wireless AP diagnostics does not have a ping facility, try pinging the IP address of the primary and secondary RADIUS servers from a network node that is attached to the same subnet as the wireless AP.

If the ping from the network node succeeds and the ping from the wireless AP does not, examine the IP configuration of the wireless AP to ensure that it has been configured with the correct IP address, subnet mask, and default gateway for the attached wired subnet. If neither ping works, troubleshoot the lack of IP connectivity between the attached subnet and the RADIUS servers.

> **Note** The ping test is not necessarily a definitive test of IP reachability. There might be routers in the path between the wireless AP and the RADIUS server that are filtering ICMP traffic, or the RADIUS server might be configured with packet filters or IPSec to discard ICMP traffic.

To ensure that RADIUS traffic is reaching the primary and secondary RADIUS servers, use a network sniffer such as Network Monitor on the Internet Authentication Service (IAS) RADIUS servers to capture the RADIUS traffic sent from and to the wireless AP during an authentication attempt. For more information about Network Monitor, see Chapter 16.

RADIUS Server Configuration If RADIUS traffic is reaching the primary and secondary IAS RADIUS servers, verify that the primary and secondary IAS RADIUS servers are configured with a RADIUS client that corresponds to the wireless AP, including the following:

- The IP address of the wireless AP's interface on the wired network

- The destination UDP ports for RADIUS traffic sent by the wireless AP (UDP port 1812 for RADIUS authentication traffic and UDP port 1813 for RADIUS accounting traffic)

- The shared secret configured at the wireless AP

Check the system event log for authentication failure events corresponding to connection attempts to the wireless AP. To view the failed authentication events, use the Event Viewer to view the events in the system event log with the Source of IAS and the Event ID of 2.

IPSec for RADIUS Traffic If you are using IPSec to encrypt the RADIUS traffic sent between the wireless AP and the IAS RADIUS server, check the IPSec settings on both the wireless AP and IAS server to ensure that they can successfully negotiate security associations and authenticate each other.

More Info For more information about how to configure IPSec policies in Windows Server 2003 to provide protection for RADIUS traffic, see Help and Support Center for Windows Server 2003. For more information about how to configure IPSec settings for a wireless AP, see your wireless AP's product documentation.

WPA Configuration

If your wireless AP is WPA-capable and you want to use WPA for wireless security, ensure that WPA is enabled. For a Small Office/Home Office (SOHO) configuration using WPA and preshared key authentication, ensure that the correct preshared key is configured.

Unable to Communicate Beyond the Wireless AP

The wireless AP is a transparent bridge and Layer 2 switching device, forwarding packets between the wired network to which it is attached and the connected wireless clients. If wireless clients can connect and authenticate, but cannot reach locations beyond the wireless AP, one or more of the following may be happening.

- **The wireless AP is not forwarding frames as a bridge.** All transparent bridges support the *spanning tree protocol*, which is used to prevent loops in a bridged section of the network. The spanning tree protocol uses a series of multicast messages to communicate bridge configuration information and automatically configure bridge interfaces to forward frames or block forwarding to prevent loops. While the spanning tree algorithm is determining forwarding and blocking interfaces, the bridge is not forwarding frames. Check the wireless AP's forwarding status and bridge configuration.

- **The wireless AP is not configured with the correct virtual LAN identifiers (VLAN IDs).** Many wireless APs support VLANs, a grouping of ports and interfaces so that they appear on the same link or subnet. Each group is assigned a separate VLAN ID. Verify that the VLAN IDs for your wireless client ports and your wired interfaces are correctly configured. For example, you might use one VLAN ID for authenticated wireless clients (that connects them to the organization intranet) and a separate VLAN ID for guest wireless clients (that connects them to an alternate subnet or the Internet).

Summary

The tools for troubleshooting wireless APs commonly consist of panel indicators, site survey software, SNMP support, and on-board diagnostics. If wireless clients cannot see the wireless AP, ensure that the wireless AP is beaconing with the correct information, is configured for the correct channel, and has the correct coverage volume. If wireless clients are unable to authenticate with the wireless AP, verify the configuration of 802.1X, RADIUS, and WPA. If wireless clients are unable to reach locations beyond the wireless AP, verify that the wireless AP is forwarding frames as a bridge and that the VLAN IDs are correctly configured.

Chapter 16
Troubleshooting the Authentication Infrastructure

If you have multiple wireless APs and are unable to authenticate with any of them, then you might have a problem with your authentication infrastructure, which consists of your Internet Authentication Service (IAS) servers, public key infrastructure (PKI), and Active Directory directory service accounts. In this chapter, we examine IAS troubleshooting tools, common issues with IAS authentication and authorization, validation of certificate and password-based authentications, and common problems with obtaining authenticated wireless access.

IAS Troubleshooting Tools

To help you gather information to troubleshoot problems with IAS, the following tools are available:

- IAS event logging and Event Viewer snap-in
- Network Monitor
- SChannel logging
- Tracing
- SNMP agent
- Performance Logs and Alerts snap-in

IAS Event Logging and Event Viewer Snap-In

To troubleshoot IAS authentication attempts using events in the Microsoft Windows event logs, ensure that event logging is enabled for all types of IAS events (such as rejected, discarded, and successful authentication events). Event logging for all these types of events are enabled by default for both Windows Server 2003 IAS and Windows 2000 IAS. For more information, see Chapter 4, "RADIUS, IAS, and Active Directory."

IAS events are stored in the system event log, which can be viewed from the Event Viewer snap-in. Here is an example of the description for a successful authentication event (Source: IAS, Event ID: 1):

```
User client@example.com was granted access.
Fully-Qualified-User-Name = example.com/Users/Client
NAS-IP-Address = 10.7.0.4
NAS-Identifier = <not present>
Client-Friendly-Name = Building 7 Wireless AP
Client-IP-Address = 10.7.0.4
NAS-Port-Type = Wireless-IEEE 802.11
NAS-Port = 6
Policy-Name = Wireless Remote Access Policy
Authentication-Type = EAP
EAP-Type = Smart Card or other Certificate
```

To view the failed authentication events, use the Event Viewer to view the events with the Source of IAS and the Event ID of 2.

Viewing the IAS events in the system event log is one of the most useful troubleshooting tools for obtaining information about failed authentications. The IAS events are also helpful when troubleshooting remote access policies. When you have multiple remote access policies configured, the Policy-Name field in the event description records the name of the remote access policy that either accepted or rejected the connection attempt.

Network Monitor

You can use Microsoft Network Monitor—available in Microsoft Systems Management Server or the Windows 2000 Server and Windows Server 2003 families—or a commercial packet analyzer (also known as a network sniffer) to capture and view RADIUS authentication and accounting messages that are sent to and from an IAS RADIUS server or an IAS RADIUS proxy. Network Monitor includes a RADIUS parser, which you can use to view the attributes of a RADIUS message and troubleshoot connection issues.

Network Monitor is useful for checking to see whether RADIUS messages are being exchanged, and for determining the RADIUS attributes of each message.

SChannel Logging

Secure channel (SChannel) logging is the logging of detailed information for SChannel events in the system event log. By default, only SChannel error messages are recorded. To log errors, warnings, informational, and successful events, set the HKEY_LOCAL_MACHINE\System\CurrentControlSet\Control\SecurityProviders\SCHANNEL\EventLogging registry value to 4 (as a DWORD type). With SChannel logging recording all events, it is possible to obtain more information about the certificate exchange and validation process on the IAS server.

Tracing

As described in Chapter 14, "Troubleshooting the Windows Wireless Client," Windows Server 2003 and Windows 2000 have an extensive tracing capability that creates tracing files that describe the internal behavior of Windows components during the authentication and authorization process. This information is typically useful only to Microsoft support engineers, who might request that you create trace files for a connection attempt during their investigation of a support issue.

You can enable the components in Windows Server 2003 to log tracing information to files by using the **netsh** command for specific components or for all components.

To enable and disable tracing for a specific component, the command is

netsh ras set tracing *component* enabled | disabled

in which *component* is a component in the list of components found in the registry under HKEY_LOCAL_MACHINE\SOFTWARE\Microsoft\Tracing. For example, to enable tracing for the IASRAD component, the command is

netsh ras set tracing iasrad enabled

Although you can enable tracing for individual components of IAS, it is easier to turn tracing on for all the IAS components at once. Microsoft support engineers typically want see all the trace files, rather than the trace file for an individual component. To enable tracing for all components, the command is

netsh ras set tracing * enabled

To disable tracing for all components, the command is

netsh ras set tracing * disabled

The log files that are generated are stored in the *SystemRoot*\tracing folder.

Tip   Tracing consumes system resources and should be used sparingly during the investigation of a support issue. After the trace is done or the problem is identified, you should disable tracing. Do not leave tracing enabled on multiprocessor computers.

SNMP Agent

You can use the Simple Network Management Protocol (SNMP) agent software included with Windows 2000 Server and Windows Server 2003 to monitor status information for your IAS server from an SNMP console. IAS supports the RADIUS Authentication Server MIB (RFC 2619) and the RADIUS Accounting Server MIB (RFC 2621). Use Control Panel-Add/Remove Programs to install the SNMP agent as an optional management and monitoring tool.

The SNMP agent can be used in conjunction with your existing SNMP-based network management infrastructure to monitor your IAS RADIUS servers or proxies.

Performance Logs And Alerts Snap-In

You can use the Performance Logs And Alerts snap-in to monitor counters, create logs, and set alerts for specific IAS components and program processes. You can also use charts and reports to determine how efficiently your server uses IAS and to both identify and troubleshoot potential problems.

You can use the Performance Logs And Alerts snap-in to monitor counters within the following IAS-related performance objects:

- IAS Accounting Clients
- IAS Accounting Proxy
- IAS Accounting Server
- IAS Authentication Clients
- IAS Authentication Proxy
- IAS Authentication Server
- IAS Remote Accounting Servers
- IAS Remote Authentication Servers

For more information about how to use the Performance Logs And Alerts snap-in, see Windows 2000 Server Help or the Help and Support Center for Windows Server 2003.

Troubleshooting IAS Authentication and Authorization

To troubleshoot the most common issues with IAS authentication and authorization, verify the following:

- The wireless AP can reach the IAS servers.

  To test this, try to ping the IP address of the wireless AP's interface on the wired network from each of the IAS servers. Additionally, ensure that Internet Protocol security (IPSec) policies, IP packet filters, and other mechanisms that restrict network traffic are not preventing the exchange of RADIUS messages between the wireless AP and its configured IAS servers. RADIUS traffic to the IAS servers uses a source IP address of the wireless AP, a destination IP address of the IAS server, and a destination User Datagram Protocol (UDP) port of 1812 for authentication messages and destination UDP port 1813 for accounting messages. RADIUS traffic from the IAS servers uses a source IP address of the IAS server, a destination IP address of the wireless AP, and a source UDP port of 1812 for authentication messages and source UDP port 1813 for accounting messages. These examples assume that you are using the RADIUS UDP ports defined in RFC 2865 and 2866 for RADIUS authentication and accounting traffic.

- Each IAS server/wireless AP pair is configured with a common RADIUS shared secret.

  Each IAS server/wireless AP pair does not necessarily have to use a unique RADIUS shared secret, but it must use the same value for the RADIUS shared secret. For example, when you copy the IAS configuration from one IAS server to another, the shared secret must be the same for the IAS server/ wireless AP pair for the IAS server that the configuration is being copied from to each IAS server/wireless AP pair for the IAS servers the configuration is being copied to.

- The IAS servers can reach a global catalog server and an Active Directory domain controller.

  The IAS server uses a global catalog server to resolve the user principal name (UPN) of the computer or user certificate or the Microsoft Challenge Handshake Authentication Protocol version 2 (MS-CHAP v2) account name to the distinguished name of the corresponding account in Active Directory. The IAS server uses an Active Directory domain controller to validate the credentials of the computer and user account and obtain account properties to evaluate authorization.

- The computer accounts of the IAS servers are members of the RAS and IAS Servers security group for the appropriate domains.

  Adding the IAS server computer accounts to the RAS and IAS Servers security group for the appropriate domains is normally done during the initial configuration of the IAS server. To add the IAS server computer account to the appropriate domains, you can use the **netsh ras add registeredserver** command.

- The user or computer account is not locked out, expired, or disabled; or the time the connection is being made corresponds to the permitted logon hours.

- The user account has not been locked out by remote access account lockout.

  Remote access account lockout is an authentication counting and lockout mechanism designed to prevent an online dictionary attack against a user's password. If remote access account lockout is enabled, you can reset account lockout for the account by deleting the HKEY_LOCAL_MACHINE\SYSTEM\CurrentControlSet\Services\Remote-Access\Parameters\AccountLockout*DomainName:AccountName* registry value on the IAS server.

More Info For more information about remote access account lockout, see Chapter 4.

- The connection is authorized. For authorization, the parameters of the connection attempt must:

  - Match all the conditions of at least one remote access policy.

  - Be granted remote access permission through the user account (set to Allow Access), or if the user account has the Control Access Through Remote Access Policy option selected, the remote access permission of the first matching remote access policy must be set to Grant Remote Access Permission.

  - Match all the settings of the profile. Verify that the authentication settings of the profile have EAP-TLS or PEAP-MS-CHAP v2 enabled and properly configured.

  - Match all the settings of the dial-in properties of the user or computer account.

  To obtain the name of the remote access policy that rejected the connection attempt, ensure that IAS event logging is enabled for rejected authentication attempts and use the Event Viewer to view the events that have the Source of IAS and Event ID set to 2. In the text of the event message, look for the remote access policy name in the Policy-Name field.

- If you have just changed your Active Directory domain from mixed-mode to native-mode, IAS servers can no longer authenticate valid connection requests. You must restart every domain controller in the domain in order for the change to replicate.

Troubleshooting Certificate-Based Validation

Troubleshooting certificate validation for EAP-TLS authentication consists of verifying the wireless client's computer and user certificates and the computer certificates of the IAS servers (as discussed in the following sections).

Validating the Wireless Client's Certificate

In order for an IAS server to validate the certificate of a wireless client, the following must be true for each certificate in the certificate chain sent by the wireless client:

- The current date is within the validity dates of the certificate.

  When certificates are issued, they are issued with a range of valid dates, before which they cannot be used and after which they are considered expired.

- The certificate has not been revoked.

  Issued certificates can be revoked at any time. Each issuing certification authority (CA) maintains a list of certificates that should no longer be considered valid by publishing an up-to-date certificate revocation list (CRL). By default, the IAS server checks all the certificates in the wireless client's certificate chain (the series of certificates from the wireless client certificate to the root CA) for revocation. If any of the certificates in the chain have been revoked, certificate validation fails. This behavior can be modified with registry settings described later in this chapter.

  To view the CRL distribution points for a certificate in the Certificates snap-in (as shown in Figure 16-1), double-click the certificate in the contents pane, click the Details tab, and then click the CRL Distribution Points field.

Figure 16-1. *The CRL Distribution Points field.*

  The certificate revocation validation works only as well as the CRL publishing and distribution system. If the CRL is not updated often, a certificate that has been revoked can still be used and considered valid because the published CRL that the IAS server is checking is out of date.

- The certificate has a valid digital signature.

  CAs digitally sign certificates they issue. The IAS server verifies the digital signature of each certificate in the chain (with the exception of the root CA certificate) by obtaining the public key from the certificate's issuing CA and mathematically validating the digital signature.

The wireless client certificate must also have the Client Authentication certificate purpose (also known as Enhanced Key Usage [EKU]) and must contain either a UPN of a valid user account or a fully qualified domain name (FQDN) of a valid computer account in the Subject Alternative Name field of the certificate.

To view the EKU for a certificate in the Certificates snap-in (as shown in Figure 16-2), double-click the certificate in the contents pane, click the Details tab, and then click the Enhanced Key Usage field.

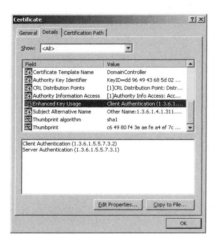

Figure 16-2. *The Enhanced Key Usage field.*

To view the Subject Alternative Name field for a certificate in the Certificates snap-in (as shown in Figure 16-3), double-click the certificate in the contents pane, click the Details tab, and then click the Subject Alternative Name field.

Figure 16-3. *The Subject Alternative Name field.*

Finally, to trust the certificate chain offered by the wireless client, the IAS server must have the root CA certificate of the issuing CA of the wireless client certificate installed in its Trusted Root Certification Authorities Local Computer store.

> **Note** In addition to performing normal certificate validation, the IAS server verifies that the identity sent in the initial EAP-Response/Identity message is the same as the name in the Subject Alternative Name property of the received certificate. This prevents a malicious user from masquerading as a different user or computer from that specified in the EAP-Response/Identity message.

By default, IAS performs certificate revocation checking on the certificate received from the wireless clients. The following registry settings in HKEY_LOCAL_MACHINE\SYSTEM\CurrentControlSet\Services\RasMan\PPP\EAP\13 on the IAS server can modify certificate revocation behavior:

- **IgnoreNoRevocationCheck**   When set to 1, IAS accepts EAP-TLS authentications, even when it does not perform or cannot complete a revocation check of the client's certificate chain (excluding the root certificate). Typically, revocation checks fail because the certificate does not include CRL information.

  IgnoreNoRevocationCheck is set to 0 (disabled) by default. IAS rejects an EAP-TLS authentication unless it can complete a revocation check of the client's certificate chain (including the root certificate) and verify that none of the certificates have been revoked.

  Set IgnoreNoRevocationCheck to 1 to accept EAP-TLS authentications when the certificate does not include CRL distribution points, such as those from third-party CAs.

- **IgnoreRevocationOffline**   When set to 1, IAS accepts EAP-TLS authentications, even when a server that stores a CRL is not available on the network. IgnoreRevocationOffline is set to 0 by default. IAS rejects an EAP-TLS authentication unless it can access CRLs and complete a revocation check of their certificate chain and verify that none of the certificates has been revoked. When it cannot connect to a location that stores a CRL, EAP-TLS considers the certificate to have failed the revocation check.

  Set IgnoreRevocationOffline to 1 to prevent certificate validation failure due to poor network conditions that inhibit revocation checks from completing successfully.

- **NoRevocationCheck**   When set to 1, IAS does not perform a revocation check on the wireless client's certificate. The revocation check verifies that the wireless client's certificate and the certificates in its certificate chain have not been revoked. NoRevocationCheck is set to 0 by default.

- **NoRootRevocationCheck**   When set to 1, IAS does not perform a revocation check of the wireless client's root CA certificate. This entry eliminates only the revocation check of the client's root CA certificate. A revocation check is still performed on the remainder of the wireless client's certificate chain. NoRootRevocationCheck is set to 0 by default.

  You can use NoRootRevocationCheck to authenticate clients when the root CA certificate does not include CRL distribution points, such as those from third-party CAs. Also, this entry can prevent certification-related delays that occur when a certificate revocation list is offline or is expired.

All these registry settings must be added as a DWORD (a registry data type composed of hexadecimal data with a maximum allotted space of 4 bytes) type and have the valid values of 0 or 1. The Windows wireless client does not use these settings.

Validating the IAS Server's Certificate

In order for the wireless client to validate the certificate of the IAS server, the following must be true for each certificate in the certificate chain sent by the IAS server:

- The current date must be within the validity dates of the certificate.

  When certificates are issued, they are issued with a range of valid dates, before which they cannot be used and after which they are considered expired.

- The certificate has a valid digital signature.

  CAs digitally sign certificates they issue. The wireless client verifies the digital signature of each certificate in the chain, with the exception of the root CA certificate, by obtaining the public key from the certificate's issuing CA and mathematically validating the digital signature.

Additionally, the IAS server computer certificate must have the Server Authentication EKU (object identifier [OID] 1.3.6.1.5.5.7.3.1). To view the EKU for a certificate in the Certificates snap-in, double-click the certificate in the contents pane, click the Details tab, and then click the Enhanced Key Usage field.

Finally, to trust the certificate chain offered by the IAS server, the wireless client must have the root CA certificate of the issuing CA of the IAS server certificate installed in its Trusted Root Certification Authorities Local Computer store.

Notice that the wireless client does not perform certificate revocation checking for the certificates in the certificate chain of the IAS server's computer certificate. The assumption is that the wireless client does not yet have a physical connection to the network and therefore cannot access a Web page or other resource in order to check for certificate revocation.

Troubleshooting Password-Based Validation

Troubleshooting password validation with PEAP-MS-CHAP v2 authentication consists of verifying the wireless client's username and password credentials and the computer certificates of the IAS servers.

Validating the Wireless Client's Credentials

When you are using PEAP-MS-CHAP v2 for authentication, the name and password as sent by the wireless client must match the credentials of a valid account. The successful validation of the MS-CHAP v2 credentials by the IAS server depends on the following:

- The domain portion of the name corresponds to a domain that is either the domain of the IAS server or a domain that has a two-way trust with the domain of the IAS server.

- The account portion of the name corresponds to a valid account in the domain.

- The password is the correct password for the account.

To verify user account credentials, have the user of the wireless client log on to their domain using a computer that is already connected to the network, such as with an Ethernet connection (if possible). This process demonstrates whether there is a problem with the user's credentials or if the problem lies in the configuration of the authentication infrastructure.

Validating the IAS Server's Certificate

In order for the wireless client to validate the certificate of the IAS server for PEAP-MS-CHAP v2 authentication, the following must be true for each certificate in the certificate chain sent by the IAS server:

- The current date must be within the validity dates of the certificate.

  When certificates are issued, they are issued with a range of valid dates, before which they cannot be used and after which they are considered expired.

- The certificate has a valid digital signature.

  CAs digitally sign certificates they issue. The wireless client verifies the digital signature of each certificate in the chain, with the exception of the root CA certificate, by obtaining the public key from the certificate's issuing CA and mathematically validating the digital signature.

Additionally, the IAS server computer certificate must have the Server Authentication EKU (OID 1.3.6.1.5.5.7.3.1). To view the EKU for a certificate in the Certificates snap-in, double-click the certificate in the contents pane, click the Details tab, and then click the Enhanced Key Usage field.

Finally, to trust the certificate chain offered by the IAS server, the wireless client must have the root CA certificate of the issuing CA of the IAS server certificate installed in its Trusted Root Certification Authorities Local Computer store.

Common Authentication Problems

The most common problem with wireless connectivity is that wireless clients cannot be successfully authenticated. There are many configurations and components that could be at fault. When troubleshooting any problem, it is helpful to use a logical approach. Some questions to ask include the following:

- What works?

- What does not work?

- How are the things that do and do not work related?

- Have the things that do not work ever worked?

- If so, what has changed since it last worked?

One of the first places to look for troubleshooting information is the system event log on the IAS server that received the RADIUS Access-Request message for the event corresponding to the failed authentication. If there is an event, use the text of the event message as a basis for correcting the problem or performing additional troubleshooting. If attempting to correct the problem based on the event message text does not fix the problem, use the information in this section or in the "Troubleshooting IAS Authentication and Authorization" section of this chapter for additional troubleshooting ideas and directions.

If there is no event, troubleshoot the lack of connectivity or the inability to exchange RADIUS messages between the wireless AP and the IAS server. Check for packet filtering in intermediate routers and the incorrect configuration of intermediate RADIUS proxies (if any).

The following are common problems with wireless connectivity and authentication that can be caused by the authentication infrastructure:

- No wireless clients can be authenticated (includes both EAP-TLS and PEAP-MS-CHAP v2-based wireless clients)

  If no wireless clients can be authenticated, do the following:

  - Verify that all the IAS servers and the wireless APs have symmetric reachability for RADIUS traffic. *Symmetric reachability* means that the IAS server can reach the wireless AP and the wireless AP can reach the IAS server.

- Verify that Active Directory global catalog and domain controller computers are available and have symmetric reachability with the IAS servers.

- Verify that the computer certificates on the IAS servers have not expired.

- Verify that there is a matching remote access policy against which the wireless authentication requests are being evaluated. If there is no matching policy, all wireless authentication requests are rejected. If there is a matching policy, investigate the remote access policies conditions, remote access permission, and profile properties for the correct settings.

- No EAP-TLS-based wireless clients can be authenticated.

  If EAP-TLS-based wireless clients cannot be authenticated (but PEAP-MS-CHAP v2-based wireless clients can), do the following:

  - Verify that the CRL locations, as specified in the wireless client user or computer certificate chains, are available to the IAS servers and are symmetrically reachable. If the IAS servers cannot access the CRLs, EAP-TLS authentication fails by default. This behavior can be modified with the IgnoreRevocationOffline registry setting previously described.

  - Verify that the CRLs available to the IAS servers have not expired. If the CRLs available to the IAS servers have expired, EAP-TLS authentication fails. If any of them have expired, manually publish new CRLs using either the Certification Authority snap-in (if you are using a Windows CA) or the appropriate tool (if you are using a third-party CA).

  - Verify that the remote access policy used for wireless connections is configured to allow EAP-TLS authentication.

  - Verify that the correct computer certificate is selected in the properties of the Smart Card or Other Certificate dialog box in the profile properties of the remote access policy used for wireless connections.

  - Verify that the root CA certificate for the issuing CA of the wireless client user or computer certificate is installed in the Trusted Root Certification Authorities Local Computer store on the IAS server.

  - Verify that the root CA certificate for the issuing CA of the IAS server certificate is installed in the Trusted Root Certification Authorities Local Computer store on the wireless client computers.

- No PEAP-MS-CHAP v2-based wireless clients can be authenticated.

  If PEAP-MS-CHAP v2-based wireless clients cannot be authenticated (but EAP-TLS-based wireless clients can), do the following:

  - Verify that the remote access policy used for wireless connections is configured to allow PEAP authentication with the MS-CHAP v2 EAP type.

- Verify that the correct computer certificate is selected in the properties of the Protected EAP Properties dialog box in the profile properties of the remote access policy used for wireless connections.

- Verify that the root CA certificate for the issuing CA of the IAS server certificate is installed in the Trusted Root Certification Authorities Local Computer store on the wireless client computers.

- Individual wireless clients cannot be authenticated.

    If an individual wireless client cannot be authenticated, do the following:

    - Verify that the account exists, is enabled, and is not locked out (via account properties or remote access account lockout); and that the connection is being attempted during allowed logon times.

    - Verify that the connection attempt for the user or computer account matches a remote access policy. For example, if you are using a group-based remote access policy, verify that the user or computer account is a member of the group specified in the Windows Groups condition of the appropriate remote access policy.

    - Verify that the root CA certificate for the issuing CA of the IAS server certificate is installed in the Trusted Root Certification Authorities Local Computer store on the wireless client computer.

- For an EAP-TLS-based wireless client, verify that the computer or user certificate meets the conditions described in the "Validating the Wireless Client's Certificate" section of this chapter.

- For a PEAP-MS-CHAP v2-based wireless client, investigate whether the wireless client's account password has expired and verify that the Allow Client to Change Password After It Has Expired check box on the EAP MS-CHAP v2 Properties dialog box is enabled on the IAS servers.

Summary

The tools for troubleshooting wireless connection problems from the IAS server consist of the IAS event logging and Event Viewer snap-in, Network Monitor, tracing, the SNMP agent, and the Performance Logs And Alerts snap-in. To troubleshoot IAS authentication and authorization, verify account settings, IAS server settings, and remote access policy settings. To troubleshoot certificate-based validation, validate the properties of the wireless client and IAS server certificate chains. To troubleshoot password-based validation, validate the credentials of the wireless client and the properties of the IAS server certificate chain.

Part IV
Appendixes

Appendix A
Wireless Deployment Best Practices

The following sections describe recommendations and best practices for deploying wireless networks.

Security

When designing for secure wireless connectivity, use the following best practices:

- Use one of the following combinations of encryption and authentication for secure wireless in an organization network:

  - Wired Equivalent Privacy (WEP) and Extensible Authentication Protocol-Transport Layer Security (EAP-TLS)

  - WEP and Protected EAP (PEAP)-Microsoft Challenge Handshake Authentication Protocol version 2 (MS-CHAP v2)

  - Wi-Fi Protected Access (WPA)/Temporal Key Integrity Protocol (TKIP) and EAP-TLS

  - WPA/TKIP and PEAP-MS-CHAP v2

- For the Small Office/Home Office (SOHO) wireless network without a Remote Authentication Dial-In User Service (RADIUS) server, the following combinations of encryption and authentication are recommended:

  - WEP with a static WEP key and open system authentication

  - WPA/TKIP and WPA with pre-shared key

- For the strongest authentication configuration, wireless clients should have HKEY_LOCAL_MACHINE\Software\Microsoft\EAPOL\Parameters\General\Global\AuthMode set to 1. This setting enforces the use of a user certificate and user authentication after the user has successfully logged on. Computers running Windows XP (SP1 and later) and Windows Server 2003 have AuthMode set to 1 by default. Computers running Windows XP (prior to SP1) have AuthMode set to 0 by default.

- To prevent rogue wireless access points (APs) from being attached to your wired network, use Ethernet switches that support 802.1X authentication for network ports that are accessible to users.

- If you are using EAP-TLS authentication, do not also use PEAP-TLS. Allowing both protected and unprotected authentication traffic for the same type of network connection renders the protected authentication traffic susceptible to spoofing attacks.

PKI

When installing a public key infrastructure (PKI), use the following best practices:

- Plan your PKI before deploying certification authorities (CAs).

- For enterprise organizations, the root CA should be offline, and its signing key should be secured by a Hardware Security Module (HSM) and kept in a vault to minimize potential for key compromise.

- Enterprise organizations should not issue certificates to users or computers directly from the root CA; instead, they should deploy the following:

  - An offline root CA

  - Offline intermediate CAs

  - Online issuing CAs (using Windows 2000 or Windows Server 2003 Certificate Services as an enterprise CA)

  This CA infrastructure provides flexibility and insulates the root CA from attempts to compromise its private key by malicious users. The offline root and intermediate CAs do not have to be Windows CAs. Issuing CAs can be subordinates of a third-party intermediate CA. The offline CA needs to be placed online on a preset period to publish the certificate revocation list (CRL), or else all certificate revocation checks will fail.

- Medium-sized organizations should use a two-level hierarchy consisting of root CA/issuing CAs. Small organizations can use a single CA that is both the root CA and the issuing CA.

- Back up the CA database, the CA certificate, and the CA keys to protect against the loss of critical data. The CA should be backed up on a regular basis (daily, weekly, monthly) based on the number of certificates issued over the same interval. The more certificates issued, the more frequently you should back up the CA.

- Train your users to back up their keys. Otherwise, they will have problems imaging new machines.

- You should review the concepts of security permissions and access control in Windows because enterprise CAs issue certificates based on the security permissions of the certificate requester.

For the certificates used for wireless access, use the following best practices:

- If you are using EAP-TLS authentication, use both user and computer certificates for both user and computer authentication.

- To install computer certificates in an Active Directory directory service environment, use autoenrollment.

  This process requires the use of a Windows 2000 or Windows Server 2003 Certificate Services server as an enterprise CA at the issuer CA level.

- To install user certificates in a Windows Server 2003 Active Directory environment, use autoenrollment of user certificates.

  This process requires the use of a Windows Server 2003, Enterprise Edition, or Windows Server 2003, Datacenter Edition, Certificate Services server as an enterprise CA at the issuer CA level. Only computers running Windows XP and Windows Server 2003 support autoenrollment of user certificates.

- To install user certificates when you do not have a Windows Server 2003 Active Directory environment, use a CAPICOM script.

  Alternately, use a CAPICOM script to install both computer and user certificates.

- Because certificate revocation checking can prevent wireless access due to the unavailability or expiration of CRLs for each certificate in the certificate chain, design your PKI for high availability of CRLs. For instance, configure multiple CRL distribution points for each CA in the certificate hierarchy and configure publication schedules so that the most current CRL is always available.

- Although it is possible to import a certificate by double-clicking a certificate file that is stored in a folder or sent in an email message, this works only for certificates created with Windows CAs. This method does not work for third-party CAs. The recommended method of importing certificates is to use the Certificates snap-in.

Wireless APs

When choosing and deploying wireless APs, use the following best practices:

- Use wireless APs that support 802.1X, 128-bit WEP, and the use of both multicast/global and unicast session encryption keys. Optionally, choose wireless APs that support WPA.

- Change the administration configuration of the wireless AP, such as administrator-level usernames and passwords, from its default configuration.

- If you are installing wireless APs in the plenum area (the space between the ceiling tiles and the ceiling), you must obtain plenum-rated wireless APs to comply with fire safety codes.

- To minimize interference on the 802.11b wireless frequencies in the S-Band Industrial, Scientific, and Medical (ISM) frequency band, overlapping coverage areas should have a five-channel separation. For example, to get the most channels in the United States, use channels numbers 1, 6, and 11.

- If you are using Simple Network Management Protocol (SNMP) to manage or configure wireless APs, change the default SNMP community name. If possible, use wireless APs that support SNMPv2.

Wireless Network Adapters

When choosing and deploying wireless network adapters, use the following best practices:

- Use wireless network adapters whose drivers support the Wireless Zero Configuration (WZC) service.

- Use wireless network adapters that support 128-bit WEP encryption keys and both multicast/global and unicast session keys. Optionally, use wireless adapters that support WPA.

- For easier deployment, use wireless network adapters that have Plug and Play drivers already included with Windows XP or that are available through Windows Update (*http://www.windowsupdate.com*).

- Avoid installing wireless configuration utilities that are provided with the wireless network adapter; use the WZC service.

Active Directory

When configuring Active Directory directory service for wireless access, use the following best practices:

- If you have a native-mode domain and are using a group-based wireless remote access policy, use universal groups and global groups to organize your wireless accounts into a single group. Additionally, set the remote access permission on computer and user accounts to Control Access Through Remote Access Policy.

- If you are using a Windows 2000 or Windows Server 2003 enterprise CA as an issuing CA, use the Computer Configuration Automatic Certificate Request Settings Group Policy setting to automatically issue computer certificates to all domain members.

  Ensure that all appropriate domain system containers are configured for automatic enrollment of computer certificates, either through the inheriting of group policy settings of a parent system container or explicit configuration.

- If you are using a Windows Server 2003, Enterprise Edition, or Windows Server 2003, Datacenter Edition, enterprise CA as an issuing CA, create a user certificate template and use the User Configuration Autoenrollment Settings Group Policy setting to automatically issue user certificates to all domain members.

  Ensure that all appropriate domain system containers are configured for automatic enrollment of user certificates, either through the inheriting of group policy settings of a parent system container or explicit configuration.

RADIUS

When deploying your RADIUS infrastructure for wireless access, use the following best practices:

- If supported by your wireless APs, use Internet Protocol security (IPSec) and Encapsulating Security Payload (ESP) to provide data confidentiality for RADIUS traffic between the wireless AP and the Internet Authentication Service (IAS) servers and between IAS servers. Use Triple Data Encryption Standard (3DES) encryption and, if possible, certificates for Internet Key Exchange (IKE) main mode authentication. IPSec settings for RADIUS traffic sent between IAS servers can be configured using Group Policy and assigned at the Active Directory system container level. For more information about IPSec, see the Help and Support Center for Windows Server 2003.

- To provide the maximum security for unprotected RADIUS traffic, choose RADIUS shared secrets that are random sequences of upper- and lowercase letters, numbers, and punctuation marks at least 22 keyboard characters long.

  If possible, use a random character-generation program to determine shared secrets to configure on the IAS server and the wireless AP.

- Use as many different RADIUS shared secrets as possible. The actual number of RADIUS shared secrets depends on configuration constraints and management considerations.

  For example, IAS allows the configuration of RADIUS shared secrets on a per-client or per-server basis. However, many wireless APs allow for the configuration of a single RADIUS shared secret for both primary and secondary RADIUS servers. In this case, a single RADIUS shared secret is used for two different RADIUS client–RADIUS server pairs: the wireless AP with its primary RADIUS server and the wireless AP with its secondary RADIUS server. Additionally, if you are using the **netsh aaaa show** and **netsh exec** commands to copy the configuration of one IAS server (designated as the primary configuration server) to another (designated as the secondary configuration server), the RADIUS shared secret for each wireless AP/primary IAS server pair must be the same as the RADIUS shared secret for each wireless AP/secondary IAS server pair.

Because the Windows Server 2003, Enterprise Edition, and Windows Server 2003, Datacenter Edition, versions of IAS allows you to configure a range of IP addresses to define a single RADIUS client (for example, all the wireless APs on a single subnet in a single building), all the wireless AP/IAS server pairs defined by this single RADIUS client are configured with the same RADIUS shared secret.

- When there are separate account databases, such as different Active Directory forests or domains that do not have two-way trusts, you must use a RADIUS proxy between the wireless APs and the RADIUS servers providing the authentication and authorization processing.

  Windows Server 2003 IAS supports RADIUS proxy functionality through the configuration of connection request policies and remote RADIUS server groups. For this example, connection request policies are created to match different portions of the User-Name RADIUS attribute corresponding to each account database (such as different Active Directory forests). RADIUS messages are forwarded to a member of the corresponding remote RADIUS server group matching the connection request policy.

- To balance the load of RADIUS traffic between the primary and secondary IAS servers (regardless of whether they are acting as a RADIUS server or RADIUS proxy), configure half of the wireless APs with the primary IAS server as their primary RADIUS server and the secondary IAS server as their secondary RADIUS server; configure the other half with the secondary IAS server as their primary RADIUS server and the primary IAS server as their secondary RADIUS server.

- Investigate whether the wireless APs need RADIUS vendor-specific attributes (VSAs) and configure them during the configuration of the remote access policy on the Advanced tab of the remote access policy profile.

- If you manage the remote access permission of user and computer accounts on a per-account basis, use remote access policies that specify a connection type. If you manage the remote access permission through the remote access policy (the recommended method), use remote access policies that specify a connection type and group.

- If you change the IAS server configuration in any way, use the Internet Authentication Service snap-in to change the configuration of the IAS server that is designated as the primary configuration server and then copy the configuration of the primary configuration server to the secondary IAS server.

Performance

When designing for performance, use the following best practices:

- Do not overload your wireless APs with too many connected wireless clients. Although most wireless APs can theoretically support hundreds of wireless connections, the practical limit is 20–25 connected clients, due to the effective bandwidth usable by each wireless client.

- For higher-density situations, lower the signal strength of the wireless APs to reduce the coverage area, thereby allowing more wireless APs to fit in a specific space and more wireless bandwidth to be distributed to more wireless clients.

- To minimize the authentication and authorization latency of wireless authentication requests, install IAS on domain controllers.

Scalability

When designing for scalability, use the following best practice:

- For a large amount of authentication traffic within an Active Directory forest, use a layer of RADIUS proxies running Windows Server 2003 IAS between the wireless APs and the RADIUS servers.

  By default, an IAS RADIUS proxy balances the load of RADIUS traffic across all the members of a remote RADIUS server group on a per-authentication basis and uses failover and failback mechanisms. Members of a remote RADIUS server group can also be individually configured with priority and weight settings so that the IAS RADIUS proxy favors specific RADIUS servers.

Appendix B
Wireless ISPs and Windows Provisioning Services

Public-access wireless hotspots are a high-growth area in wireless networking. Wireless Internet service providers (WISPs) are deploying public hotspots at thousands of locations around the world to provide their customers with many points of wireless-based network access. There are several challenges that wireless users and WISPs face in using hotspots, however. Recognizing this, Microsoft plans to update the Microsoft Windows XP wireless service to help address these challenges.

The challenges faced by wireless users and WISPs include the following:

- The current security model for WISP sign-up and usage is insecure.

  Hotspot wireless access points (APs) are typically configured for open system authentication and with Wired Equivalent Privacy (WEP) encryption disabled.

- Users without additional hotspot client software cannot easily detect hotspots.

  Users cannot gain information about the WISP or search for the WISP's hotspot locations. If they sign up at one hotspot, they are not necessarily configured to use other hotspots of the same WISP.

- Additional hotspot client software typically conflicts with the wireless client software built into the operating system of the wireless client.

  Additional hotspot client software helps the user access the hotspots of that specific WISP's network. However, installing it might cause conflicts with the existing wireless client software, such as the Microsoft Windows XP Wireless Zero Configuration (WZC) service. As a result, information technology departments within organizations are reluctant to deploy hotspot client software to their users. Additionally, updates to the WISP configuration usually require updates to the wireless client software.

- WISPs lack common methods to sign up new users and update the configurations of existing users.

Users are typically required to launch a Web browser such as Microsoft Internet Explorer to sign up to the WISP service and for subsequent logins. Each WISP has a different set of configuration screens that users must navigate to sign up for wireless service and different methods of updating the configuration of the installed WISP client software.

Windows XP Wireless Provisioning Services

To help solve these issues for WISPs and wireless users, Windows XP is being extended with Wireless Provisioning Services, an update to the existing wireless service in Windows XP. This update allows wireless users to seamlessly detect, sign up, get provisioned, and use wireless hotspots through a common user interface and configuration update method.

Provisioning is the process of sending the wireless client a set of configuration information about the WISP's network that includes items such as the names of Service Set Identifiers (SSIDs), 802.1X settings, authentication settings, and WISP locations. This configuration information is used for subsequent automated connection to the hotspots of the WISP. Wireless Provisioning Services for Windows XP allows provisioning entities such as WISPs to send Extensible Markup Language (XML)–formatted configuration information to the wireless client for both initial sign-up and ongoing configuration changes.

WISPs that will be supporting Wireless Provisioning Services for Windows XP must deploy an infrastructure to support provisioning, sign-up, and authentication of prospective and existing customers to allow them to connect to the network.

More Info Wireless Provisioning Services for Windows XP was in development at the time of the writing of this book. For more information about Wireless Provisioning Services for Windows XP and the requirements for WISP infrastructure, see the white papers, resources, and the link to the Wireless Provisioning Services update at *http://www.microsoft.com/wifi*.

Appendix C
Setting Up Secure Wireless Access in a Test Lab

This appendix describes how to configure secure wireless access using IEEE 802.1X with Protected Extensible Authentication Protocol-Microsoft Challenge Handshake Authentication Protocol version 2 (PEAP-MS-CHAP v2) and Extensible Authentication Protocol-Transport Layer Security (EAP-TLS) authentication in a test lab using a wireless access point (AP) and four computers. Of the four computers, one is a wireless client; one is a domain controller, certification authority (CA), and Dynamic Host Configuration Protocol (DHCP) and Domain Name System (DNS) server; one is a Web and file server; and one is an Internet Authentication Service (IAS) server that is acting as a Remote Authentication Dial-in User Service (RADIUS) server.

Note The following instructions are for configuring a test lab using a minimum number of computers. Individual computers are needed to separate the services provided on the network and to clearly show the desired functionality. This configuration is neither designed to reflect best practices nor is it designed to reflect a desired or recommended configuration for a production network.

PEAP-MS-CHAP v2 Authentication

The infrastructure for the wireless test lab network consists of four computers performing the following roles:

- A computer running Microsoft Windows Server 2003, Enterprise Edition, named DC1 that is acting as a domain controller, a DNS server, a DHCP server, and a CA.

- A computer running Microsoft Windows Server 2003, Standard Edition, named IAS1 that is acting as a RADIUS server.

- A computer running Windows Server 2003, Standard Edition, named IIS1 that is acting as a Web and file server.

- A computer running Microsoft Windows XP Professional and Windows XP Service Pack 1 (SP1) named CLIENT1 that is acting as a wireless client.

Additionally, a wireless AP is present that provides connectivity to the Ethernet intranet network segment for the wireless client.

Figure C-1 shows the configuration of the wireless test lab.

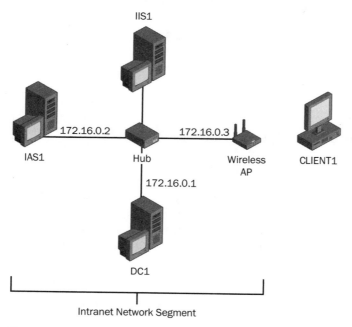

Figure C-1. *Configuration of the wireless test lab.*

The wireless test lab represents a network segment in a corporate intranet. All computers on the corporate intranet, including the wireless AP, are connected to a common hub or Layer 2 switch. Private addresses of 172.16.0.0/24 are used on the intranet network segment.

IIS1 and CLIENT1 obtain their IP address configuration using DHCP. The following sections describe how to configure each of the components in the test lab. To reconstruct this test lab, configure the computers in the order presented.

DC1

DC1 is a computer running Windows Server 2003, Enterprise Edition, which is performing the following roles:

- A domain controller for the example.com domain.
- A DNS server for the example.com DNS domain.
- A DHCP server for the intranet network segment.
- The enterprise root certification authority (CA) for the example.com domain.

Note   Windows Server 2003, Enterprise Edition, is used so that autoenrollment for both user and computer certificates for EAP-TLS authentication can be configured. This is described in the "EAP-TLS Authentication" section of this appendix.

To configure DC1 for these services, do the following:

- Perform basic installation and configuration
- Configure the computer as a domain controller
- Raise the domain functional level
- Install and configure DHCP
- Install Certificate Services
- Add computers to the domain
- Add users to the domain
- Add groups to the domain
- Add users to WirelessUsers group
- Add client computers to WirelessUsers group

▶ **To perform basic installation and configuration**

1. Install Windows Server 2003, Enterprise Edition, as a standalone server.

2. Configure the TCP/IP protocol with the IP address of 172.16.0.1 and the subnet mask of 255.255.255.0.

▶ **To configure the computer as a domain controller**

1. Click Start, click Run, type **dcpromo.exe**, and then click OK to start the Active Directory Installation Wizard.

2. Run the Active Directory Installation Wizard (Dcpromo.exe) to create a new domain named example.com in a new forest. Install the DNS service when prompted.

▶ **To raise the domain functional level**

1. Open the Active Directory Domains And Trusts snap-in from the Administrative Tools folder, and then right-click the domain computer dc1.example.com.

2. Click Raise Domain Functional Level, and then select Windows Server 2003 on the Raise Domain Functional Level page.

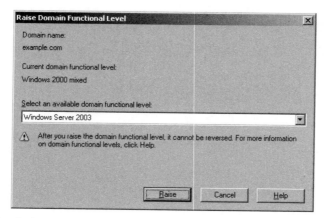

3. Click Raise, click OK, and then click OK again.

▶ **To install and configure DHCP**

1. Install Dynamic Host Configuration Protocol (DHCP) as a Networking Services component by using Add Or Remove Programs in Control Panel.

2. Open the DHCP snap-in from the Administrative Tools folder and then highlight the DHCP server, dc1.example.com.

3. Click Action, and then click Authorize to authorize the DHCP service.

4. In the console tree, right-click dc1.example.com, and then click New Scope.

5. On the Welcome page of the New Scope Wizard, click Next.

6. On the Scope Name page, type **CorpNet** in Name.

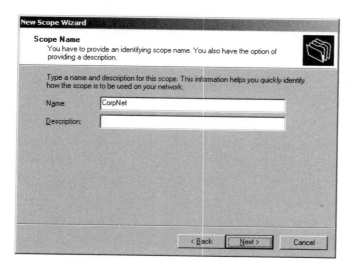

7. Click Next. On the IP Address Range page, type **172.16.0.10** in Start IP Address, type **172.16.0.100** in End IP Address, and type **24** in Length.

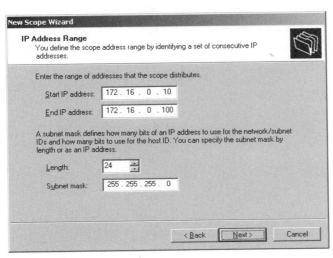

8. Click Next. On the Add Exclusions page, click Next.

9. On the Lease Duration page, click Next.

10. On the Configure DHCP Options page, click Yes, I Want To Configure These Options Now.

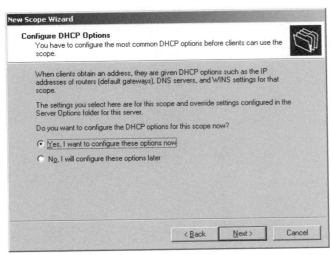

11. Click Next. On the Router (Default Gateway) page, click Next.

12. On the Domain Name and DNS Servers page, type **example.com** in Parent Domain. Type **172.16.0.1** in IP Address, and then click Add.

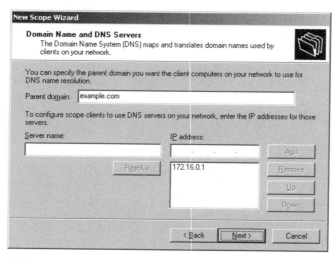

13. Click Next. On the WINS Servers page, click Next.

14. On the Activate Scope page, click Yes, I Want To Activate This Scope Now.

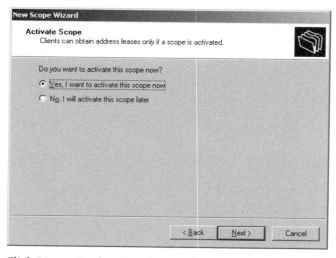

15. Click Next. On the Completing the New Scope Wizard page, click Finish.

▶ **To install Certificate Services**

1. In Control Panel, open Add Or Remove Programs, and then click Add/ Remove Windows Components.

2. In the Windows Components Wizard page, select Certificate Services, and then click Next.

3. On the next Windows Components Wizard page, select Enterprise root CA.

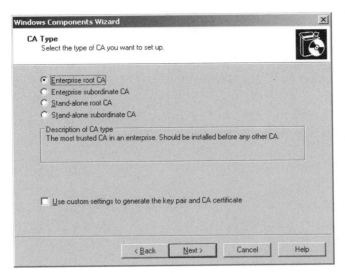

4. Click Next. Type **Example CA** in the Common Name For This CA field, and then click Next. On the Certificate Database Settings page, make no changes.

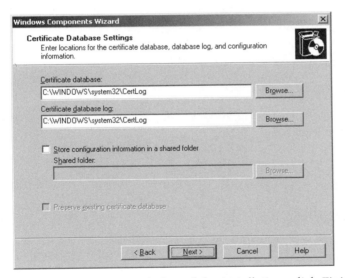

5. Click Next. Upon completion of the installation, click Finish.

▶ **To add computers to the domain**

1. Open the Active Directory Users And Computers snap-in.

2. In the console tree, expand example.com.

3. Right-click Users, click New, and then click Computer.

4. In the New Object – Computer dialog box, type **IAS1** in Computer Name.

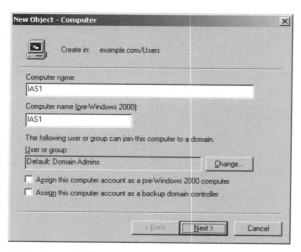

5. Click Next. In the Managed dialog box, click Next. In the New Object – Computer dialog box, click Finish.

6. Repeat steps 3-5 to create additional computer accounts with the following names: IIS1 and CLIENT1.

▶ **To add users to the domain**

1. In the Active Directory Users And Computers console tree, right-click Users, click New, and then click User.

2. In the New Object – User dialog box, type **WirelessUser** in First Name and type **WirelessUser** in User Logon Name.

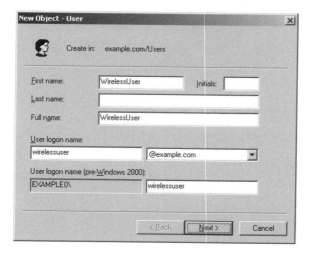

3. Click Next.

4. In the New Object – User dialog box, type a password of your choice in Password and Confirm Password. Clear the User Must Change Password At Next Logon check box.

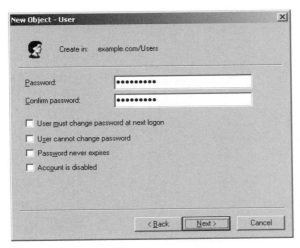

5. In the New Object – User dialog box, click Finish.

▶ **To add groups to the domain**

1. In the Active Directory Users And Computers console tree, right-click Users, click New, and then click Group.

2. In the New Object – Group dialog box, type **WirelessUsers** in Group Name, and then click OK.

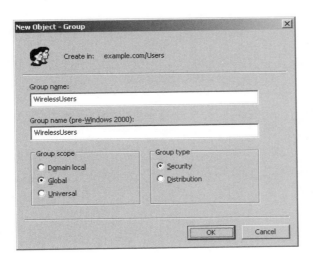

▶ **To add users to WirelessUsers group**

1. In the details pane of the Active Directory Users And Computers, double-click WirelessUsers.

2. Click the Members tab, and then click Add.

3. In the Select Users, Contacts, Computers, Or Groups dialog box, type **wirelessuser** in Enter The Object Names To Select.

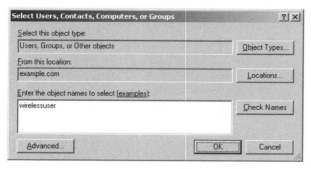

4. Click OK. In the Multiple Names Found dialog box, click OK. The WirelessUser user account is added to the WirelessUsers group.

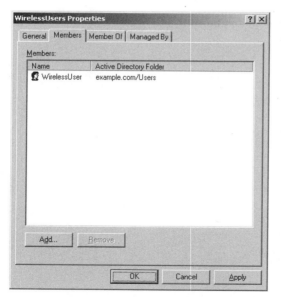

5. Click OK to save changes to the WirelessUsers group.

▶ To add client computers to WirelessUsers group

1. Repeat steps 1 and 2 in the preceding "To add users to WirelessUsers group" procedure.

2. In the Select Users, Contacts, Computers, or Groups, type **client1** in Enter The Object Names To Select.

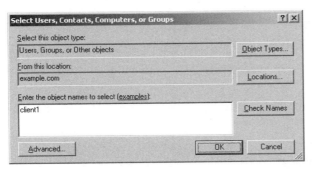

3. Click Object Types. In the Object Types dialog box, clear the Users check box and the Groups check box, and then select the Computers check box.

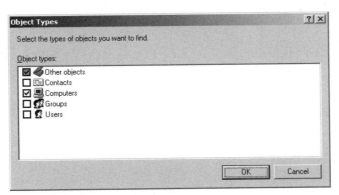

4. Click OK twice. The Client1 computer account is added to the WirelessUsers group.

Note   Adding client computers to the WirelessUsers group allows computer authentication. Computer authentication is needed so that the computer can attach to the wireless network, obtain an IP address configuration, locate Active Directory domain controllers, download the latest Computer Configuration Group Policy settings, and perform other computer startup processes.

IAS1

IAS1 is a computer running Windows Server 2003, Standard Edition that is providing RADIUS authentication and authorization for the wireless AP. To configure IAS1 as a RADIUS server, do the following:

- Perform basic installation and configuration

- Install and configure Internet Authentication Service

- Create the Certificates (Local Computer) console

- Request a computer certificate

- Add the wireless AP as a RADIUS client

- Create and configure remote access policy

▶ **To perform basic installation and configuration**

1. Install Windows Server 2003, Standard Edition, as a member server named IAS1 in the example.com domain.

2. For the intranet local area connection, configure the TCP/IP protocol with the IP address of 172.16.0.2, the subnet mask of 255.255.255.0, and the DNS server IP address of 172.16.0.1.

▶ **To install and configure Internet Authentication Service**

1. Install Internet Authentication Service as a Networking Services component by using Add Or Remove Programs in Control Panel.

2. In the Administrative Tools folder, open the Internet Authentication Service snap-in.

3. Right-click Internet Authentication Service, and then click Register Server in Active Directory. When the Register Internet Authentication Server In Active Directory dialog box appears, click OK.

▶ **To create the Certificates (Local Computer) console**

1. Click Start, click Run, type **mmc**, and then click OK.

2. On the File menu, click Add/Remove Snap-in, and then click Add.

3. Under Snap-in, double-click Certificates, click Computer account, and then click Next.

4. Click Local Computer, click Finish, click Close, and then click OK. The Certificates (Local Computer) snap-in is shown in the following figure.

Note PEAP with MS-CHAP v2 requires computer certificates on the IAS servers but not on the wireless clients. Autoenrollment of computer certificates for the IAS servers can be used to simplify a deployment. However, in this section, a certificate is manually requested for the IAS1 computer because the autoenrollment of the certificates is not yet configured. This is described in the "EAP-TLS Authentication" section of this appendix.

▶ To request a computer certificate

1. Right-click the Personal folder, click All Tasks, click Request New Certificate, and then click Next.

2. Click Computer for the Certificate Types, and then click Next.

3. Type **IAS Server1 Certificate** in Friendly Name.

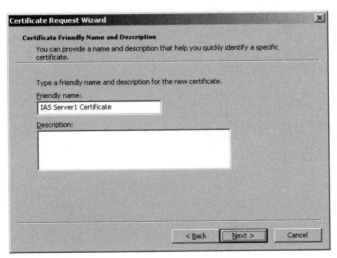

4. Click Next. On the Completing The Certificate Request Wizard page, Click Finish.

5. A "The certificate request was successful" message is displayed. Click OK.

▶ **To add the wireless AP as a RADIUS client**

1. In the console tree of the Internet Authentication Service snap-in, right-click RADIUS Clients, and then click New RADIUS Client.

2. In the Name And Address page of the New RADIUS Client wizard, for Friendly Name, type **WirelessAP**. In Client Address (IP Or DNS), type **172.16.0.3**, and then click Next.

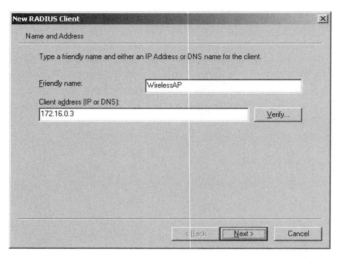

3. In the Additional Information page of the New RADIUS Client Wizard, for Shared Secret, type a shared secret for the wireless AP, and then type it again in Confirm Shared Secret.

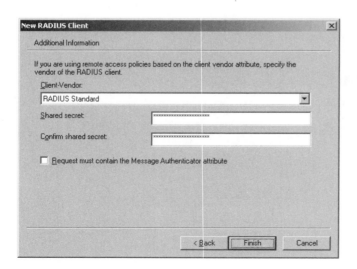

4. Click Finish.

► **To create and configure remote access policy**

1. In the console tree of the Internet Authentication Service snap-in, right-click Remote Access Policies, and then click New Remote Access Policy.

2. On the Welcome To The New Remote Access Policy Wizard page, click Next.

3. On the Policy Configuration Method page, type **Wireless access to intranet** in Policy Name.

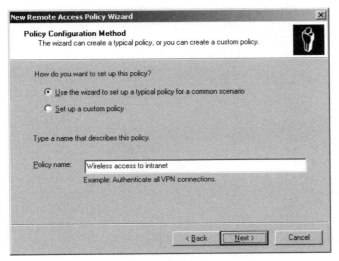

4. Click Next. On the Access Method page, select Wireless.

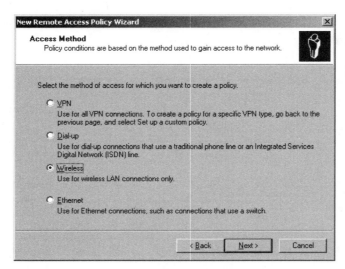

5. Click Next. On the User Or Group Access page, select Group.

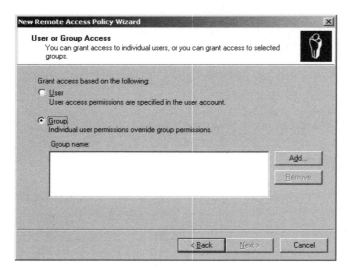

6. Click Add. In the Select Groups dialog box, type **wirelessusers** in the Enter The Object Names To Select box. Verify that example.com is listed in the From This Location field.

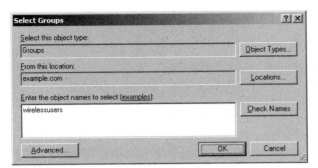

7. Click OK. The WirelessUsers group in the example.com domain is added to the list of groups on the User Or Group Access.

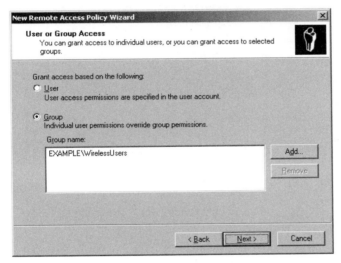

8. Click Next. On the Authentication Methods page, the Protected EAP (PEAP) authentication is selected by default and configured to use PEAP-MS-CHAP v2.

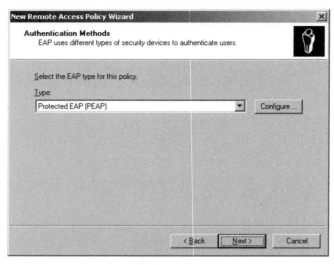

9. Click Next. On the Completing The New Remote Access Policy page, click Finish.

IIS1

IIS1 is a computer running Windows Server 2003, Standard Edition, and Internet Information Services (IIS). It provides Web and file server services for intranet clients. To configure IIS1 as a Web and file server, do the following:

- Install and configure IIS
- Configure a shared folder

▶ To install and configure IIS

1. On IIS1, install Windows Server 2003, Standard Edition, as a member server named IIS1 in the example.com domain.

2. Install Internet Information Services (IIS) as a subcomponent of the Application Server component by using the Windows Components Wizard of Add or Remove Programs.

▶ To configure a shared folder

1. On IIS1, use Windows Explorer to create a new share for the root folder of the C drive using the share name ROOT with the default permissions.

2. To determine whether the Web server is working correctly, start Internet Explorer on IAS1. If the Internet Connection Wizard prompts you, configure Internet connectivity for a LAN connection. In Internet Explorer, in Address, type **http://IIS1/iisstart.htm**. You should see an "under construction" Web page.

3. To determine whether file sharing is working correctly, on IAS1, click Start, Run, type **\\IIS1\ROOT**, and then click OK. You should see the contents of the root folder of the C drive on IIS1.

Wireless AP

Configure the wireless AP for the following:

1. The network name, also known as the Service Set Identifier (SSID), of WIR_TST_LAB.

2. The IP address of 172.16.0.3 with the subnet mask of 255.255.255.0 on the Ethernet interface.

3. IEEE 802.1X authentication with WEP enabled.

4. For the primary RADIUS server: the IP address 172.16.0.2, the UDP port of 1812, and the shared secret, which must match the shared secret previously configured on the IAS server for the RADIUS client corresponding to the wireless AP.

CLIENT1

CLIENT1 is a computer running Windows XP Professional SP1 that acts as a wireless client and obtains access to intranet resources through the wireless AP. To configure CLIENT1 as a wireless client, do the following:

- Perform basic installation and configuration

- Install a wireless network adapter

- Configure a wireless network connection

▶ **To perform basic installation and configuration**

1. Connect CLIENT1 to the intranet network segment using an Ethernet cable connected to the hub.

2. On CLIENT1, install Windows XP Professional as a member computer named CLIENT1 of the example.com domain.

3. Install Windows XP SP1. SP1 must be installed in order to have PEAP support.

If you have not yet installed the wireless network adapter, then complete the steps in the next section, "To install a wireless network adapter." If your computer already has a wireless network adapter installed, go to the next section titled "To configure a wireless network connection."

▶ **To install a wireless network adapter**

1. Shut down the CLIENT1 computer.

2. Disconnect the CLIENT1 computer from the intranet network segment.

3. Restart the CLIENT1 computer, and then log on using the local administrator account.

4. Install the wireless network adapter.

▶ **To configure a wireless network connection**

1. Log off and then log on by using the WirelessUser account in the example.com domain.

2. Wait until you are prompted to select the wireless network in the notification area of the desktop.

3. In the Available Wireless Networks field, select WIR_TST_LAB, and then click Advanced.

4. In the Wireless Network Connection Properties dialog box, select WIR_TST_LAB, and then click Configure.

5. On the Association tab, verify that both Data Encryption (WEP Enabled) and The Key Is Provided For Me Automatically are selected.

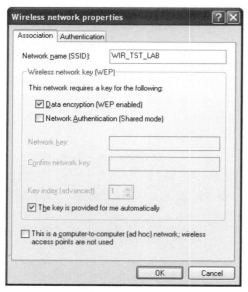

6. On the Authentication tab, configure the WIR_TST_LAB wireless network for PEAP-MS-CHAP v2 authentication.

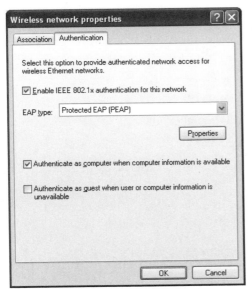

7. Click OK. After authentication is successful, check the TCP/IP configuration for the wireless adapter by using Network Connections. It should have an address from the DHCP scope 172.16.0.10-172.16.0.100.

8. To test functionality to the Web server between CLIENT1 and IIS1 over the wireless connection, start Internet Explorer on CLIENT1.

9. If prompted by the Internet Connection Wizard, configure it for a LAN connection. In Address, type **http://IIS1/iisstart.htm**. You should see an "under construction" Web page.

10. On CLIENT1, click Start, click Run, type **\\IIS1\ROOT**, and then click OK. You should see the contents of the root folder of the C drive on IIS1.

EAP-TLS Authentication

Extensible Authentication Protocol-Transport Layer Security (EAP-TLS) authentication requires computer and user certificates on the wireless client, the addition of EAP-TLS as an EAP type to the remote access policy for wireless access, and a reconfiguration of the wireless network connection.

DC1

To configure DC1 to provide autoenrollment for computer and user certificates, do the following:

- Create a Certificate Templates snap-in

- Create a certificate template for wireless users

- Configure a certificate template

- Enable a certificate template and user and computer certificate autoenrollment

▶ **To create a Certificate Templates snap-in**

1. Click Start, click Run, type **mmc**, and then click OK.

2. On the File menu, click Add/Remove Snap-in, and then click Add.

3. Under Snap-in, double-click Certificate Templates, click Close, and then click OK.

4. In the console tree, click Certificate Templates. All of the certificate templates will be displayed in the details pane.

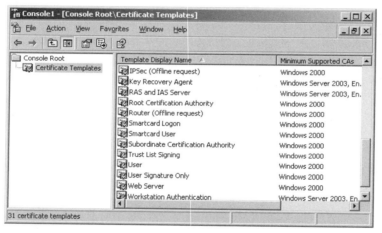

▶ **To create a certificate template for wireless users**

1. In the details pane of the Certificate Templates snap-in, click the User template.

2. On the Action menu, click Duplicate Template.

3. In the Template Display Name field, type **Wireless User Certificate Template**.

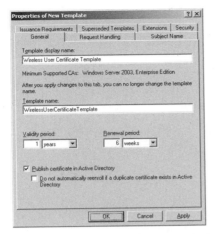

▶ To configure a certificate template

1. In the Properties Of New Template dialog box, make sure that the Publish Certificate In Active Directory check box is selected.

2. Click the Security tab.

3. In the Group Or User Names field, click Domain Users.

4. In the Permissions For Domain Users list, select the Read, Enroll, and Autoenroll check boxes.

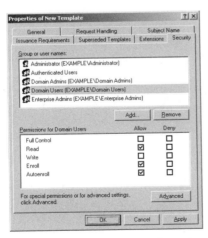

5. Click the Subject Name tab and ensure that Include E-Mail Name In Subject Name and E-mail Name boxes are cleared.

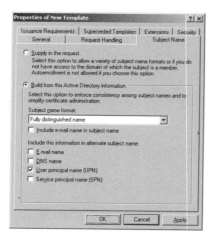

Note These two options are disabled for this test tab configuration because an e-mail name was not entered for the WirelessUser account in the Active Directory Users and Computers snap-in.

6. Click OK.

▶ **To enable the certificate template and user and computer certificate autoenrollment**

1. Open the Certification Authority snap-in.

2. In the console tree, expand Example CA, and then click Certificate Templates.

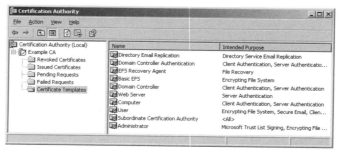

3. On the Action menu, point to New, and then click Certificate To Issue.

4. Click Wireless User Certificate Template.

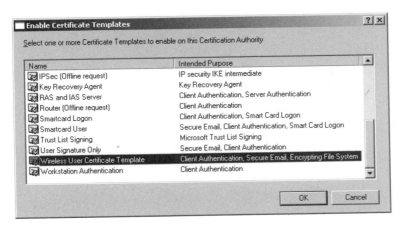

5. Click OK.

6. Open the Active Directory Users And Computers snap-in.

7. In the console tree, double-click Active Directory Users And Computers, right-click the example.com domain, and then click Properties.

8. On the Group Policy tab, click Default Domain Policy, and then click Edit. This opens the Group Policy Object Editor snap-in.

9. In the console tree, expand Computer Configuration, Windows Settings, Security Settings, and Public Key Policies, and then click Automatic Certificate Request Settings.

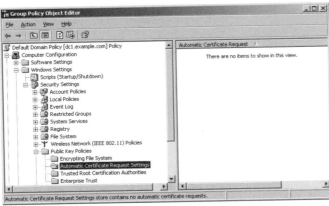

10. Right-click Automatic Certificate Request Settings, point to New, and then click Automatic Certificate Request.

11. On the Welcome To The Automatic Certificate Request Setup Wizard page, click Next.

12. On the Certificate Template page, click Computer.

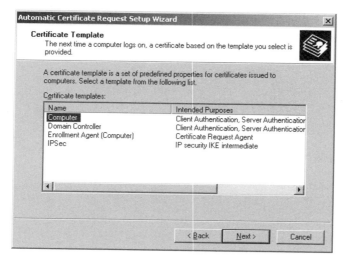

13. Click Next. On the Completing The Automatic Certificate Request Setup Wizard page, click Finish. The Computer certificate type now appears in the details pane of the Group Policy Object Editor snap-in.

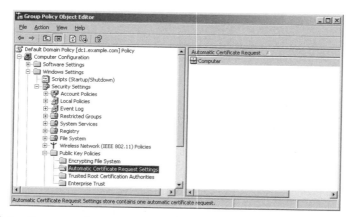

14. In the console tree, expand Computer Configuration, Windows Settings, Security Settings, and Public Key Policies.

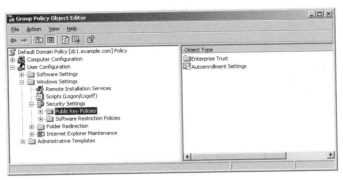

15. In the details pane, double-click Autoenrollment Settings.

16. Click Enroll Certificates Automatically. Select the Renew Expired Certificates, Update Pending Certificates, And Remove Revoked Certificates check box. Select the Update Certificates That Use Certificate Templates check box.

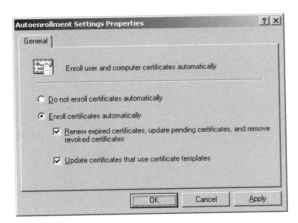

17. Click OK.

IAS1

To configure IAS1 to use EAP-TLS authentication, perform the following steps:

1. Open the Internet Authentication Service snap-in.

2. In the console tree, click Remote Access Policies.

3. In the details pane, double-click Wireless Access To Intranet. The Wireless Access To Intranet Properties dialog box is displayed.

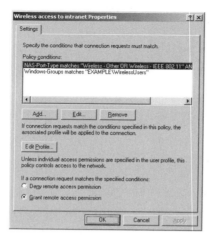

4. Click Edit Profile, and then click the Authentication tab.

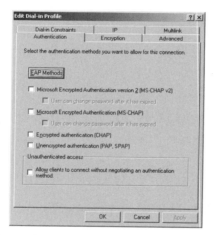

5. On the Authentication tab, click EAP Methods. The Select EAP Providers dialog box is displayed.

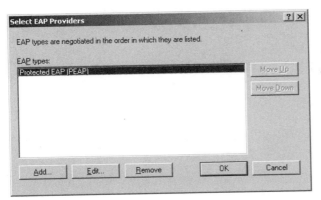

6. Click Add. The Add EAP dialog box is displayed.

7. Click Smart Card Or Other Certificate, and then click OK. The Smart Card Or Other Certificate type is added to the list of EAP providers.

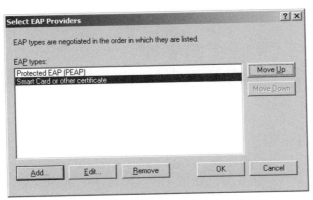

8. Click Edit. The Smart Card Or Other Certificate Properties dialog box is displayed.

9. The properties of the computer certificate issued to the IAS1 computer are displayed. This step verifies that IAS has an acceptable computer certificate installed to perform EAP-TLS authentication. Click OK.

10. Click Move Up to make the Smart Card Or Other Certificate EAP provider the first in the list.

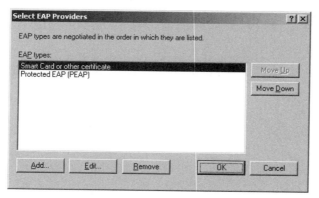

11. Click OK to save changes to EAP providers. Click OK to save changes to the profile settings.

12. Click OK to save changes to the remote access policy.

This will allow the Wireless access to intranet remote access policy to authorize wireless connections using the EAP-TLS authentication method.

CLIENT1

To configure CLIENT1 to use EAP-TLS authentication, perform the following steps:

1. Update computer and user configuration Group Policy settings and obtain a computer and user certificate for the wireless client computer immediately, by typing **gpupdate** at a command prompt. You must be logged on to the domain, either via your previously-created PEAP-MS-CHAP v2 wireless connection or by connecting to the hub.

2. To obtain properties for the WIR_TST_LAB wireless network click Start, click Control Panel, double-click Network Connections, and then right-click your wireless network connection.

3. Click Properties, click the Wireless Networks tab, click WIR_TST_LAB, and then click Configure.

4. On the Authentication tab, select Smart Card Or Other Certificate for the EAP type.

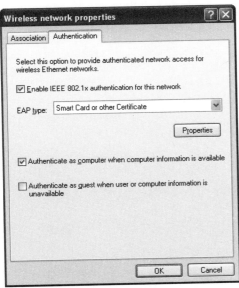

5. Click OK to exit the Wireless Network Properties dialog box, and then click OK to exit the Wireless Network Connection Properties dialog box.

6. The wireless network connection reconnects using EAP-TLS authentication.

Summary

This appendix described in detail the steps required to configure secure wireless access using PEAP-MS-CHAP v2 and EAP-TLS in a test lab with a wireless AP and four computers.

Index

Numerics

A

B

C

Joseph Davies is a Microsoft Corporation employee working as a Program Manager for Content Development on the Networking and Communications team in the Windows product group. He has been a technical writer and instructor of TCP/IP and networking technology topics for over 10 years. He wrote Windows 2000, Windows XP, and Windows Server 2003 product documentation, and Microsoft Resource Kit chapters on TCP/IP, routing, remote access, virtual private networking, Internet Authentication Server (IAS), IPSec, and IPv6. He has written numerous white papers about IEEE 802.11 wireless deployment, IPv6, and Windows XP home networking, and he is the author for the monthly TechNet Cable Guy column (*http://www.microsoft.com/technet*). He is author of Understanding IPv6 (Microsoft Press, 2003) and co-author of *Microsoft Windows Server 2003 TCP/IP Protocols and Services Technical Reference* (Microsoft Press, 2003) and *Microsoft Windows 2000 TCP/IP Protocols and Services Technical Reference* (Microsoft Press, 1999).

Get a **Free**
e-mail newsletter, updates,
special offers, links to related books,
and more when you

register online!

Register your Microsoft Press® title on our Web site and you'll get a FREE subscription to our e-mail newsletter, *Microsoft Press Book Connections.* You'll find out about newly released and upcoming books and learning tools, online events, software downloads, special offers and coupons for Microsoft Press customers, and information about major Microsoft® product releases. You can also read useful additional information about all the titles we publish, such as detailed book descriptions, tables of contents and indexes, sample chapters, links to related books and book series, author biographies, and reviews by other customers.

Registration is easy. Just visit this Web page and fill in your information:

http://www.microsoft.com/mspress/register

Microsoft®

- -